THE
CONFIDENT
WOMAN
DEVOTIONAL

THE CONFIDENT WOMAN

DEVOTIONAL

365 DAILY DEVOTIONS

JOYCE MEYER

NEW YORK   BOSTON   NASHVILLE

All Scripture quotations, unless otherwise indicated, are taken from the *Amplified® Bible.* Copyright © 1954, 1958, 1962, 1964, 1965, 1987 by The Lockman Foundation. Used by permission. (www.Lockman.org)

Scriptures noted NKJV are taken from the *New King James Version.* Copyright ©1979, 1980, 1982 by Thomas Nelson, Inc., Publishers.

Scriptures noted NLT are taken from the *Holy Bible, New Living Translation.* Copyright © 1996. Used by permission of Tyndale House Publishers, Inc., Wheaton, Illinois 60189. All rights reserved.

Scriptures noted THE MESSAGE are taken from *The Message.* Copyright © 1993, 1994, 1995, 1996, 2000, 2001, 2002. Used by permission of NavPress Publishing Group.

Literary development: Koechel Peterson & Associates, Inc., Minneapolis, Minnesota.

Portions of this book have been adapted from *The Confident Woman,* copyright © 2006; *Approval Addiction,* copyright © 2005; *How to Succeed at Being Yourself,* copyright © 1999; *The Battle Belongs to the Lord,* copyright © 2002; *Eight Ways to Keep the Devil Under Your Feet,* copyright © 2002; *Straight Talk,* copyright © 2004, and other miscellaneous books by Joyce Meyer, published by FaithWords. Also Discs 3 and 5 of the *How to Be a Confident Woman* CD set (C294), copyright © 2006 by Joyce Meyer, published by Joyce Meyer Ministries.

FaithWords
Hachette Book Group
237 Park Avenue
New York, NY 10017

www.faithwords.com.

Printed in the United States of America

Originally published in hardcover by FaithWords.

First Joyce Meyer Ministries Edition: November 2010
10   9   8   7   6   5   4   3   2

FaithWords is a division of Hachette Book Group, Inc.
The FaithWords name and logo are trademarks of Hachette Book Group, Inc.

ISBN 978-0-446-56885-2

Introduction

Women are a precious gift from God to the world. They are creative, sensitive, compassionate, intelligent, talented, and, according to the Bible, equal to men.

But many of us have lost the confidence God wants us to enjoy. Many of us have been left with vague feelings that we are somehow "less" than men. Less valuable. Less worthy. The end result is a society filled with insecure people, which causes great difficulty in personal relationships and is one of the reasons divorce is so prevalent today.

During my childhood, I endured many years of sexual abuse, which profoundly affected my confidence and the image I carried inside of myself. Inwardly I was very fearful, but outwardly I presented myself as a tough, bold person who couldn't care less what others thought of her. I created a "pretend me" so no one could discover the "real me." I was filled with shame and condemnation over something a man had done to me, and for many years I held a rather low opinion of men as a result.

Today, however, I believe I am a well-balanced woman. I have a wonderful husband and four grown children. I am the president and founder of a worldwide media ministry that is helping millions of people find salvation through Jesus Christ, as well as freedom and wholeness in their lives. My husband, children, and I all work together in the ministry.

I have learned a lot on my journey about what "true confidence" is and about overcoming my need to please everyone, and it is my desire that the readings of this devotional will help you become the woman God intends you to be. His desire is that you be bold, courageous, confident, respected, admired, promoted, sought after, and, most of all, loved.

God has a wonderful plan for your life, and I pray that reading these devotions will help you enter it more fully than ever before. You can hold your head up high and be filled with confidence about yourself and your future. You can be bold and step out to do new things—even things no man or woman has ever done before. You have what it takes!

THE
CONFIDENT
WOMAN
DEVOTIONAL

Jesus Came

In the fourth watch [between 3:00–6:00 a.m.] of the night, Jesus came to them, walking on the sea. And when the disciples saw Him walking on the sea, they were terrified and said, It is a ghost! And they screamed out with fright. But instantly He spoke to them, saying, Take courage! I AM! Stop being afraid!

—MATTHEW 14:25–27

As was true of the twelve disciples, you are full of capabilities, gifts, and talent. God's enablement of His grace and presence is with you. So what are you doing with your life? Are you like the eleven disciples who stayed in the boat, or are you like Peter, who when Jesus was passing by said, "Lord, I want to walk on the water with You!" Do you have a vision for your life and want to do something greater than what you're doing? Are you going to just sit in the boat and shake and quake and watch the rest of the world go by, or will you be one of those rare individuals who jumps out of the boat and refuses to live afraid?

It's up to you what you're going to do with your life. Fear is always going to come against you. But listen to Jesus' words: "Take courage! I AM! Stop being afraid!" It's time to step out and do the thing you desire to do.

Lord, I praise You that You come to me and extend Your presence and Your helping hand. Like Peter, I want to be a water walker. Amen.

Had Enough?

And Peter answered Him, Lord, if it is You, command me to come to You on the water.   —MATTHEW 14:28

When I tell you to join Peter and get out of the boat, you may wonder what your boat is. Your boat may be a lot of different things. What is your place of comfort, safety, and ease? It could be a place of misery, but yet, somehow or other, you've gotten comfortable in your own misery—so comfortable that you wouldn't do anything about it even if you could. You may have gotten addicted to dysfunction. The sad thing is that most people yield to the fear and remain stuck in life.

Maybe your boat consists of people whose approval you crave, who rule all of your decisions and who bind your life to their lives. If they approve of it, you do it, and if they don't like it, you don't. You may be so addicted to getting your approval from other people that you let everyone else run your life, and you're too afraid to confront them and stand up to them. Are you going to sit in your miserable little boat for the rest of your life and be unhappy? Or are you ready to say, "I've had enough of this! I am ready to step out with confidence and follow God fully!"

———————

Lord, I need to see You and hear Your voice over and above the storms in my life. Help me to break free of anything that is holding me back from doing Your will. Amen.

What Is Confidence?

Hezekiah trusted in, leaned on, and was confident in the Lord, the God of Israel; so that neither after him nor before him was any one of all the kings of Judah like him.   —2 KINGS 18:5

What is confidence? I believe confidence is all about being positive concerning what you can do—and not worrying over what you can't do. A confident person is open to learning, because she knows that her confidence allows her to walk through life's doorways, eager to discover what waits on the other side. She knows that every new unknown is a chance to learn more about herself and unleash her abilities.

Confident people do not concentrate on their weaknesses; they develop and maximize their strengths. For example, on a scale of one to ten, I might be a three when it comes to playing the piano. Now, if I were to practice long and hard—and if my husband could put up with the racket—I could, maybe, transform myself into a middle-of-the road, level-five pianist. However, as a public speaker, I might be an eight. So, if I invested my time and effort into this ability, I might just be able to get to a level ten. When you look at it this way, it's easy to see where you need to invest your efforts.

What are your strengths? If you don't know, ask God to show you.

———————————

Lord, if Hezekiah could learn to lean upon and be confident in You, I know that it's also possible for me. Enable me to recognize, develop, and maximize my strengths rather than concentrating on my weaknesses. Amen.

Believe in Your Value

Because you are precious in My sight and honored, and because I love you, I will give men in return for you and peoples in exchange for your life. Fear not, for I am with you.   —ISAIAH 43:4–5

Take a minute and look into your heart. How do you feel about yourself? If your answer does not agree with God's Word, I encourage you to begin today renewing your mind about yourself.

See yourself as God sees you. Study God's Word and you will find out that you are precious, created in your mother's womb by God's own hand. You are not an accident. Even if your parents told you they never really wanted you, I can assure you that God wanted you. You are valuable, you have worth, you are gifted, you are talented, and you have a purpose on this earth.

Not only must we ask God for things He has promised us but we must receive them (John 16:24). If you feel unworthy, you probably won't ask, and even if you do, you won't receive by faith. Don't let feelings rule you anymore. Take a step of faith and start improving your quality of life today. Believe that you make good decisions, that you are a valuable person with a great future, and something good is going to happen to you today!

Lord, I ask You to imprint Your love into the depths of my heart. I believe that You have a great future for me and that I can walk in Your purpose for my life. Amen.

Cracked Pots

*We possess this precious treasure [the divine Light of the Gospel]
in [frail, human] vessels of earth, that the grandeur and exceeding
greatness of the power may be shown to be from God and not from
ourselves.*   —2 CORINTHIANS 4:7

God works through jars of clay, or what I often call "cracked pots."
This means we are flawed, so when people look at us and see amazing things happening, they know it must be God at work because it
certainly could not be us. I believe anyone who really knows me does
not have any difficulty realizing the work I am doing on earth today
certainly must be God at work in and through me. They give Him the
glory, not me, because they see my imperfections and know my limitations. God chooses the weak and foolish things on purpose so no
mortal can have pretense for glorying in His presence (1 Corinthians
1:27–29).

Imagine a pot with a lamp in it and a lid on it. Even though it may
be filled with light, no one can see the light within it. Yet if the pot is
cracked, the light will shine through the cracks. In this same way, God
works through our imperfections.

Can you love a cracked pot? God can! It is godly to love yourself in a
balanced, healthy way. It is ungodly to reject and despise yourself.

———————————

**Lord, You and I are both well aware of my imperfections. I ask
You to shine Your light through my life, and know that You get
every ounce of glory for it. Amen.**

With God's Help

For if you keep silent at this time, relief and deliverance shall arise for the Jews from elsewhere, but you and your father's house will perish. And who knows but that you have come to the kingdom for such a time as this and for this very occasion?

—ESTHER 4:14

One of the most confident women we find in the Bible is Esther, who rescued her people from certain death at the hands of an evil and hateful man. Though her beauty didn't hurt, it was her character and quiet confidence that helped her find favor with the king, Xerxes. She took a great risk when she made her way to Xerxes' inner court uninvited. But God honored her and the prayers that the other Jews were praying, and Xerxes received her warmly. In the end, Esther saved her people from perishing.

Confidence is holding on to a strong faith in God, a faith that is backed up with a complete knowledge and understanding that with God's help you can do anything. Fear brings a lack of confidence in God and in you. It is a destructive, debilitating belief that "you can't." As a woman, you can do amazing things, but you will have to become confident. Replace your fears with confidence and watch what God can do. God always does His part, making seemingly impossible things possible!

Lord, with Your help, Esther saved her people, and with Your help, I can do the impossible. I look forward to the great things You are going to do in my life. Amen.

Take Care of Yourself

And Asa did right in the eyes of the Lord, as did David his father [forefather]. . . . Also Maacah his mother he removed from being queen mother, because she had an image made for [the goddess] Asherah. Asa destroyed her image, burning it by the brook Kidron.
—1 KINGS 15:11, 13

Country singer Wynonna Judd knows what can happen when you don't think about yourself. At seventeen, she had accepted Christ, but the whirlwind years of fame and fortune had created a deep sense of insecurity for her. She felt like she had to take care of everyone. She worked through two pregnancies so she could ensure that the thirty families of her crew would continue to have an income; she ate when she felt empty inside, and she spent enormous amounts of money on her family and friends.

The need to please everyone eventually caught up with her, and in 2004, Wynonna found herself overweight, out of money, guilt-stricken, and close to losing her 525-acre farm. She had to surrender to God and start taking care of herself again. She's now twenty pounds lighter, she's cut back her excessive spending, and she's learned to say no.

Women in particular want to please people, especially their family, but they need to be very aggressive in standing against getting out of balance in this area.

You must take care of yourself in order to take care of anyone else.

———————

Lord, it's challenging to know when I need to pull back and restore my own self. Help me to serve and give while staying in balance. Amen.

The Heart of a King

When the queen of Sheba heard of [the constant connection of] the fame of Solomon with the name of the Lord, she came to prove him with hard questions (problems and riddles).... When she had come to Solomon, she communed with him about all that was in her mind.

—1 KINGS 10:1–2

Wrong gender, great ruler—that about sums up the life of Queen Elizabeth I of England. Elizabeth ruled what came to be known as the "Golden Age" of history until 1603. In 1588, King Philip II sent the great Spanish Armada to conquer England once and for all. As the Armada was approaching, Elizabeth said to her troops at Tillbury, "I know I have the body of a weak and feeble woman, but I have the heart and stomach of a king, and of a king of England too; and think foul scorn that Parma or Spain, or any prince of Europe should dare to invade the borders of my realm." At the end of her reign, she said to her people, "Though God hath raised me high, yet this I count the glory of my crown: that I have reigned with your love."

I love the fact that Queen Elizabeth followed her heart and ignored her deficits. God will always strengthen those who are willing to look their weaknesses in the face and say, "You cannot stop me."

Lord, give me the heart of a king in the things that You call me to do. I will not allow my weaknesses to stop me from fulfilling my destiny. Amen.

Be Extraordinary

*My frame was not hidden from You when I was being formed in
secret [and] intricately and curiously wrought [as if embroidered
with various colors] in the depths of the earth [a region of darkness
and mystery].*   —PSALM 139:15

Celebrate the fact that you're not exactly like everyone else. You are
special! You are unique! You are the product of twenty-three chromo-
somes from your father and twenty-three from your mother. Scientists
say there is only one chance in 10/2,000,000,000 of your parents having another child just like you. The combination of attributes that you
have cannot be duplicated. You need to explore the development of
your uniqueness and make it a matter of high priority.

It does not increase your value when you find that you can do something that nobody else you know can do, nor does it diminish your
value when you are with people who can do things that you cannot do.
Our worth is not found in being different or the same as others, it is
found in God.

Thousands of years ago the Greek philosopher Aristotle suggested
that each human being is bred with a unique set of potentials that yearn
to be fulfilled. Don't settle for "average" or "getting by." You may have
some limitations, but you can be extraordinary if you decide to be.

**Lord, it's a joy to know that my worth is found in You and that
I don't have to compare myself with others. I celebrate the fact
that I am unique, one of a kind, and that You have something
special for my life. Amen.**

Say "Yes!"

And you will be hated by all for My name's sake, but he who perseveres and endures to the end will be saved.
—MATTHEW 10:22

As a young boy in school, Henry Ward Beecher learned a lesson in self-confidence that he never forgot. He was called upon to recite in front of the class. He had hardly begun when the teacher interrupted with an emphatic, "No!" He started over and again the teacher thundered, "No!" Humiliated, Henry sat down.

The next boy rose to recite and had just begun when the teacher shouted, "No!" This student, however, kept on with the recitation until he completed it. As he sat down, the teacher responded, "Very good!"

Henry was irritated. "I recited just as he did," he complained to the teacher. But the instructor replied, "It is not enough to know your lesson; you must be sure. When you allowed me to stop you, it meant that you were uncertain. If the entire world says, 'No!' it is your business to say, 'Yes!' and prove it."

The world says "No!" in a thousand ways. And each "No!" you hear has the potential to erode your confidence bit by bit until you quit altogether. You just need to be bold enough to say "Yes!" when the world says "No!" God is for you, and with Him on your side you absolutely cannot lose.

———————————

Lord, I'm glad You're here at my side. Because You are for me, I have the confidence to say "Yes," knowing that I can't lose. Amen.

Know Your Strengths

That is why I would remind you to stir up (rekindle the embers of, fan the flame of, and keep burning) the [gracious] gift of God, [the inner fire] that is in you.   —2 TIMOTHY 1:6

An important thing in gaining confidence is that you must absolutely know your strengths. What are you good at? Do you even know? Have you seriously thought about it or have you been so busy thinking about what you are not good at that you have not even noticed your abilities? Remember, God does not make junk. After God created the entire world and Adam and Eve, He looked at all of it and said, "It is very good!"

Make a list of what you are good at and read it out loud to yourself at least three times a day until you gain confidence in your abilities. Thinking about what you're good at is not conceited; it is preparation to do your job with confidence. I know that anything I am good at is because God has gifted me in that area, and I thank Him all the time for the abilities He has equipped me with.

I encourage you to be bold enough to do this. Make positive affirmations to yourself every day about your qualities. Jesus came to take care of what you could not do, so let Him do His job and thank Him for it.

Lord, thank You for the abilities You have given me. I recognize them, and I ask You to show me the best way I can use them. Amen.

Take the Step

[Jesus] *said, Come! So Peter got out of the boat and walked on the*
water, and he came toward Jesus.   —MATTHEW 14:29

Perhaps the boat you need to get out of is your past. Sometimes we
get so addicted to murmuring about the past and blaming the past for
everything that we miss our whole future. You're not going to enjoy your
future, and you're not going to enjoy your right now, if all you can do
is be guilty and ashamed and afraid of your past. What is it that you're
afraid somebody will find out that will cause them to turn against you?

Anything you have to keep hidden has power over you. You are not
going to ever be free if you just keep running away from your past. You
have to confront and deal with it. No one is going to come along and
do it for you. Jesus is calling you out of the boat. God has given you His
power, and His Spirit is dwelling in you, so you can do things that are
hard to do. You can do anything you need to do. He isn't going to get
into your boat and make you feel better. Get it out of your system. Get
out of the boat of your past.

Lord, I will not stay stuck in my past. By Your grace, the past
has been forgiven, and I have a new life in You. If there's
something in my past that needs to be dealt with, show me
how to do it in the right way. Amen.

Never Stop Trying

*Therefore, my beloved brethren, be firm (steadfast), immovable,
always abounding in the work of the Lord [always being superior,
excelling, doing more than enough in the service of the Lord],
knowing and being continually aware that your labor in the Lord
is not futile [it is never wasted or to no purpose].*

—1 CORINTHIANS 15:58

A confident woman recovers from setbacks. We don't need to see
setbacks as failures. A person is not a failure because she tried some
things that did not work out. She fails only when she stops trying. Most
of the people who are huge successes failed on their way to success.
Instead of allowing mistakes to stop you, let them train you. I always
say that if I step out and try something and it does not work, at least I
know not to do that again.

Many people are confused about what they are to do with their lives.
They don't know what God's will is for them; they are without direction. I felt the same way once, but I discovered my destiny by trying
several things, experiencing some disappointments—but it all worked
out well in the end. I quickly found where I fit when I was asked to
teach God's Word at church. I thank God that I was confident enough
to step out and discover what was right for me.

Will you "step out" today?

**Lord, I'm excited to be able to step out and try new things,
even if they don't work. Help me to discover my role of service
for You, the work You have called me to do. Amen.**

Worry Is a Waste

Therefore I tell you, stop being perpetually uneasy (anxious and worried) about your life, what you shall eat or what you shall drink; or about your body, what you shall put on. Is not life greater [in quality] than food, and the body [far above and more excellent] than clothing?   —MATTHEW 6:25

Once you allow the spirit of fear to take hold of your life, you open the door to other spirits that want to grip your heart and cause you to freeze up, unable to move forward in confidence and assurance. Worry and dread are both relatives of the spirit of fear. Or look at it this way: Fear is the parent, and worry and dread are the children. The Bible clearly teaches that God's children are not to worry. When we worry, we rotate our minds around and around a problem and come up with no answers. The more we do it, the more anxious we feel.

Worry starts with our thoughts, but it affects our moods and even our physical bodies. A person can worry so much that it makes them feel depressed and sad. Worry places stress on your entire system and causes a lot of physical ailments, such as headaches, tension in muscles, and stomach problems. It's no wonder that 80 percent of chronic worriers also have a poor self-image—their confidence has been eaten up by fear and doubt!

Resist worry and fear. They accomplish nothing and are of the enemy.

————————

Lord, You know what I'm worrying about even as I pray. Help me to see through the lie that I am believing and to replace it with truth. Amen.

Give God Everything

If we [freely] admit that we have sinned and confess our sins, He is faithful and just (true to His own nature and promises) and will forgive our sins [dismiss our lawlessness] and [continuously] cleanse us from all unrighteousness [everything not in conformity to His will in purpose, thought, and action].   —1 JOHN 1:9

I don't know about you, but every day I tell the Lord, "Father, You are looking at a desperate woman. I need You, Lord. Without You I can do nothing."

The Bible teaches us that if we admit our sins and confess them, He will forgive us and cleanse us from all unrighteousness. Start by freely admitting all your faults. Hold nothing back. Admit them to God and to people. Don't make excuses or place blame elsewhere. As you do this, you will experience a new freedom, and your relationship with Jesus and with people will improve greatly. I have found that if I tell people my faults before they find them on their own, neither one of us is as bothered by them. Be open with people. Most people respect and admire honesty and openness. It is what we try to hide that comes back to haunt us.

Invite Jesus into every area of your life. Don't hide your faults from Him. He knows all about them anyway. Don't hold anything back; give God everything!

———————————

Lord, I ask You to come into every area of my life. I confess my sins and faults to You and ask Your forgiveness. Cleanse me from all unrighteousness and make me whole. Amen.

Start Enjoying You

You shall not covet your neighbor's house, your neighbor's wife, or his manservant, or his maidservant, or his ox, or his donkey, or anything that is your neighbor's. —EXODUS 20:17

Other people can be examples to us but should never be our standard or a reason for us to covet who they are. The Bible says in Romans 8:29 that we are destined to be molded into the image of Jesus Christ and share inwardly His likeness. Another Scripture says that we have the mind of Christ (1 Corinthians 2:16). We can think, speak, and learn to behave as Jesus did, and He certainly did not ever compare Himself with anyone or desire to be anything other than what His Father had made Him to be. He lived to do the Father's will, not to compete with others and compare Himself with them.

I encourage you to be content with who you are. That does not mean that you cannot make progress and continually improve, but when you allow other people to become a law (rule or regulation), you are continually disappointed. God will never help you be someone else. Remember that being "different" is good; it is not a bad thing. Celebrate your uniqueness and rejoice in the future God has planned for you. Be confident and start enjoying you!

Lord, the world continually tries to conform me to be like everyone else. I thank You for making me different. Help me to be content with who I am. Amen.

Confronting Fear

*Do not be afraid of sudden terror, nor of trouble from the wicked
when it comes; for the LORD will be your confidence, and will keep
your foot from being caught.*   —PROVERBS 3:25–26 NKJV

I once heard a story of a village where the children were told, "Whatever you do, don't go near the top of the mountain. It's where the monster lives." One day, some brave young men decided they wanted to see the monster and defeat it. Halfway up the mountain, they encountered a huge roar and a terrible stench. Half the men ran down the mountain, screaming. The other half of the group got farther up the mountain and noticed the monster was smaller than they had expected—but it continued to roar and emit such a stench that all but one man ran away. As he took another step forward, the monster shrank to the size of a man. Another step, and it shrank again. It was still hideously ugly and stank, but the man could actually pick it up and hold it in the palm of his hand. He said to the monster, "Who are you?" In a tiny, high-pitched voice, the monster squeaked, "My name is Fear."

If you follow God's plan for conquering fear, you will find one day that the things that frightened you the most were really nothing at all.

———————————

**Lord, help me to begin to confront the fears I've been running
away from. I want to silence the roars that keep me from moving ahead with my life. Amen.**

Faith to Do It

For by the grace (unmerited favor of God) given to me I warn
everyone among you not to estimate and think of himself more
highly than he ought [not to have an exaggerated opinion of his
own importance], but to rate his ability with sober judgment, each
according to the degree of faith apportioned by God to him.

—ROMANS 12:3

When God told Abraham to leave his home and relatives, Abraham first had to go out before God would show him the destination (Genesis 12:1). As was true of Abraham, God has given each of us "a measure of faith." For whatever we need to do, we have the faith to do it; but for faith to work, we have to release our faith, and the way we release it is to go in obedience. We have to go with our dreams despite all the "what ifs" and the doubts from the enemy. When we make our step, God shows up.

I cried a swimming pool of tears to get to where I am, and no one was cheering for me, but I am happy and I love my life today. I remember when I woke up in the morning and wished it was time to go to bed, but not anymore.

Don't live another week where you never follow your dreams and heart.

Remember: God's rewards are overwhelming.

―――――――――

Lord, You have given me a measure of faith, and I want to live according to it. Help me to follow my heart today and not be hesitant with doubts. Amen.

God Can Fix It

And we know that all things work together for good to those who love God, to those who are the called according to His purpose.
—ROMANS 8:28 NKJV

A confident woman is not afraid to get out of her boat and shake things up. I'm not talking about doing whatever you want to do, but what you think God is leading you to do. If your heart is right, if you've done your best to seek God and done what you know to do to hear from God, and you feel like what's come to you is right, you've got to step out and find out.

I'm not afraid to make mistakes, because I know that God knows I'm doing all that I know how to do, and that I'm on a journey. I'm not where I need to be, but thank God I am not where I used to be. I'm more excited about my progress than depressed about how far I have to go. God approves of me. He doesn't approve of everything I do, but He approves of me because I love Him and my faith is in Him, and I'm doing the best I can to follow Him. You can be bold to step out for Him and try new things and do new things. God is God. He can fix it if you make a mistake.

———————

Lord, I take great confidence from the fact that You have the power to work all things together for good, even my mistakes. I delight in Your approval of my life. Amen.

God Has the Answers

But the Lord replied to her by saying, Martha, Martha, you are
anxious and troubled about many things; there is need of only one
or but a few things. Mary has chosen the good portion [that which is
to her advantage], which shall not be taken away from her.

—LUKE 10:41–42

Life has its bumps and potholes in the road. Why would anyone want to worry about tomorrow's problems? What we worry about frequently never happens anyway, and if it is going to happen, worrying won't prevent it. Worry does not make you escape your trouble; it only makes you unfit to deal with it when it comes.

God is our help in trouble (Psalm 46:1). With worry, you are on your own. When you worry, which do you worry about—what might happen or what might not happen? For worriers, the Scots have a proverb: "What may be, may not be."

A confident woman does not worry because she sees the future differently than women who are worriers. She confidently believes that with God's help she can do whatever she needs to do no matter what it is. Her positive attitude enables her to expect good things in the future, not bad ones. Confidence is the fruit of trusting God. When we trust Him, we may not have all the answers, but we are confident that He does.

Lord, thank You that You didn't leave me on my own to try to cope with all of life. I step ahead knowing that You know the way and that You'll lead me all the way. Amen.

Free from the Past

For as the heavens are high above the earth, so great are His mercy and loving-kindness toward those who reverently and worshipfully fear Him. As far as the east is from the west, so far has He removed our transgressions from us.   —PSALM 103:11–12

Millions of people destroy their lives by feeling guilty about something that is in the past and that they cannot do anything about. When God forgives our sin, He also removes the guilt. But just as we must receive His forgiveness, we must also receive freedom from guilt and not let the emotion of guilt control us. If God says we are forgiven and pronounced not guilty, we should believe His Word more than how we feel.

We frequently hear people say, "I will feel guilty about that the rest of my life." I have heard people say, "I will never get over what I have done." God's Word says that when He forgives us, He forgets the offense, and there is no more penalty for sin where there is complete remission of it (Hebrews 10:17–18). Why decide that you will feel guilty the rest of your life when God has provided a way for you to live free from the guilt?

Don't let your past failures leave you hopeless about your future success. Your future has no room in it for the failures of the past.

———————

Lord, by Your grace I am forgiven of the past as well as the guilt that wants to linger. I will not allow my past failures to spoil the future You have for me. Amen.

Freedom to Be Ourselves

Why are you cast down, O my inner self? And why should you moan over me and be disquieted within me? Hope in God and wait expectantly for Him, for I shall yet praise Him, my Help and my God.   —PSALM 42:5

Ask twenty-first-century women, "How do you feel about yourself?" and many will confess, "I hate myself." Or perhaps their opinion of themselves is not that severe, but they will admit they really don't like themselves.

Our world has created a false, unrealistic image of what women are supposed to look like and act like. But the truth is that not every woman was created by God to be skinny, with a flawless complexion and long flowing hair. Not every woman was intended to juggle a career as well as all of the other duties of being a wife, mother, citizen, and daughter. Single women should not be made to feel they are missing something because they are not married. Married women should not be made to feel they must have a career to be complete. We must have the freedom to be our individual selves.

Many women hate themselves and have no self-confidence because they have been abused, rejected, abandoned, or in some way damaged emotionally. Women need to experience a revival of knowing their infinite worth and value.

Ask God to help you be your unique self.

———————————

Lord, You know exactly how I feel about myself. You know how deeply I've been influenced by the messages of our culture and how confusing it is. Help me to discover the truth of my worth and value in Your eyes. Amen.

God Is Our Leader

I am the Vine; you are the branches. Whoever lives in Me and
I in him bears much (abundant) fruit. However, apart from Me
[cut off from vital union with Me] you can do nothing.

—JOHN 15:5

Imagine you're a member of a basketball team, captained by a point guard who is the most talented player in the world. Not only can this athlete outplay anyone else on the court, she can also bring out the best in her teammates. You can enter each game with confidence, knowing that your team leader has the knowledge and skill to lead you to victory. Sure, you will need to do your part, fulfill your role on the team, but even if you have an off game, your superstar will have you covered. She's got your back. And, as each game unfolds, you find that your leader's confidence is contagious. You can play boldly, because your captain inspires you.

So, if I say I am confident, I don't mean that I am confident in myself or my abilities. I mean that I am confident in my leader, God, and the gifts, talents, and knowledge He has placed in me. Without Him we are nothing, but with Him we can be champions, because He brings out the best in us.

———————

Lord, I'm delighted that You have welcomed me by grace onto Your team. I am glad that my confidence has been grounded in You and what You've done for me rather than in myself. I will enjoy being a branch of Your Vine today. Amen.

Secure in Christ

May Christ through your faith [actually] dwell (settle down, abide, make His permanent home) in your hearts! May you be rooted deep in love and founded securely on love. —EPHESIANS 3:17

An addiction is something that controls people—something they feel they cannot do without or something they do to alleviate pain or pressure. It is what people run to when they are hurting or feel lonely. It comes in many varieties, such as drugs, alcohol, gambling, sex, shopping, eating, work—and, yes, even approval. Like any addict, insecure people look for a "fix" when they get shaky. They need someone to reaffirm them and assure them everything is all right and they are acceptable. When a person has an addiction, the things they are addicted to are on their mind most of the time. Therefore, if a woman is an approval addict, she will have an abnormal concern and an abundance of thoughts about what people think of her.

The good news is that none of us has to suffer with insecurity; there is a cure for the approval addict. The Word of God says we can be secure and confident through Jesus Christ. That means we are free to be ourselves and become all we can be in Him.

————————

Lord, teach me what it means to be rooted deep in Your love and to be secure in my relationship with Jesus. You know my weaknesses and everything that seeks to control my life. You know the "fixes" that I have tried. Help me to know my freedom in Christ. Amen.

Draw the Line

So the king said to me, Why do you look sad, since you are not sick?...Then I was very much afraid....The king said to me, For what do you ask? So I prayed to the God of heaven.
—NEHEMIAH 2:2–4

When a boss demands so much of an employee that it is ruining her home life, her spiritual life, and perhaps her health, she is not being rebellious if she confronts the boss and states plainly what she can and cannot do. She actually would incur guilt if she did not.

God expects a person to put her marriage, her family, her home, her spiritual life, and her health before her job. If she loses her job as a result of proper confrontation, God will help her get a better one. It is sad when a person lives in so much fear of the loss of money and reputation that she allows herself to lose her health, the respect of her family, and a good relationship with God. It is sad to have the approval of someone, such as a boss, but to be out of the will of God. If you have been allowing someone to control you, you should ask yourself what price you are paying to have that person's approval. Don't play the games you have to play in order to have everyone's approval.

Lord, when it comes to doing Your will, I trust You to help me to draw the line and stand for the right values. I will stand with You. Amen.

God Forgets

I, even I, am He Who blots out and cancels your transgressions, for My own sake, and I will not remember your sins. Put Me in remembrance [remind Me of your merits]; let us plead and argue together. Set forth your case, that you may be justified (proved right).   —ISAIAH 43:25–26

God holds nothing against you if you are sincerely sorry for what you have done in the past and are trusting in the blood of Jesus to cleanse you from your former wickedness. The minute you repent, God forgives and forgets, so why not follow His example and receive His forgiveness and forget it yourself?

A confident woman does not live in the past; she lets go of it and looks to the future. It may be that you have a decision to make right now. Maybe you failed someone, or had an abortion, or committed adultery, stole something, lied, or did any number of terrible things. But God's question to you is, what are you going to do today? Will you live the rest of your life serving God and following His plan for you? If you are ready to make that commitment, there is nothing in your past that has enough power to hold you back.

Lord, help me to forget what You have forgotten regarding my past. I thank You that by Your grace I can let the past go and concentrate on the future. Show me Your plans for the days ahead. Amen.

Joy Stealers

For my sighing comes before my food, and my groanings are poured out like water. For the thing which I greatly fear comes upon me, and that of which I am afraid befalls me. I was not or am not at ease, nor had I or have I rest, nor was I or am I quiet, yet trouble came and still comes [upon me].   —JOB 3:24–26

People dread many things, and most don't even realize what dread does to them. It sucks the joy right out of the present moment. The life God has provided for us through Jesus Christ is a precious gift, and we should enjoy every moment of it.

Dread is insidious and can insert itself into even the most innocuous of circumstances. For example, once I was getting a facial and enjoying it extremely. I glanced at the door and saw my clothes hanging on the hook and thought, *Oh, I dread getting up and putting on my clothes and driving all the way home.* Then I realized I was letting dread do its dirty work again. It was stealing the joy of the present moment.

Pray and ask God to show you every time you begin to dread any task or something lurking in your future that you're not quite sure of. Merely eliminating dread from your life will release more of your God-given confidence and help you experience more joy.

———————————

Lord, make me aware of what I dread. It's such a part of my life that it's easy to not even notice. Help me to retain my joy and walk in all the confidence You've given me. Amen.

Confidently Take Action

*If you walk in My statutes and keep My commandments and do
them, I will give you rain in due season, and the land shall yield her
increase and the trees of the field yield their fruit. . . . I will give peace
in the land; you shall lie down and none shall fill you with dread or
make you afraid.*   —LEVITICUS 26:3–4, 6

How often do you find yourself putting off things that you dread
doing? Maybe it's that stack of laundry or those bills that need to be
paid. Train yourself not to dread unpleasant tasks but instead to tackle
them first. The sooner in the day you do the things you don't prefer
doing, the more energy you have to do them. If you wait until the end
of the day, it will be worse than doing your tasks earlier. Dread causes
us to procrastinate, but if you're ever going to do something, now is the
best time!

Putting something off does not make it go away; it only allows the
dread more time to torment you. You can dread or you can confidently
take action. As Christians with the power of the Holy Spirit inside of
us, surely we can manage to do an unpleasant task without dreading
it and with a good attitude. God's power is not available just to make
unpleasant things in our lives go away; it is frequently available to walk
us through them courageously.

Lord, by Your grace and power I am determined to take action
over the areas of life where I procrastinate. Help me to stop
the torment of holding back and give me courage to do the
things I must. Amen.

Hold on to Your Dreams

So it was year after year; whenever Hannah went up to the Lord's house, Peninnah provoked her...And [Hannah] was in distress of soul, praying to the Lord and weeping bitterly. She vowed, saying, O Lord of hosts, if You will indeed look on the affliction of Your handmaid and [earnestly] remember, and not forget Your handmaid but will give me a son, I will give him to the Lord all his life; no razor shall touch his head.   —1 SAMUEL 1:7, 10–11

Mary Fairfax Somerville (1780–1872) completed all of one year at a women's boarding school and is considered one of the greatest scientists of her day—but she had to learn her science the hard way. The only daughter of a Scottish admiral, she studied the Elements by Euclid and an algebra text obtained from her brother's tutor. From this unpromising beginning, she worked her way up to Newton's *Principles* and went on to study botany, astronomy, higher mathematics, and physics. Her textbook *Mechanism* became a standard in astronomy and higher mathematics for most of the nineteenth century, and *Physical Geography* caused her to be recognized throughout Europe. She became an honorary member of the Royal Astronomical Society.

Mary proved that there is always a way for the determined woman. She did not give up in the face of difficulties and what seemed to be insurmountable disadvantages. Don't give up your dreams either. Keep pressing forward!

———————————

Lord, I will not give up on the dreams You have put in my heart. I will keep pressing forward and praying until it comes to pass. Amen.

Anointed

Jesse sent and brought him. David had a healthy reddish complexion and beautiful eyes, and was fine-looking. The Lord said [to Samuel], Arise, anoint him; this is he. Then Samuel took the horn of oil and anointed David in the midst of his brothers; and the Spirit of the Lord came mightily upon David from that day forward.

—1 SAMUEL 16:12–13

When I think of the word *anointed*, I think of something being rubbed all over. We are anointed (rubbed all over) with God's power. He has anointed us with the presence and power of the Holy Spirit to help us live life in a supernatural way.

Even as spiritual people, we must deal with ordinary natural things all the time. Think about how messy your closet, garage, or basement is—it didn't get that way overnight, and it probably won't get cleaned up without some time and effort. Does a messy area of your home aggravate you every time you see it, yet you put off cleaning it up because you dread it? If so, it is time for change. I want you to attack those messes boldly and have the confidence that you can have order in your life and home. You have the power of God in your life. You are able to clean up anything in your life and do it with joy!

Lord, I receive Your Spirit afresh today and ask for Your anointing presence. Help me to bring all of my life into order and live up to the light You have given to me. Amen.

Experience True Joy

There is no fear in love [dread does not exist], but full-grown (complete, perfect) love turns fear out of doors and expels every trace of terror! For fear brings with it the thought of punishment, and [so] he who is afraid has not reached the full maturity of love [is not yet grown into love's complete perfection]. —1 JOHN 4:18

Under-confidence is a condition; it might even be considered a sickness. And just like many other sicknesses, under-confidence is caused by a deficiency of one thing (confidence) and too much of another— fear. I refer to fear as an emotional virus because it begins as a thought, then affects your emotions and behaviors—just like a flu virus might invade your body via a handshake or a sneeze and then make you feel miserable all over.

Fear is a dangerous virus, because a fearful person has no confidence and can never reach her potential in life. She won't step out of her comfort zone to do anything—especially something new or different. Fear is a cruel ruler, and its subjects live in constant torment.

It breaks my heart when I see people living fearfully, because without confidence, people can never know and experience true joy. The Holy Spirit of God Himself is grieved, because He has been sent into our lives to help us fulfill our God-ordained destinies.

Ask God today to replace your fear with faith.

Lord, I am sick and tired of living in fear and all of its repercussions in my life. I welcome the Holy Spirit to come into my life and equip me to fulfill my destiny. Amen.

Living Large

Do not [earnestly] remember the former things; neither consider the things of old. Behold, I am doing a new thing! Now it springs forth; do you not perceive and know it and will you not give heed to it? I will even make a way in the wilderness and rivers in the desert.

—ISAIAH 43:18–19

I truly believe this moment can be life-changing for you—that it will help you step out onto the path of your true life. The life that has been waiting for you since the beginning of time—and the one you may have been missing due to fear and intimidation. Satan is the master of intimidation, but once you realize that he is the one behind all your hesitation, you can take authority over him by simply placing confidence in Jesus Christ and stepping out boldly to be all you can be. God told Joshua, "Fear not, for I am with you." He is sending you that same message today: FEAR NOT! God is with you, and He will never leave you or forsake you.

Abraham was told, "God is with you in everything you do" (Genesis 21:22). That sounds like large living to me. Are you ready for a larger life, one that leaves you feeling satisfied and fulfilled? I believe you are, and I want to do everything I can to help you on your journey.

———————

Lord, I make my bold confession that I am thrilled to have You with me today and forever. Today is another step in my journey. Help me to live large. Amen.

Confidence Is Contagious

*Forty years old was I when Moses the servant of the Lord sent me
from Kadesh-barnea to scout out the land. And I brought him a
report as it was in my heart. But my brethren who went up with me
made the hearts of the people melt; yet I wholly followed the Lord my
God.*   —JOSHUA 14:7–8

I know what it is like to live in fear. Fear can actually make you sick
to your stomach. It can make you so tense and nervous that everyone
around you notices that something is wrong; it's that evident in your
facial expressions and your body language. What's more, just as confidence is contagious, so is the lack of self-confidence. When we possess
no inner confidence, no one else has confidence in us either. Imagine
a timid, cowering basketball player, standing in the corner of the court
with her arms wrapped around herself. Is anyone going to pass her the
ball? Is anybody going to call out plays to her?

When we think people are rejecting us, we feel hurt by them. The
basketball player in the example above might think that her teammates
hate her or have something against her. But, for fearful, under-confident
people, the root of the problem is that they are rejecting themselves.
They are rejecting the person God intended them to be.

**Lord, I want to wholly follow You no matter where You lead
me. I believe that You made me for who I am and I accept that
by faith. Your creation is good. Thank You. Amen.**

Over the Walls

For You, O Lord, are my Lamp; the Lord lightens my darkness. For by You I run through a troop; by my God I leap over a wall. As for God, His way is perfect; the word of the Lord is tried. He is a Shield to all those who trust and take refuge in Him.

—2 SAMUEL 22:29–31

Katie Brown is a world champion and multiple gold medalist "difficulty climber." She says, "My faith in God doesn't get rid of my healthy fear or caution when climbing extreme heights, but it does help me deal with it. It takes away a lot of the pressure, because you know that God's not going to condemn you if you don't win. So there's nothing to worry about. When I see others competing, I wonder how I could compete if I didn't have faith in God."

The "walls" you face in your life might be emotional or relational. And it's okay to feel intimidated or frightened by the walls in your life. As Katie notes, it would be unhealthy not to appreciate the significance of a major challenge. But you can rest secure in the truth that God will not condemn you if you can't get to the top of your wall—or if it takes you hundreds of attempts. God is more concerned in your faithful effort—an effort built on your confidence in His love for you.

Lord, You know the walls I face. Give me strength to leap over them . . . even if it takes a hundred tries. Amen.

Launch Out

When He had stopped speaking, He said to Simon, "Launch out into the deep and let down your nets for a catch."

—LUKE 5:4 NKJV

The only way we ever reach our final destination and succeed at being our true selves is to take many, many steps of faith. Stepping out into the unknown—into something we have never done before—can leave us shaking in our boots. Because of feelings of fear, many people never "step out," therefore they never "find out" what they are capable of.

I believe we are very close to the time when Jesus will return for His Church, and I don't think He has time to spend months and months convincing each of us to obey when He wants us to step out into something. I believe the more we progress into what we call "the last days," the more God is going to require radical steps of obedience.

Many people are missing the will of God for their lives because they are "playing it safe." I don't want to come to the end of my life and say, "I was safe, but I'm sorry."

The world has a little saying: "Better safe than sorry." I am not sure that always works in God's economy. If I had tried to be safe all the time, I am sure I would not be where I am today.

God asks us to take risks. What risks will you take in order to obey God?

———————————

Lord, there truly is no safe place apart from being with You, walking in Your will for my life. I refuse to play it safe as long as I know what You want. Amen.

Fail Forward

*Do not, therefore, fling away your fearless confidence, for it carries
a great and glorious compensation of reward. For you have need
of steadfast patience and endurance, so that you may perform and
fully accomplish the will of God, and thus receive and carry away
[and enjoy to the full] what is promised.*   —HEBREWS 10:35–36

I believe that failing is part of every success. As John Maxwell says,
"We can fail forward." History is filled with examples of people who
are famous for doing great things—yet if we study their lives, we find
that they failed miserably before they succeeded. Some of them failed
numerous times before they ever succeeded at anything. Their real
strength was not their talent as much as it was their tenacity. A person
who refuses to give up will always succeed, eventually.

Henry Ford failed and went broke five times before he succeeded.

NBA superstar Michael Jordan was once cut from his high school
basketball team.

After his first audition, screen legend Fred Astaire received the following assessment from an MGM executive: "Can't act. Slightly bald.
Can dance a little."

Best-selling author Max Lucado had his first book rejected by
fourteen publishers before finding one that was willing to give him a
chance.

A so-called football expert once said of two-time Super Bowl-
winning coach Vince Lombardi, "He possesses minimal football
knowledge. Lacks motivation."

Remember: failure is simply a detour on the road to success.

———————

**Lord, people have written me off as well, and I've failed and
will fail, but I will keep moving forward. I will be tenacious!
Amen.**

Doors Will Open

Naaman, commander of the army of the king of Syria . . . was a leper. The Syrians had gone out in bands and had brought away captive out of the land of Israel a little maid, and she waited on Naaman's wife. She said to her mistress, Would that my lord were with the prophet who is in Samaria! For he would heal him of his leprosy.

—2 KINGS 5:1–3

Elizabeth Fry (1780–1845) was a Quaker minister and European prison reformer. The mother of ten children, Mrs. Fry was invited to do social work in England's Newgate prison. She said she found "half naked women, struggling together . . . with the most boisterous violence. . . . I felt as if I were going into a den of wild beasts." Mrs. Fry did nothing sophisticated to initiate reform but began reading her Bible to prisoners. She went on to such innovations as suggesting that men and women be segregated in prison, that more violent offenders be kept from the less violent, and that prisoners be employed in some useful work. Her influence ranged throughout France and the British Colonies.

If you will do what you can do, God will do what you cannot do. Doors will open, a way will be made, and creative ideas will come. You will also inspire others to do what they can do, and even though each person can only do a little, together we can make a big difference.

Lord, help me to do what I can do in whatever circumstance I am to bring about good. If You can use a little maid in exile, You can use me. Amen.

Seeing the Invisible One

By faith he forsook Egypt, not fearing the wrath of the king; for he endured as seeing Him who is invisible. —HEBREWS 11:27 NKJV

A shining example of perseverance is renowned pastor John Wesley. Let's take a peek into his diary:

Sunday, A.M., May 5—Preached in St. Anne's. Was asked not to come back any more.

Sunday, A.M., May 12—Preached in St. Jude's. Can't go back there, either.

Sunday, A.M., May 19—Preached in St. Somebody Else's. Deacons called a special meeting and said I couldn't return.

Sunday, P.M., May 19—Preached on street. Kicked off street.

Sunday, A.M., May 26—Preached in meadow. Chased out of meadow as bull was turned loose during service.

Sunday, A.M., June 2—Preached out at the edge of town. Kicked off the highway.

Sunday, P.M., June 2—Afternoon, preached in a pasture. Ten thousand people came out to hear me.

Mr. Wesley ultimately succeeded because he had a classic case of confidence. A refusal to give up is one of the components of confidence. I encourage you to keep trying, and if at first you don't succeed, try, try, again!

———

Lord, I know the secret to my success lies in seeing You . . . even though You're invisible. Give me eyes of faith that behold You in the midst of my days, even today. Amen.

Created by God

God said, Let Us [Father, Son, and Holy Spirit] make mankind in Our image, after Our likeness, and let them have complete authority over the fish of the sea, the birds of the air, the [tame] beasts, and over all of the earth, and over everything that creeps upon the earth. So God created man in His own image, in the image and likeness of God He created him; male and female He created them.

—GENESIS 1:26–27

God created women, and He said that everything He created was very good. Learn to believe about yourself what God says about you, not what other people have said about you. God created you, and He looked at you and proclaimed, "Very good!" You are one of God's works of art, and Psalm 139 states all of His works are wonderful. Therefore, you must be wonderful!

God never intended for women to be less than men in anyone's estimation. Neither are they above men. Both genders should work together for the common good of all. The competitive spirit that exists in our society today between men and women is downright foolish. When women began to realize they would have to fight for their rights, some of them became extreme in their attitudes. It seems that we imperfect human beings always live in the ditch on one side or the other. The key to peace between the sexes is balance.

Lord, plant Your words of life in my soul and help me make them real. I want to live up to Your "very good." Amen.

Get Moving

Elijah said to Elisha, Ask what I shall do for you before I am taken from you. And Elisha said, I pray you, let a double portion of your spirit be upon me. He said, You have asked a hard thing. However, if you see me when I am taken from you, it shall be so for you.

—2 KINGS 2:9–10

Just as under-confidence comes with its list of symptoms, the same is true of confidence. A confident woman believes she is loved, valuable, cared for, and safe in God's will. When we feel secure, it's easy to step out and take a chance on failing in order to try to succeed. When we know we are loved for ourselves and not just for our accomplishments or performance, we no longer need to fear failure. We realize that failing at something does not make us a failure at everything. We are free to explore and find out what we are best suited to do. We are free to find our own niche in life, which is not possible without stepping out.

Trial and error is the road to success, and you can't drive that road as long as your car is parked. So get moving, and God will direct you. When people are confident, they try things, and they keep trying until they find a way to be successful in what God has called them to do.

———————————

Lord, I want to explore all that You have for me, and I accept there may be failures. Show me the way to be successful for You. Amen.

Be Yourself

But by the grace of God I am what I am, and His grace toward me was not in vain; but I labored more abundantly than they all, yet not I, but the grace of God which was with me.

—1 CORINTHIANS 15:10 NKJV

A person without confidence is like an airplane sitting on a runway with empty fuel tanks. The plane has the ability to fly, but without some fuel, it's not getting off the ground. Confidence is our fuel. Our confidence, our belief that we can succeed, gets us started and helps us finish every challenge we tackle in life. Without confidence, a woman will live in fear and never feel fulfilled.

Confidence allows us to face life with boldness, openness, and honesty. It enables us to live without worry and to feel safe. It enables us to live authentically. We don't have to pretend to be somebody we're not, because we are secure in who we are—even if we're different from those around us. I firmly believe that confidence gives us permission to be different, to be unique. God has created every person in a unique way, yet most people spend their lives trying to be like someone else—and feeling miserable as a result. Trust me on this: God will never help you be some other person. He wants you to be you!

———————————

Lord, I want to be able to say confidently that by Your grace I am what am. I confess that Your grace has never been in vain in my life, and I ask You for more grace. Amen.

Christ Is Our Confidence

For we [Christians] are the true circumcision, who worship God
in spirit and by the Spirit of God and exult and glory and pride
ourselves in Jesus Christ, and put no confidence or dependence
[on what we are] in the flesh and on outward privileges and physical
advantages and external appearances.   —PHILIPPIANS 3:3

God is merciful toward us and wants to bless and prosper us. He sees our heart attitude and our faith in Jesus. When we have confidence in God and His love and kindness, we can progress to living confidently and enjoying the life He wants for us. Note that I said confidence in God, not in ourselves. Usually, people think of confidence as self-confidence, such as TV self-help gurus or athletes promote when urging us to "Believe in yourself!"

I beg to differ. I want to make it clear, right from the start, that our confidence must be in Christ alone, not in ourselves, not in other people, not in the world or its systems. The Bible states that we are sufficient in Christ's sufficiency (Philippians 4:13), so we might also say that we are confident through Christ's confidence. Or another way to say it would be, "We have self-confidence only because He lives in us, and it is His confidence that we draw on."

———————

Lord, I know that far too often I put my confidence in my own abilities, or other people, or the place I work to provide for my needs. I fix my eyes upon You. You alone are worthy of being my confidence. Amen.

Think Positively

Finally, brethren, whatever things are true, whatever things are noble, whatever things are just, whatever things are pure, whatever things are lovely, whatever things are of good report, if there is any virtue and if there is anything praiseworthy—meditate on these things.   —PHILIPPIANS 4:8 NKJV

I once interviewed a minister and his wife on our ministry's television program. I asked the man what his weaknesses were. His answer: "You know, I don't concentrate on them. I am sure I have some, but I couldn't tell you right now what they are because I just don't focus on them." I laughingly replied that I would ask his wife later. I was sure she would know his weaknesses, even if he didn't. When she joined us later in the broadcast, I promptly popped that question to her. She replied, "To me, my husband is perfect; I don't focus on his weaknesses. He has so many strengths that I just focus on them and help him be all he can be."

It didn't take me long to understand why these two were so happy and upbeat all the time—and why they had such a wonderful marriage. Confident people make it a habit to think and act positively. Therefore, they enjoy life, and they accomplish a lot.

Focus on the positives today and see how your perspective changes.

———————————

Lord, it seems as though it's a lot easier to see others' negatives rather than their positives. Help me to see others through Your eyes, especially my loved ones and those with whom I am closest. I want to bless and support them as You do. Amen.

Begin Again

On the day after the Passover the Israelites went out [of Egypt] with a high hand and triumphantly in the sight of all the Egyptians, while the Egyptians were burying all their firstborn whom the Lord had struck down among them. —NUMBERS 33:3–4

Are you doing what you really believe you should be doing at this stage in your life, or have you allowed fear and a lack of confidence to prevent you from stepping out into new things—or higher levels of old things? If you don't like your answer, then let me give you some good news: It is never too late to begin again! Don't spend one more day living a narrow life that has room for only you and your fears. Make a decision right now that you will learn to live boldly, aggressively, and confidently. Don't let fear rule you any longer.

It's important to note that you can't just sit around and wait for fear to go away. You will have to feel the fear and take action anyway. Or, as John Wayne put it, "Courage is being scared to death, but saddling up anyway." In other words, courage is not the absence of fear; it is action in the presence of fear. Bold people do what they know they should do—not what they feel like doing.

———————————

Lord, show me any narrowness in my life and help me to take the steps of faith that break the rule of fear over my life. Amen.

When You Feel Afraid

Though fear had come upon them because of the people of those countries, they set the altar on its bases; and they offered burnt offerings on it to the LORD, both the morning and evening burnt offerings. They also kept the Feast of Tabernacles, as it is written.

—EZRA 3:3–4 NKJV

Just because ordinary people take steps to accomplish extraordinary things does not mean that they do not feel fear. I believe the Old Testament hero Esther felt fear when she was asked to leave her familiar, comfortable life and enter the king's harem so she could be used by God to save her nation. I believe Joshua felt fear when, after Moses died, he was given the job of taking the Israelites into the Promised Land. I know I had fear when God called me to quit my job and prepare for ministry. I still remember my knees shaking and my legs feeling so weak that I thought I would fall down. I remember the fear I felt then, but it frightens me more now to think of how my life would have turned out had I not faced the fear and pressed forward to do God's will.

Fear does not mean you are a coward. It only means that you need to be willing to feel the fear and do what you need to do anyway.

———————————

Lord, thank You for the many examples in Your Word of individuals who stepped forward in faith despite their fears. Help me to do the same. Amen.

Safe in Christ

But now [in spite of past judgments for Israel's sins], thus says the
Lord, He Who created you, O Jacob, and He Who formed you, O
Israel: Fear not, for I have redeemed you [ransomed you by paying
a price instead of leaving you captives]; I have called you by your
name; you are Mine.   —ISAIAH 43:1

A sense of security is something everyone needs and desires. Security enables us to enjoy healthy thinking and living. It means we feel safe, accepted, and approved of. When we are secure, we approve of ourselves, we have confidence, and we accept and love ourselves in a balanced way.

You can't seek out your destiny when you've let fear slam and lock the door of your life. Instead, you cower behind the door, filled with self-hatred, condemnation, fear of rejection, fear of failure, and fear of others. Many victims of fear end up being people pleasers, prone to being controlled and manipulated by others. They give up the right to be themselves and usually spend their lives trying to be what they think they ought to be in someone else's eyes.

Sadly, when we try to be something or someone we are not intended to be, we stifle ourselves and God's power in us. Without confidence, even simple accomplishments are beyond our grasp. When we have confidence, we can reach truly amazing heights.

———————————

Lord, You have redeemed me and called me by name. I am
Yours. I refuse to allow fear to lock the door on my life. Thank
You that I don't have to be a people pleaser. Amen.

The New and Living Way

Therefore, brethren...we have full freedom and confidence to enter into the [Holy of] Holies [by the power and virtue] in the blood of Jesus, by this fresh (new) and living way which He initiated and dedicated and opened for us.   —HEBREWS 10:19–20

Believing we are made right with God through our faith in Jesus Christ is a new and living way, one that gives us freedom, boldness, and confidence. Trying to follow the law (trying to do everything right) in order to earn acceptance ministers death (every kind of misery) to us. Grace is God's power coming to us free of charge to help us do with ease what we could never accomplish on our own. Grace is freeing! It puts the burden to perform on God, rather than on us. As believers in Jesus Christ, our work is to believe while God works on our behalf.

I cannot make myself acceptable to all people, and neither can you, but we can believe God will give us favor with the people He wants us involved with. Sometimes we try to have relationships with people God does not even want us to be associated with. Knowing who we are in Christ sets us free from the need to impress others. Once we know who we are and accept ourselves, we no longer have anything to prove.

If God is for you, who can be against you?

———————————

Lord, thank You today for Your grace and all the freedom it brings. I ask You to help me to be free in my relationships as well. Give me favor with the right people. Amen.

Supernatural Rest

Let us therefore be zealous and exert ourselves and strive diligently to enter that rest [of God, to know and experience it for ourselves], that no one may fall or perish by the same kind of unbelief and disobedience [into which those in the wilderness fell].

—HEBREWS 4:11

Trust is confidence; confidence gives us boldness, and boldness does not allow fear to hinder its progress. Boldness is action in the face of fear. Babies naturally trust, but as they have experiences in life, sadly, they learn how to fear. They learn that everything and everyone in their life is not stable. People and circumstances change. A child may trust that mom and dad will always love each other and be together. But if mom and dad get a divorce, the child's world comes crashing in because something they never even conceived could happen did happen.

As children continue to mature and encounter various disappointing circumstances, they either distrust more and more, or they learn how to trust God who never changes and is always faithful. This does not mean that God always does what we expect Him to do or even what we want Him to do, but He is good. Trusting Him brings a supernatural rest into our soul that allows us to enjoy life and live free from the tyranny of fear.

———————————

Lord, all of life is changing constantly, except for You. You are ever faithful, and I enter into the supernatural rest that only comes through completely trusting in You. Bless Your name forever and ever. Amen.

Different Is Good

The sun is glorious in one way, the moon is glorious in another way, and the stars are glorious in their own [distinctive] way; for one star differs from and surpasses another in its beauty and brilliance.

—1 CORINTHIANS 15:41

Like the sun, the moon, and the stars, God has created us to be different from one another, and He has done it on purpose. Each of us meets a need, and we are all part of God's overall plan. When we try to be like others, we lose ourselves, and we grieve the Holy Spirit. God wants us to fit into His plan, not to feel pressured trying to fit into everyone else's plans. It is all right to be different.

We should be free to love and accept ourselves and one another without feeling pressure to compare or compete. Secure people who know God loves them and has a plan for them are not threatened by the abilities of others. They enjoy what other people can do, and they enjoy what they can do.

We are all born with different temperaments, different physical features, different fingerprints, different gifts and abilities. God gave us gifts and wants us to focus on our potential instead of our limitations. Our goal should be to find out what we individually are supposed to be, and then succeed at being that.

Lord, I am so glad that I can be free to love and accept others rather than compete with or compare myself with them. Thank You for making me unique. Amen.

A Spokesperson for God

Now Deborah, a prophetess, the wife of Lappidoth, judged Israel at that time. She sat under the palm tree of Deborah between Ramah and Bethel in the hill country of Ephraim, and the Israelites came up to her for judgment.   —JUDGES 4:4–5

Whether we look at Miriam, Deborah, Esther, and Ruth in the Old Testament or Mary the mother of Jesus, Mary Magdalene, or Priscilla in the New Testament, we easily see that God has always used women in ministry. For instance, Deborah was a prophetess and a judge. As a prophetess, she was a spokesperson for God. As a judge, she made decisions on God's behalf.

When God needed someone to save the Jews from the destruction that wicked Haman had planned for them, He called upon Esther (Esther 4:14). If God is against using women, why didn't He call a man for this job? Esther sacrificed her plans as a young woman and allowed herself to be taken into the king's harem in order to be in a position to speak on behalf of God's people when the time came to do so. Because of her obedience, God gave her favor with the king, and she exposed a plot to kill all of the Jews. She saved her nation and became a queen who held a high position of leadership in the land and cared for the poor. How does God want to use you? Will you let him?

———————

Lord, help me to be a spokesperson for You today. Wherever You put me, I will do whatever it takes to represent Your great name. Amen.

The Simplicity of Faith

*But [now] I am fearful, lest that even as the serpent beguiled Eve
by his cunning, so your minds may be corrupted and seduced from
wholehearted and sincere and pure devotion to Christ.*

—2 CORINTHIANS 11:3

Believing God really is simple, yet we make it very complicated. The
Bible says we must become as little children or we will not enter the
kingdom of God (Matthew 18:3). Little children are simple. They usually believe what adults whom they trust tell them. They don't try to
figure everything out; they simply believe. Hebrews 4 teaches us that
we can enter the rest of God through believing (v. 3). It says we should
be zealous and exert ourselves and strive diligently to enter the rest of
God. We should have knowledge of it and experience it for ourselves
(v. 11). Those who have entered the rest of God have ceased from the
weariness and pain of human labors (v. 10). They are not tied up in
knots; they are relaxed, secure, and free to be themselves.

We can even enter the rest of God concerning what people think of
us and whether they approve of us. We can become so secure in Christ
that as long as we know our heart is right, we know whatever people
think of us is between them and God and not our concern.

**Lord, it is good news that I can rest in You. I come as a child
in simple faith in You and what You have done for me. That is
enough for me. I rest in You. Amen.**

Shine

Let your light so shine before men that they may see your moral
excellence and your praiseworthy, noble, and good deeds and
recognize and honor and praise and glorify your Father Who is
in heaven.   —MATTHEW 5:16

Some people never realize the fulfillment of their dreams because they always play it safe. Although safety is necessary, too much of it is merely another manifestation of fear.

What if Henry Ford had simply been content to run a sawmill instead of going on to pursue being an engineer and ultimately one of our nation's first automobile creators? What if Alexander Graham Bell had listened to his friends and family and focused on the telegraph instead of his telephone invention? What if Jonas Salk, the scientist who discovered the vaccine for polio, had followed his initial "safe" inclination to go into law instead of medical research?

Always living in the safe zone of life and never taking chances actually makes one a thief and a robber. You might think that statement is a bit strong, but the truth is always strong, and the truth also makes us free. If you spend your life keeping yourself safe, you rob everyone else of your gifts and talents simply because you are too afraid to step out and be willing to find out what you can do in life.

Step out of your safe zone and let God surprise you.

Lord, I want my life to shine in such a way that You get the glory. I know that involves using my gifts and talents. Help me to be my best. Amen.

God's Guarantee

Have not I commanded you? Be strong, vigorous, and very
courageous. Be not afraid, neither be dismayed, for the Lord your
God is with you wherever you go.   —JOSHUA 1:9

Notice the emphasis that God places on Himself. Joshua was to keep his eyes on God and His command. He was not to get entangled in other things that might frighten him; he was to stay focused on his goal. If he obeyed God, he would not only help himself, he would also have the privilege of leading multitudes of people into a better life.

And just in case he needed one last encouragement, God basically repeats Himself in saying He would be with Joshua. I believe His discourse to Joshua is evidence that there would naturally be reasons for him to fear and become dismayed and want to turn back. When we take steps of faith to make progress in life, there is no guarantee that we will not experience opposition. But we do have God's guarantee that He will always be with us, and that is truly all we need. We don't need to know what God is going to do, how He is going to do it, or when He is going to do it. We only need to know that He is with us.

———————————

Lord, of all the blessings in life, the greatest one I ask You for is that You will be with me as You were with Joshua. I can do without a lot of things, but not without You. Amen.

Do What You Can

Do not be deceived and deluded and misled; God will not allow
Himself to be sneered at (scorned, disdained, or mocked by mere
pretensions or professions, or by His precepts being set aside).
[He inevitably deludes himself who attempts to delude God.] For
whatever a man sows, that and that only is what he will reap.
                                                                —GALATIANS 6:7

Get up and start doing whatever you can do to get the messes in your
life cleaned up. If they are marriage messes, do your part. Don't worry
about what your spouse is not doing; just do your part and God will
reward you. If you have a financial mess, stop spending and start paying off your debts. Get an extra job for a period of time if you need
to. If you are not able to do that, ask God to show you what you can
do. Remember, you cannot have a harvest without first sowing seed of
some kind.

A lot of laziness is rooted in fear. People are so afraid to do something that they form a habit of doing nothing. They sit idly by and
become jealous of the people who have the life they would like to have.
They fail to realize that "Things cannot work out for them if they don't
work!"

Remember: "If you do what you can do, God will do what you cannot do."

———————————

**Lord, I will begin to sow whatever I can to change the messes
of my life. I cannot clean them up without Your help, but I can
do my part. Amen.**

Determination

Persecutions, sufferings . . . I endured, but out of them all the Lord
delivered me. Indeed all who delight in piety and are determined
to live a devoted and godly life in Christ Jesus will meet with
persecution [will be made to suffer because of their religious stand].
—2 TIMOTHY 3:11–12

In the beginning of my ministry, I had a dream that I was driving my car and approaching a flooded bridge. I stopped, looking first at the water-covered bridge, back where I had been, and to the side of the road, trying to decide if I should park, retreat, or keep moving forward. Then I woke up.

God used that dream to show me that there will always be opposition when pressing toward a goal. There will always be opportunity to park and go no farther or turn around and give up. It was up to me to decide each time if I would give up or go on. That dream has helped me many times to press on when difficulties came and I was tempted to quit. I have decided that even though I don't always do everything right, I will never quit! Determination will get you a lot further than talent. So if you feel you lack in talent, take heart. All you need to win in life is more determination than anyone else you know.

Lord, today may have its challenges, but I am determined to press on following Your will. By Your grace, I will go the distance and never quit. Amen.

Whatever You Face

And the Lord turned and looked at Peter. And Peter recalled the Lord's words, how He had told him, Before the cock crows today, you will deny Me thrice. And he went out and wept bitterly [that is, with painfully moving grief].   —LUKE 22:61–62

The apostle Peter was a man who began with phony boldness. He thought he was bold, but in reality he was forward, presumptuous, rude, and foolish on many occasions. Peter was usually the first one to speak, but what he said was often prideful and completely out of place. Peter thought more highly of himself than he should have. He needed to trade his self-confidence for confidence in God.

Jesus tried to warn Peter that he would deny Him three times in a very short period of time, but Peter thought that was absolutely impossible. After Jesus allowed Himself to be captured, Peter was recognized as one of His disciples. He immediately denied that he even knew Him. Peter continued on with the same fearful response until he quickly denied Christ three times. Peter, who appeared to be so bold, fell apart in fear during a real crisis (Luke 22).

What are you facing right now? Are there threatening circumstances looming in front of you? If so, remember that God is with you and He will never leave you or forsake you.

Lord, it's always humbling to read about Peter's denial. I need the strength that comes from You more than I can possibly realize. Help me to draw so close to You today that I can face any challenge. Amen.

Steps of Faith

There was a certain man there who had suffered with a deep-seated and lingering disorder for thirty-eight years. When Jesus noticed him lying there [helpless], knowing that he had already been a long time in that condition, He said to him, Do you want to become well?

—JOHN 5:5–6

Maybe you've had so much fear in your life for so long that you can't see how you can ever be free from it. I have experienced a lot of fear in my own life, and I know it takes a lot of courage to face what you fear the most. But God's promises are not for a specially selected few people; they are for everyone. If God can help anyone at all, He can help you face your fears. God's promises offer hope and an opportunity for a new life for you—a life lived boldly and aggressively instead of by fear and uncertainty.

I can assure you that taking the steps of faith you need to do in order to enjoy a life of freedom is definitely not as difficult as staying in bondage for the rest of your life. We need to remember that God is our partner and realize that He has a part and we have a part. When we do our part, praying and stretching our spiritual muscles in faith, each time we confront fear, it becomes smaller and smaller.

Lord, show the steps of faith I must take to break any bondages of fear in my life. I cling to Your promises to live with boldness and certainty. Amen.

God's Approval

Now am I trying to win the favor of men, or of God? Do I seek to please men? If I were still seeking popularity with men, I should not be a bond servant of Christ (the Messiah).   —GALATIANS 1:10

There is an epidemic of insecurity in our society today. Many people are insecure and feel bad about themselves, which steals their joy and causes major problems in all their relationships.

I know the effect insecurity can have on lives because I experienced it myself. Those who have been hurt badly often seek the approval of others to try to overcome their feelings of rejection and low self-esteem. They suffer from those feelings and use the addiction of approval to try to remove the pain. They are miserable if anyone seems to not approve of them in any way or for any reason, and they are anxious about the disapproval until they feel they are once again accepted. They may do almost anything to gain the approval they feel they have lost—even things their conscience tells them are wrong. For example, if a person is met with disapproval when she declines an invitation, she might change her plans and accept the invitation just to gain approval. She compromises herself for the sake of feeling approved.

Remember whose approval you should truly seek—God's.

Lord, it's true that You are the only one whom I need to please. Today, help me to not compromise myself or be a slave to pleasing others, no matter what I feel. I seek Your favor alone. Amen.

Learn to Say No

The messenger who went to call Micaiah said to him, Behold now, the prophets unanimously declare good to the king. Let your answer, I pray you, be like theirs, and say what is good. But Micaiah said, As the Lord lives, I will speak what the Lord says to me.

—1 KINGS 22:13–14

Anyone who says yes to everyone all the time is headed for trouble. When people want you to do something, they definitely won't be happy if you tell them no, but sooner or later you must decide if you're going to spend your life making other people happy at the expense of never being happy yourself.

There should always be times when we do things for other people just because we want to make them happy, even if the thing they want is not what we would prefer doing. To live that way all the time, however, is not healthy emotionally or in any other way.

Sometimes you have to say no to others in order to say yes to yourself, otherwise you will end up bitter and resentful. A confident woman can say no when she needs to. She can endure people's displeasure and is able to reason that if the disappointed person truly wants a relationship with her, he or she will get over their disappointment and want her to be free to make her own decisions.

Lord, give me the courage to say no to others when pleasing them will only damage me. I cannot live to please others. Amen.

Circle of Friends

*And Ruth said, Urge me not to leave you or to turn back from
following you; for where you go I will go, and where you lodge I will
lodge. Your people shall be my people and your God my God. Where
you die I will die, and there will I be buried. The Lord do so to me,
and more also, if anything but death parts me from you.*

—RUTH 1:16–17

A confident woman knows that she is loved. She does not fear being
unloved, because she knows first and foremost that God loves her
unconditionally. To be whole and complete, we need to know that we
are loved. Everyone desires and needs love and acceptance from God
and others. Although not everyone will accept and love us, some will.
I encourage you to concentrate on those who do love you and forget
about those who don't. God certainly does love us, and He can provide others who do as well—if we'll look to Him and stop making bad
choices about whom we bring into our circle of inclusion.

I believe we need to have what I call "divine connections." In other
words, pray about your circle of friends. Don't just decide what social
group you want to be part of and then try to get into it. Instead, follow
the leading of the Holy Spirit in choosing with whom you want to asso-
ciate closely.

**Lord, I ask You to bring the right friends into my life. Give
me wisdom to know whom to welcome into my circle of
friends. Amen.**

Destined by Love

*Even as [in His love] He chose us [actually picked us out for Himself
as His own] in Christ before the foundation of the world, that we
should be holy (consecrated and set apart for Him) and blameless
in His sight, even above reproach, before Him in love. For He
foreordained us (destined us, planned in love for us) to be adopted
(revealed) as His own children through Jesus Christ.*

—EPHESIANS 1:4–5

There are women who feel so bad about themselves that they get
involved with men who will hurt them because they believe that is all
they deserve. You need to be around safe people, not people who continue to wound you. God will help you learn to recognize those people
if you listen to His wisdom.

The first place to start if you need to be loved is with God. He is a
Father who wants to shower love and blessings upon His children. If
your natural father did not love you properly, you can now get from
God what you missed in your childhood. Love is the healing balm that
the world needs, and God offers it freely and continuously. His love is
unconditional. He does not love us IF; He simply and for all time loves
us. He does not love us because we deserve it; He loves us because He
is kind and wants to.

———————————

**Lord, Your eternal love surrounds me today, and I receive it
with a heart full of praise. I am secure in Your love and kindness, given to me unconditionally. Amen.**

The Foundation of Love

See what [an incredible] quality of love the Father has given (shown, bestowed on) us, that we should [be permitted to] be named and called and counted the children of God! And so we are! The reason that the world does not know (recognize, acknowledge) us is that it does not know (recognize, acknowledge) Him.

—1 JOHN 3:1

Many people fail at marriage because they don't love themselves, and therefore they have nothing to give in the relationship. They spend most of their time trying to get from their spouses what only God can give them, which is a sense of their own worth and value. In my case, although I didn't even know what love was, I married a boy of nineteen simply because I was afraid no one would ever want me. He had problems of his own and did not really know how to love me—so the pattern of pain in my life continued. I was repeatedly hurt in that relationship, which ended in divorce after five years.

Receiving the free gift of God's unconditional love is the beginning of our healing, and the foundation for our new life in Christ. We cannot love ourselves unless we realize how much God loves us, and if we don't love ourselves, we cannot love other people. We can only maintain good, healthy relationships with this foundation of love in our lives.

Lord, I am amazed that You love me and desire me to be Your daughter. I receive Your love today and choose to love myself. Amen.

Believe and Receive

Yes, I have loved you with an everlasting love; therefore with lovingkindness I have drawn you.

—JEREMIAH 31:3 NKJV

There is only one thing you can do with a free gift, and that is receive it and be grateful. I urge you to take a step of faith right now and say out loud, "God loves me unconditionally, and I receive His love!" It took me a long time to fully accept His love. When you feel unlovable, it is hard to get it through your head and down into your heart that God loves you perfectly—even though you are not perfect and never will be as long as you are on the earth. You may have to say it a hundred times a day, like I did for months, before it finally sinks in, but when it does it will be the happiest day of your life. To know that you are loved by someone you can trust is the best and most comforting feeling in the world. God will not only love you that way, but He will also provide other people who will truly love you. When He does provide, be sure to remain thankful for those people. Having people who genuinely love you is one of the most precious gifts in the world.

God loves you! God loves you! God loves you! Believe it and receive it!

Lord, I declare Your everlasting love for me. You have drawn me with loving-kindness, and I believe and receive it. Amen.

Covered with Armor

Put on God's whole armor [the armor of a heavy-armed soldier which God supplies], that you may be able successfully to stand up against [all] the strategies and the deceits of the devil.

—EPHESIANS 6:11

When Adam and Eve sinned in the Garden of Eden, the first thing they did was run away and try to hide from the presence of God. It didn't work for them, and it won't work for us either. God had to intervene with a plan for their redemption, and He has one for us.

Take a look at Ephesians 6 and notice what battle armor God provides us with. He tells us to stand firm with a belt of truth, a breastplate of righteousness, shoes of the gospel of peace, a shield of faith, a helmet of salvation, and the sword of the Spirit, and to pray at all times in the Spirit. Notice there's nothing provided to protect our backside! That's because God never intended us to run from our enemies. His plan was and still is that with Him at our side we confront any issue in our life that is a problem. People are so skilled at not facing real issues, and they're even better at trying to cover them up by living make-believe lives and inventing false personalities. It is time to take a stand and confront fear!

Lord, life is more than a struggle; it's a spiritual battle with evil enemies set upon my destruction. Equip me with Your armor that I might take my stand and never run. Amen.

Do It Afraid

For [the Spirit which] you have now received [is] not a spirit of slavery to put you once more in bondage to fear, but you have received the Spirit of adoption [the Spirit producing sonship] in [the bliss of] which we cry, Abba (Father)! Father!

—ROMANS 8:15

We should strive to do everything with a spirit of faith. Faith is confidence in God and a belief that His promises are true. When a person begins to walk in faith, Satan immediately tries to hinder her through many things, including fear. Faith will cause a person to go forward, to try new things, and to be aggressive. I believe fear is the main evil force that Satan uses against people. Fear causes people to bury their talents due to fear of failure, judgment, or criticism. It causes them to draw back in misery and live in torment.

God wants to teach us to walk in the Spirit, not the flesh, and that includes emotions. Unless we make a firm decision to "fear not," we will never be free from the power of it. I encourage you to be firm in your resolve to do whatever you need to do, even if you have to "do it afraid!" To "do it afraid" means to feel the fear and do what you believe you should do anyway. The only thing we really need to do is fear God reverentially.

Lord, thank You for sending the Holy Spirit into my life. I will walk with You by faith today and live as a child of the King. Amen.

Encourage Yourself

David was greatly distressed, for the men spoke of stoning him because the souls of them all were bitterly grieved, each man for his sons and daughters. But David encouraged and strengthened himself in the Lord his God. David said to Abiathar the priest, . . . bring me the ephod.   —1 SAMUEL 30:6–7

God corrects and chastises us when we need it, but He also encourages us along the way. This is how we should raise our children. As a matter of fact, Paul said in his letter to the Colossians that fathers were not to place undue and unnecessary chastisement on their children, lest it discourage them, make them feel inferior, frustrate them, and break their spirits (Colossians 3:21). If God gives earthly fathers that instruction, then He certainly will be no different toward His children.

So please remember that when discouragement comes from any source, it isn't God sending it your way! Immediately reject it, and if you have no other source of encouragement, do what David did. The Bible says that he encouraged himself in the Lord. When you feel yourself starting to lose courage, talk to yourself! Tell yourself that you have made it through difficulties in the past and you will make it again. Remind yourself of past victories. Make a list of your blessings and read them out loud anytime you feel yourself starting to sink emotionally.

Lord, I thank You for the victories You have led me through in the past. I know that You will lead me in victory today, and I can overcome. Amen.

Be Positive

[The Lord God says] And the redeemed of the Lord shall return and come with singing to Zion; everlasting joy shall be upon their heads. They shall obtain joy and gladness, and sorrow and sighing shall flee away. —ISAIAH 51:11

A confident woman is positive. Confidence and negativity do not go together. They are like oil and water; they simply do not mix. I used to be a very negative woman, but, thank God, I finally learned that being positive is much more fun and fruitful. Being positive or negative is a choice—it is a way of thinking, speaking, and acting. Either one comes from a habit that has been formed in our lives through repetitious behavior.

You may be like me. I simply got off to a bad start in life. I grew up in a negative atmosphere around negative people. They were my role models, and I became like them. I really didn't even realize my negative attitude was a problem until I married Dave in 1967. He was very positive and began asking me why I was so negative. I had never really thought about it, but as I began to observe myself, I realized that I was always that way. No wonder my life was so negative. I began to understand that I was expecting nothing good—and that is exactly what I got.

Expect good things from God today—He won't let you down.

Lord, I look to You for my joy and gladness. I ask You to drive the negativity and sighing away from my life and fill me with the joy of Your Spirit. Amen.

Bring Cheer

*But God, Who comforts and encourages and refreshes and cheers
the depressed and the sinking, comforted and encouraged and
refreshed and cheered us by the arrival of Titus. [Yes] and not only
by his coming but also by [his account of] the comfort with which he
was encouraged and refreshed and cheered as to you.*

—2 CORINTHIANS 7:6–7

Did you know that a smile is a wonderful weapon? It's so powerful you
can break ice with it! If a person is cold toward you, just start smiling
and watch them warm up. If you wear a smile, you will have friends; if
you wear a frown, all you will have is wrinkles. Smiles are a language
that even babies understand. Smiles are understood in every language.
I heard someone once say, "You are not fully dressed until you put on
your smile."

Smiling actually makes you feel better. Studies show that when you
smile, your heart rate can actually lower and your breathing slows down,
particularly if you're feeling stressed. When you get out of bed, even if
you don't feel like smiling, force yourself to smile anyway, and you will
have a happier day. A smile of encouragement at the right moment may
be the turning point for a troubled life. A smile costs nothing, but gives
much. If you are not smiling, you are like a millionaire who has money
in the bank, but no checks.

Start smiling today and don't ever stop.

———————————

Lord, I believe that You mean for me to refresh and encourage
others today. Help me to bring a smile and an uplifted spirit.
Amen.

The Priority of Prayer

You do not have, because you do not ask.   —JAMES 4:2

If you and I are going to succeed at being ourselves and succeed in life, then we must know how to pray and be willing to give prayer a place of priority in our daily lives. We have no right to expect what we have not prayed for. We have not because we fail to ask, so ask and keep on asking (Matthew 7:7).

How you ask is also important. The Bible says in James 5:16 that the fervent, effectual prayer of a righteous man makes tremendous power available. What kind of person? A righteous person! Not one who feels guilty, condemned, no good, and as if God is angry with him. Not one who is fearful, cowardly, timid, indecisive, and double-minded.

Doesn't the Bible say that our righteousness is like filthy rags and that all have sinned and come short of the glory of God? Yes, it does. But it is not our own righteousness that we wear into the prayer closet; it is the righteousness of Jesus Christ. It is that which is given to every true believer in Him. He took our sins to the cross with Him and gave us His righteousness (2 Corinthians 5:21). We can call ourselves righteous women because He gives us right standing with God through His blood sacrifice.

————————

Lord, I thank You that because of the cross I can come into Your presence and pray. I come confidently knowing that I have the righteousness of Jesus. Amen.

A Big, Rewarding Life

Only it must be in faith that he asks with no wavering (no hesitating, no doubting). For the one who wavers (hesitates, doubts) is like the billowing surge out at sea that is blown hither and thither and tossed by the wind.   —JAMES 1:6

People with low confidence are double-minded, indecisive, and constantly get frustrated with life. If they do make a decision, they are tormented by self-doubt. They second-guess themselves. As a result, they don't live boldly. They live little, narrow lives, and they miss out on the big, rewarding lives God wants them to enjoy.

You may be aware of some of God's promises for His people—promises for peace, happiness, blessings, and so on. But did you know that all of God's promises are for every person?

That's right—when it comes to fulfilling promises, God does not discriminate. However, God requires us to approach Him in faith—the deeply held confidence that God is trustworthy and will always make good on His promises. God loves you; He wants you to relax in the knowledge of that love. God wants you to experience the peace of mind that comes from resting in His love and living without the torment of fear and doubt.

———————

Lord, I hate all the second-guessing and the wavering that
come with a lack of confidence in You. I know that You
want me to enjoy a big, rewarding life, and I know that Your
promises of blessings and joy and peace are for me. By faith I
receive all that You have for me now. Amen.

Find Your Perfect Fit

[Urged on] by faith Abraham, when he was called, obeyed and went forth to a place which he was destined to receive as an inheritance; and he went, although he did not know or trouble his mind about where he was to go.   —HEBREWS 11:8

If you are doing nothing with your life because you are not sure what to do, then I recommend that you pray and begin trying some things. It won't take long before you will feel comfortable with something. It will be a perfect fit for you. Think of it this way: When you go out to buy a new outfit, you probably try on several things until you find what fits right, is comfortable, and looks good on you.

Why not try the same thing with discovering your destiny? Obviously there are some things you cannot just "try"—such as being an astronaut or the president of the United States—but one thing is for sure: You cannot drive a parked car. Get your life out of "park," and get moving in some direction. I don't suggest going deep in debt to find out if you should own a business, but you could begin in some small way, and, if it works, take it to the next level. As we take steps of faith, our destinies unfold. A confident woman is not afraid to make mistakes, and if she does, she recovers and presses on.

———————————

Lord, I want to be moving in the right direction with my life. I trust You to guide my steps as You did Abraham. Amen.

New Beginnings

I do not consider, brethren, that I have captured and made it my own [yet]; but one thing I do [it is my one aspiration]: forgetting what lies behind and straining forward to what lies ahead, I press on toward the goal to win the [supreme and heavenly] prize to which God in Christ Jesus is calling us upward.

—PHILIPPIANS 3:13–14

One of the great things about a relationship with God is that He always provides new beginnings. His Word says that His mercy is new every day. Jesus chose disciples who had weaknesses and made mistakes, but He continued working with them and helping them become all that they could be. He will do the same thing for you, if you will let Him.

Recovering from pain or disappointment of any kind is not something that just happens to some people and not to others. It is a decision! You make a decision to let go and go on. You gather up the fragments and give them to Jesus, and He will make sure that nothing is wasted (John 6:12). You refuse to think about what you have lost, but instead you inventory what you have left and begin using it. Not only can you recover, but you can also be used to help other people recover. Be a living example of a confident woman who always recovers from setbacks no matter how difficult or frequent they are.

———————————

Lord, thank You for every new beginning You are making for my life. Help me to put the past aside and move on with Your help. Amen.

Avoid Comparisons

*Not that we [have the audacity to] venture to class or [even to]
compare ourselves with some who exalt and furnish testimonials
for themselves! However, when they measure themselves with
themselves and compare themselves with one another, they are
without understanding and behave unwisely.*
—2 CORINTHIANS 10:12

Advertising is often geared to make people strive to look the best,
be the best, and own the most. If you wear "this" particular brand of
clothes, people will admire you! Try "this" new diet and lose those few
extra pounds—and then you will be accepted and noticed. The world
consistently gives us the impression that we need to be something
other than what we are.

A confident woman avoids comparisons. Confidence is not possible
as long as we compare ourselves with other people. No matter how
good we look, how talented or smart we are, or how successful we are,
there is always someone who is better, and sooner or later we will run
into her. I believe confidence is found in doing the best we can with
what we have to work with and not in comparing ourselves with others
and competing with them. Our joy should not be found in being better
than others, but in being the best we can be.

**Lord, I refuse to compare myself with others and compete to
be better than them. My only interest is to be the best I can be
with the gifts and talents You have given me. Amen.**

Love Much

Therefore I tell you, her sins, many [as they are], are forgiven her—
because she has loved much. But he who is forgiven little loves little.
And He said to her, Your sins are forgiven!　　　—LUKE 7:47–48

Mary Magdalene was a woman with a past. She had sold her love by the hour; she was a prostitute. She was called "an especially wicked sinner" by the Pharisees (Luke 7:37). At one time Jesus cast seven demons out of her (Luke 8:2).

In Luke 7:36–50, we see the account of Mary anointing Jesus' feet with a bottle of very expensive perfume, washing them with her tears, and drying them with her hair. Her act of love was seen by other people as being erotic because of her past, but Jesus knew it was an act of pure love.

When we have an unpleasant past, people often misjudge our actions, and we find ourselves trying to convince others that we are acceptable. People don't forget our past as easily as God does. The Pharisees could not understand Jesus' allowing Mary to even touch Him. Jesus said that those who have been forgiven much will love much. Mary loved Jesus greatly because He had forgiven her for her great sins. She wanted to give Him the most expensive thing she owned; she wanted to serve Him. He saw her heart, not her past.

Don't dwell on what God has forgotten.

———————

Lord, I want to love You in the way that Mary loved You.
Thank You for Your forgiveness and cleansing my heart and
soul from sin. I will give You my best. Amen.

Good Enough?

But let every person carefully scrutinize and examine and test his
own conduct and his own work. He can then have the personal
satisfaction and joy of doing something commendable [in itself
alone] without [resorting to] boastful comparison with his neighbor.
—GALATIANS 6:4

I know someone—I'll call her Pat—who was married and had three
children. She was a full-time mother and homemaker, but unless she
had help cleaning her home once a week, she struggled to get everything done and remain peaceful.

Pat had a friend named Mary who was also married and had five
children. Mary worked outside the home two days a week and did all
her own housework, cooking, and laundry with no outside help. Actually it seemed Mary was more peaceful and less temperamental than
Pat, even though she had more to do.

Pat felt very bad about herself because she just could not seem to get
everything done without help. In her thoughts and conversations, she
constantly compared herself with Mary. She put herself under so much
pressure that she became difficult to get along with. She carried a burden of guilt most of the time, and it started affecting her mood and her
health. She finally came to understand we are all different, and that is
perfectly acceptable. She did not need to be able to do what Mary did in
order to approve of herself.

Are you comparing yourself to someone else? Let go of that! God
created you, and He doesn't make mistakes!

Lord, free me from the guilt and shame that comes from com-
paring myself with others and not measuring up. I am joined
to Jesus today, and I will give Him my very best. Amen.

Accepting Weaknesses

*So for the sake of Christ, I am well pleased and take pleasure in
infirmities, insults, hardships, persecutions, perplexities and
distresses; for when I am weak [in human strength], then am I
[truly] strong (able, powerful in divine strength).*

—2 CORINTHIANS 12:10

I remember when God told me to give myself permission to be weak.
It was very hard for me because I truly despised weakness. I thought
weak people got walked on. As a result, I could not accept weaknesses
in myself. I tried to be tough in all situations. The problem was that I
did have weaknesses like everyone else, and trying to conquer all of
them was creating major stress in my life in addition to ungodly self-
hatred and self-rejection. I suffered greatly trying to overcome every
flaw I saw in myself.

God had told me to give myself permission to have weaknesses, but
it was a major step of faith. I was afraid that if I accepted weaknesses as
a part of life, they would multiply and take over. I had yet to learn that
where we stop, God begins. Instead of my weaknesses multiplying and
taking over my life, God began to strengthen me in them. He began to
flow through them. Oh, I knew my weaknesses were still in existence,
but even that knowledge caused me to lean on Him constantly and my
relationship with Him deepened.

God works with and through our weaknesses. Praise Him!

**Lord, You know my every weakness, and I know that I cannot
conquer them all. In my weaknesses, I ask You by Your grace
to make me strong. Amen.**

Walking with a Limp

And He said, Your name shall be called no more Jacob [supplanter], but Israel [contender with God]; for you have contended and have power with God and with men and have prevailed.

—GENESIS 32:28

Jacob was a man who had many weaknesses, and yet he was determined to be blessed by God. God likes that kind of determination. He actually told Jacob he had contended with God and man, and He would be glorified in him (Genesis 32:28). God can gain glory for Himself through those who will not let their personal weaknesses stop Him from flowing through them.

For God to do that through us, first we must come face to face with the fact that we have weaknesses, and then we must determine not to let them bother us. Our imperfections are not going to stop God unless we let them do so.

Jacob wrestled with the Angel of the Lord, and as a result, he always had a limp from that day forward (Genesis 32:24–32). I always say that Jacob limped off from the fight, but he limped away with His blessing. Another way to say it is this: "God will bless us even though all of us have a limp (an imperfection)." If we have our faith in God, and a heart that wants to do right, that is all that is needed.

Lord, I am glad that my imperfections cannot stop Your blessings. I don't mind walking with a limp as long as You get the glory and honor. Amen.

Shining Splendor

*Who is among you who [reverently] fears the Lord, who obeys the
voice of His Servant, yet who walks in darkness and deep trouble
and has no shining splendor [in his heart]? Let him rely on, trust in,
and be confident in the name of the Lord, and let him lean upon and
be supported by his God.*   —ISAIAH 50:10

If a person is naturally introverted or extroverted, she will always have
greater tendencies toward that natural trait—and that is not wrong.
As we have stated previously, God creates all of us differently. However, we can have the life we desire and still not deny who we are. So
search your heart and ask yourself what you believe God wants you to
do—and then do it. Where He guides, He always provides. If God is
asking you to step out into something that is uncomfortable for you, I
can assure you that when you take the step of faith, you will find Him
walking right beside you.

When you want to do something, don't let yourself think about all
the things that could go wrong. Be positive and think about the exciting things that can happen. Your attitude makes all the difference in
your life. Have a positive, aggressive, take-action attitude, and you will
enjoy your life more. Taking action may be difficult at first, but will be
worth it in the end.

———————————

**Lord, I rest in the knowledge that where You guide You also
provide. My one desire is to walk with You and to always be at
Your side. Amen.**

God's Calling

Let a woman learn in quietness, in entire submissiveness. I allow no woman to teach or to have authority over men; she is to remain in quietness and keep silence [in religious assemblies].

—1 TIMOTHY 2:11–12

In this controversial passage, it is evident that Paul was dealing with a specific situation for a specific time frame in history. As noted before, Priscilla, along with her husband, Aquila, had been a founding leader in this same church. I am not enough of a theologian to debate this problem fully. All I know is that God has always used—and still does use—women as leaders and teachers, preachers, ministers, missionaries, authors, evangelists, prophets, and so on.

Just remember that God loves you and wants to use you in powerful ways to help other people. Don't ever let anyone tell you that God cannot or will not use you, just because you are a woman. As a woman, you are creative, comforting, sensitive, and you're able to be a tremendous blessing. You can bear a lot of good fruit in your life. You don't have to merely pass through life unnoticed, always in the background. If God has called you to leadership, you should lead. If He has called you into ministry, you should minister. If He has called you to business or as a homemaker, you should boldly be all that He has called you to be.

———————————

Lord, I believe that You want to use me and that You have called and gifted me. Bless me to be a blessing. Amen.

Peace and Confidence

*I have told you these things, so that in Me you may have [perfect]
peace and confidence. In the world you have tribulation and trials
and distress and frustration; but be of good cheer [take courage;
be confident, certain, undaunted]! For I have overcome the world.
[I have deprived it of power to harm you and have conquered it for
you.]*   —JOHN 16:33

Look at each word Jesus spoke and meditate on it so that you get the
full meaning of what Jesus is saying. He is telling us that during our
lives we will have hard times, trials, and things that frustrate us, but
we don't have to let worry or depression be part of it, because He has
given us courage (if we will take it), confidence, and assurance. No
matter what comes against us, if we have confidence that we can make
it through, it won't bother us that much. It isn't really our problems that
make us unhappy; it is how we respond to them.

Jesus said to "be confident." He did not say to "feel confident." Start
today choosing to be confident in every situation and you will begin
driving fear back to Hades where it came from. When Satan tries to
give you fear, give it back to him. You wouldn't drink poison if someone
offered it to you, would you? Then stop taking fear and start choosing
courage.

————————————

**Lord, thank You that You have overcome the world. I will be
confident today because I follow You and walk in the victory
You have already won. Amen.**

Watch God Work

Moses told the people, Fear not; stand still (firm, confident, undismayed) and see the salvation of the Lord which He will work for you today. . . . The Lord will fight for you, and you shall hold your peace and remain at rest.   —EXODUS 14:13–14

We have free access to God. We can go before Him anytime we want to. We don't need a special invitation. The throne room is always open, God is always home, He is never napping or on the phone. We can go boldly, expecting Him to meet our need and do it willingly and joyfully.

No doubt millions of people pray, but the question we want answered is, how do they pray? Do they pray expectantly, boldly, fearlessly, confidently, aggressively, or ashamed, condemned, asking for barely enough to get by on, and seriously doubting if they will even get that?

You go, girl! Start praying like you have never prayed before. Believe that God wants to meet your needs because He is good, not necessarily because you are good. None of us living in a fleshly body has a perfect record. We all make mistakes, and yours probably are no worse than anyone else's. So stop beating up on yourself and start expecting God to be God in your life.

BE confident even when you don't FEEL confident and watch God work!

Lord, I am confident that You are Almighty God and You will work wonders on my behalf. I ask You to fight for me and bring me through to victory. Amen.

"Go and Tell"

Now some women were there also, looking on from a distance,
among whom were Mary Magdalene, and Mary the mother of James
the younger and of Joses, and Salome, who, when [Jesus] was in
Galilee, were in the habit of accompanying and ministering to Him;
and [there were] also many other [women] who had come up with
Him to Jerusalem.   —MARK 15:40–41

Mary Magdalene and some other women were the first to visit the
tomb on Resurrection Sunday (John 20:1). They found the tomb empty,
but an angel appeared to them and gave these instructions, "Go and
tell His disciples that He is arisen" (see Matthew 28:7). "Go and tell."
Sounds to me like the preaching of the gospel. Actually, Luke records
that when Mary and her friends found the other disciples, it was the
disciples who didn't believe that Jesus had risen from the dead and the
tomb was empty. I wonder why some of them had not already been to
the tomb? Why was it just the women who ventured out?

A woman gave birth to our Savior, and many women helped care
for and support Jesus during His life and ministry. Women were at
the cross when He died, and first at the empty tomb. God used these
women in ministry, included them in the most important events in
Jesus' life, and gave them a place of honor.

Lord, I want to be among those who "go and tell" the lost that
You rose from the dead and conquered sin and death in our
behalf. I want to be quick to serve You. Amen.

God Honors Faith

But without faith it is impossible to please and be satisfactory to
Him. For whoever would come near to God must [necessarily]
believe that God exists and that He is the rewarder of those who
earnestly and diligently seek Him [out].

—HEBREWS 11:6

For ten years, Robert and Mary Moffat labored as missionaries in Bechuanaland (now called Botswana) without a single convert. Finally, the directors of their mission board began to question the wisdom of continuing the work. The thought of leaving their post, however, brought great grief to this devoted couple, for they felt they would see people turn to Christ in due season.

They stayed, and for a year or two longer, darkness reigned. Then one day a friend in England sent word to the Moffats that he wanted to mail them a gift and asked what they would like. Trusting that, in time, the Lord would bless their work, Mrs. Moffat replied, "Send us a communion set. I am sure it will soon be needed." God honored that dear woman's faith. The Holy Spirit moved upon the hearts of the villagers, and soon a little group of six converts united to form the first Christian church in that land. The communion set from England arrived on the day before the first commemoration of the Lord's Supper in Bechuanaland.

———————

Lord, such remarkable faith and perseverance seems beyond
me. Help me to trust You with the work You want to do
through my life. I know that the day is coming when I will see
the reward for diligently seeking You. Amen.

In the Potter's Hands

But who are you, a mere man, to criticize and contradict and answer back to God? Will what is formed say to him that formed it, Why have you made me thus? Has the potter no right over the clay, to make out of the same mass (lump) one vessel for beauty and distinction and honorable use, and another for menial or ignoble and dishonorable use? —ROMANS 9:20–21

We are like a hard, cold lump of clay that is not very pliable or easy to work with. But God puts us on His potter's wheel and begins to refashion and make us because He doesn't like what we have become. Sometimes the process of molding is painful, because we do not fit the mold into which God is trying to fit us. So God keeps working on us, trimming away this bad attitude and that wrong mind-set, carefully remolding and reshaping us until gradually we are changed into His likeness.

Don't be discouraged with yourself because you have not yet arrived. You can walk in spiritual power as long as you maintain an attitude of pressing on. As long as you do your best to cooperate with God, He is pleased with you. Enjoy your life in the Spirit right now on the way to where God is shaping you. Let the Potter do His work of changing you.

———————————

Lord, it's good to be in Your hands, confident that You are working on reshaping me into Your image. I look forward to the day when You bring me to completion! Amen.

See Possibilities

The Lord said to Moses, Why do you cry to Me? Tell the people of Israel to go forward! Lift up your rod and stretch out your hand over the sea and divide it, and the Israelites shall go on dry ground through the midst of the sea.   —EXODUS 14:15–16

When God called Moses to lead the Israelites out of Egypt, Moses felt very inadequate and kept telling God what he could not do and did not have. God asked him what he had in his hand and Moses replied, "A rod." It was an ordinary rod, used for herding sheep. God told him to throw it down, implying that Moses was to give it to Him. When God gave the rod back to Moses, it was filled with miracle-working power and was used by Moses to part the Red Sea as well as for other miracles. If you will give God what you have, no matter how little and ineffective you may think it is, God will use it and give you back more than you gave Him.

In other words, it is not our abilities that God desires, but it is our availability He wants. He wants us to see possibilities, not problems. Don't spend your life thinking "if only" you had something else, then you could do something worthwhile. "If only" is a thief of what could be.

———————

Lord, I make myself available to You, just as I am. I ask You to open the doors that I might do something worthy of Your great name. Amen.

Run to God's Word

You are a hiding place for me; You, Lord, preserve me from trouble,
You surround me with songs and shouts of deliverance. Selah
[pause, and calmly think of that]! I [the Lord] will instruct you and
teach you in the way you should go; I will counsel you with My eye
upon you.   —PSALM 32:7–8

"What if" can be just as devastating as "if only"—if the "what if" is applied in a negative manner. Negatively anticipating a future experience is potentially more devastating than actually experiencing the problem.

I have a friend who was so afraid she would get heart disease that her doctor told her she was experiencing symptoms of stress induced by her fear of getting heart disease. She created her own problems by living in "what if." Anyone could be miserable with that kind of thinking. She needed to choose to think differently. She had a stronghold of fear in her mind, but she could renew her mind through studying God's Word and meditating on it. Often, people want their problems to vanish, but they are not willing to do what they need to do to help themselves. We all have fears in life, and they will show up from time to time. But we can respond by running to God's Word, which strengthens us to take steps of faith, no matter how we feel.

Lord, I am so glad that You are my hiding place and that You have the power to preserve my life. I rest in the shelter of Your wings. Amen.

A Virtuous Woman

A capable, intelligent, and virtuous woman—who is he who can find her? She is far more precious than jewels and her value is far above rubies or pearls.   —PROVERBS 31:10

Who can compete with the woman described in Proverbs 31? This woman can do it all; she's a great wife, mother, she manages the house, she runs a business, she cooks, she sews—what she doesn't seem to do is get tired! She seems absolutely perfect. I disliked her until I realized she was an example to me, a goal I could reach for. One that God Himself would help me realize if I put my trust in Him and was willing to change. I want you to consider her too and believe that you can become the confident woman you want to be. God wants each woman to be able to insert her name in this woman's story.

A good woman is hard to find; she is to be valued above rubies or pearls. Good women are precious, more precious than jewels or expensive gems. We must intentionally work to build up our husbands with thoughtful, caring questions and statements because like this verse points out, a woman who is capable, intelligent, and virtuous is a rare combination. Any man who has a wife like this should appreciate and value her tremendously.

Lord, I can't compete with this woman, but I thank You for her example. I aspire to be like her, and I trust that Your grace working in my life will lift me up higher and higher. Amen.

Be Trustworthy

The heart of her husband trusts in her confidently and relies on and believes in her securely, so that he has no lack of [honest] gain or need of [dishonest] spoil.   —PROVERBS 31:11

Trust is the glue that holds a marriage together, and the Bible says that the husband of our Proverbs 31 woman can trust her confidently. What a blessed thing to be able to say! We live in a society where so many relationships lack these qualities, so when they are present, they should be valued above all else. Confidence, trust, and security bring peace and rest to our souls. When we trust others and they trust us, it increases our confidence level.

I have confidence in my husband; I trust and feel secure in him. I enjoy these qualities in him, and I believe he can also say the same of me. He could not always say that about me. There was a time in my life when I was very unstable, but thank God He changes us as we study His Word. We can rely on the promise found in 2 Corinthians 3:18—that if we will continue in God's Word, we "are constantly being transfigured into His very own image in ever increasing splendor and from one degree of glory to another; [for this comes] from the Lord [Who is] the Spirit."

———————————

Lord, continue to use Your Word to transform me into Your image and likeness. I want to be a person whom others trust without reserve. Amen.

Be an Encourager

She comforts, encourages, and does him only good as long as there is life within her.   —PROVERBS 31:12

This woman comforts her husband and does him good as long as there is life in her. Many marriages could be saved from divorce or disappointment if a woman would take the initiative to begin comforting and complimenting her husband. The husband also has the same responsibility, but if he is not doing it, I encourage you to be willing to step out and be the first to make a move in the right direction for your marriage. A spiritually mature woman will be the first to do what is right even if nobody else is doing so. A wise, understanding, and prudent wife is a gift from the Lord (Proverbs 19:14).

We notice in our reading of Proverbs 31:10–31 that there is no mention of what the husband does other than that he praises his spouse and is well-known in the city because of his fine wife. I believe if you take the first steps of obedience, then God will also deal with your husband and you will see positive changes in him. I also believe it will increase your own level of confidence. When we compliment others, we begin to see ourselves in a better light also.

Lord, help me to be the one who takes the initiative to encourage and compliment and comfort. In all my relationships, may I be the first to give, whether or not I receive the same back. Amen.

Go the Extra Mile

She seeks out wool and flax and works with willing hands [to develop it]. She is like the merchant ships loaded with foodstuffs; she brings her household's food from a far [country].

—PROVERBS 31:13–14

Our Proverbs 31 woman is not lazy, nor does she procrastinate. She seeks (craves, pursues, and goes after with all her might) wool and flax, and works with willing hands. One thing is for sure, whether she is making her family's clothing or making things to sell at the market, she is definitely enthusiastic about it! She does not consider her work drudgery, nor is it something she dreads and complains about doing. Whatever her task, she works "at it heartily (from the soul), as [something done] for the Lord and not for men" (Colossians 3:23).

She plans good meals that include a lot of variety. She even imports things from far countries to make sure her family does not become bored with eating the same things over and over. I fed my family hamburger 1,001 different ways. I wasn't too creative. Our budget was meager, and I used that as an excuse, but once again our lady in Proverbs challenges us to go the extra mile and make things as good as possible. Making the effort to do things with excellence will always make you feel better about yourself and increase your confidence.

Lord, give me a servant's heart that is like Yours. Help me to not just do things, but to do them enthusiastically and with excellence, in a way that pleases You. Amen.

Work Your Plan

She rises while it is yet night and gets [spiritual] food for her household and assigns her maids their tasks.

—PROVERBS 31:15

She rises before daylight to spend time with God. She knows that she can never be a good wife or mother and be able to adequately provide for others unless she feeds herself with spiritual food. I am sure she reads God's Word, prays, worships, and praises and makes sure she is spiritually ready for the day. She prays, "O God, You are my God; early will I seek You; my soul thirsts for You; my flesh longs for You" (Psalm 63:1 NKJV).

She also has a plan for the day. This is so important because I don't believe we should be vague and thoughtless, merely getting up daily and waiting to see what happens. People who have this mentality rarely ever accomplish anything; they are usually frustrated and unfulfilled. Have a plan and work your plan. Be disciplined with your plan unless God shows you something else He wants you to do.

I encourage you to take charge of your life. Don't let life manage you; you manage it! Be careful about making excuses—they rob people of their destiny more than any other thing. A great confidence booster is to feel that you are doing with your life what you know you should be doing.

———

Lord, I want to take charge of my life. I know that starts with my relationship with You. I seek to know You and worship You above all else. Amen.

Consider Your Life

She considers a [new] field before she buys or accepts it [expanding prudently and not courting neglect of her present duties by assuming other duties]; with her savings [of time and strength] she plants fruitful vines in her vineyard.   —PROVERBS 31:16

This verse is very important to me. I am an aggressive person who wants to be involved in everything, but I have learned the hard way that it isn't wise or even possible. We cannot do everything and do anything well. Quality is much better than quantity. Verse 16 begins by saying she "considers" a new field before she buys it. She considers her present duties and is careful not to neglect them by taking on new ones. In other words, she seriously thinks about what she is about to do and does not act emotionally without forethought.

Oh, how much better life would be if we all took time to think about what we are about to do before we do it. It is amazing how many things I don't buy if I just go home and think about it for a while. It is amazing how one good night's sleep changes our minds. Emotions are fickle and ever changing. This is the reason why it is dangerous to do things based on high emotions without giving plenty of consideration to everything involved. Remember to think before you act.

Lord, I ask You to give me wisdom as to what I give my time and attention. Help me to be busy with the right things and to give my best to those things. Amen.

Don't Be Hasty

The thoughts of the [steadily] diligent tend only to plenteousness, but everyone who is impatient and hasty hastens only to want.

—PROVERBS 21:5

By not moving emotionally in her decisions about life, the Bible says the Proverbs 31 woman saves time and strength, which she then uses to plant fruitful vines in her vineyard (v. 16). Everything that looks good is not good, and a wise person will take time to examine things thoroughly. If you think about it, what looks good is sometimes the enemy of what is best. There may be lots of good opportunities for you to minister in your church, but that doesn't mean that each opportunity is the best choice for you.

We should choose the more excellent things and not merely settle for another good thing. I receive many good opportunities almost daily, and I have to decline most of them. I know what I am called by God to do, and I stick with my call. I encourage you to take time to think about things. Remember that "a calm and undisturbed mind and heart are the life and health of the body" (Proverbs 14:30). Don't be hasty.

———————————

Lord, I realize that not everything that glitters is gold. Give me a calm mind that refuses to be hasty when opportunities come my way. I want to be doing the best I can do. Amen.

Expand Prudently

Go from the presence of a foolish and self-confident man, for you will not find knowledge on his lips. The Wisdom [godly Wisdom, which is comprehensive insight into the ways and purposes of God] of the prudent is to understand his way, but the folly of [self-confident] fools is to deceive. —PROVERBS 14:7–8

The woman I've been considering in Proverbs 31 is in fact a prudent woman, and prudence means good management of resources. Each of us has an allotted amount of time and energy, and we should manage it in such a way that we bear the most fruit we can. Emotionally driven people usually lead frustrated lives. They are filled with creative ideas but are unable to settle down long enough to lay out a blueprint and get a solid foundation. They want instant results, and if they don't get them, they are usually off to another new project that will also fail.

I encourage you to "consider" decisions, purchases, and life choices. Be sure you expand prudently. Don't court neglect of other duties by taking on new ones, unless of course those present duties can be moved on to someone else to make room for your new venture. A sure way to lose your confidence is to have so much to do that you are not doing any of it well.

Lord, I need to know that You are my foundation, and my life is being built according to Your blueprint. Give me discernment to know Your ways and purposes. Amen.

Just Do It!

She girds herself with strength, and strengthens her arms.
—PROVERBS 31:17 NKJV

As a Christian, your body is the temple of the Holy Spirit, and you need to keep it in good condition so God can work through you the way He desires to. Being excessively tired can adversely affect us and our spiritual life. We don't have the desire or stamina to pray as we normally would. We don't present the best witness to others. It is even easier to be grouchy and unable to walk in the fruit of the Spirit when we feel tired most of the time.

I encourage you to make room in your life for exercise. In my own life, I am not where I need to be yet but I am making progress. I have finally decided that, to do what I can do is better than doing nothing at all. Find something you can enjoy and still get exercise. Try walking or playing a sport to get the exercise you need. Exercising with other people might work for you.

People who exercise regularly do tend to be more confident. For one thing, they feel better and more energetic, so they accomplish more and enjoy what they do. They usually look better, and that increases confidence. Exercise also relieves tension and stress, which will help anyone's confidence. Don't think about exercising anymore—just do it!

Lord, I acknowledge that my body is Your temple, and I want it to rightly reflect You. Help me to discipline myself and give my body the exercise it needs. Amen.

Look to the Reward

She tastes and sees that her gain from work [with and for God] is good; her lamp goes not out, but it burns on continually through the night [of trouble, privation, or sorrow, warning away fear, doubt, and distrust].   —PROVERBS 31:18

We all have times in life when we feel like giving up, and our woman in Proverbs is no different than the rest of us. However, she tastes and sees that her gain from work is good. It gives her the strength to persevere in difficult times and continue on in faith.

God gave many men and women in the Bible difficult tasks to perform, but He always promised a reward. Looking to the reward helps us endure the difficulty. The Bible states that Jesus, "for the joy [of obtaining the prize] that was set before Him, endured the cross, despising and ignoring the shame, and is now seated at the right hand of the throne of God" (Hebrews 12:2).

I encourage you not to look merely at your work but look also at the promise of reward. Take time to enjoy the fruit of your labor, and you'll be energized to finish your course. It will also build confidence as you realize that you are worth enjoying the reward of your labors, and it is indeed God's will for you.

Lord, I trust that You will give me a clear understanding of the rewards You have for me. Help me to see beyond today's challenges to where You're bringing me. Amen.

Be a Giver

She lays her hands to the spindle, and her hands hold the distaff.
She opens her hand to the poor, yes, she reaches out her filled hands
to the needy [whether in body, mind, or spirit].

—PROVERBS 31:19–20

We see our woman working again. I believe that being fruitful makes one confident. We are not created by God to waste anything He has given us, and time is certainly one of the greatest assets we have. Everyone has the same amount of time, and yet some do so many things with theirs while others do little or nothing. You will never experience confidence if you waste your life and your time.

She also takes the initiative in giving and reaches out her filled hands to the needy. In my opinion, givers are powerful people; they are happy and fulfilled. I lived a long, long time as a selfish, self-centered woman, and I was miserable all the time. I have learned over the years, though, to be an aggressive giver; I look for opportunities, and it makes my life exciting and fulfilling (see Job 29:16). There is nothing better in the world than making someone else happy. Remember that what you make happen for others, God will make happen for you. Put a smile on someone else's face and your own joy will increase.

———————————

Lord, help me to value and to make the most of my time. Fill my hands with good things to help others who are needy. Make me a powerful giver. Amen.

You Have Something

*And [God] Who provides seed for the sower and bread for eating will
also provide and multiply your [resources for] sowing and increase
the fruits of your righteousness [which manifests itself in active
goodness, kindness, and charity]. Thus you will be enriched in all
things and in every way, so that you can be generous, and [your
generosity as it is] administered by us will bring forth thanksgiving
to God.*   —2 CORINTHIANS 9:10–11

Notice that our woman in Proverbs 31 reached out her filled hands to
the needy (v. 20). When a person truly wants to give, God will give seed
to sow. Even if you don't have extra money to give, you do have something. Look around your house and start giving away everything that
you are not using or wearing. If an article of clothing has been in your
closet one year without being moved, there is a good chance you will
never wear it again. Pass it on to someone in need and God will bless
you with new things as you need them. I believe that we know giving
is the right thing to do. In our hearts we can sense joy and confidence
when we become givers and not merely takers.

It is no wonder I did not like this woman in Proverbs 31 when I first
started reading about her. She was everything I was not but needed to
become. It takes time and effort to become like her, but it's well worth
it. And it's never too late.

Lord, I truly want to be a giving person. I ask Your blessing
that I might meet the needs of others, whatever they might be.
Amen.

Invest in Yourself

Enlarge the place of your tent, and let the curtains of your habitations be stretched out; spare not; lengthen your cords and strengthen your stakes, for you will spread abroad to the right hand and to the left.   —ISAIAH 54:2–3

Note that our famous Proverbs 31 woman "makes for herself coverlets, cushions, and rugs of tapestry" (v. 22). She lived a balanced life. She did a lot for others, but she also took time to minister to herself. Many people burn out because they don't take time to refresh themselves. We feel such a need to give and do for others that we ignore our own needs or, worse, we feel guilty for even thinking about ourselves. We need to be ministered to spiritually, mentally, emotionally, and physically. Each one of these areas is important to God; He made them, and He is interested in the well-being of all of them, including our physical and emotional needs. Our confident woman made herself cushions, rugs, and clothing. Her clothes were made of the same cloth that the priests wore. In other words, she had really nice stuff. The best!

I believe we feel more confident when we look our best and take good care of ourselves. You are worth being cared for and don't ever forget it. You have value, and you should make an investment in yourself.

Lord, I believe that every aspect of my life is important to You, including how I care for myself. Help me to not think of myself too highly or too lowly. Help me to be balanced. Amen.

Pure and Fine

All her household are doubly clothed in scarlet. She makes for herself coverlets, cushions, and rugs of tapestry. Her clothing is of linen, pure and fine, and of purple [such as that of which the clothing of the priests and the hallowed cloths of the temple were made].

—PROVERBS 31:21–22

Many people have the mistaken idea that Christianity means to do for everyone else but sacrifice everything in life you might personally enjoy. I don't believe this! We will certainly be called to times of sacrifice all throughout life, and whatever God asks us to give up we should do so gladly. But we don't have to make it a contest to see just how much we can do without in life in order to try to impress and please God.

This woman had nice things, and the Bible says she made them for herself. If you are doing nothing for yourself, you need to find out what you enjoy and allow yourself the privilege of ministering to your own needs as well as everyone else's. Obviously, you should not spend money on yourself that you don't have or become excessive in doting on yourself. But giving very little attention, if any, to your own needs is not healthy, nor does it please God.

God wants to minister to yourself as well as others.

Lord, it's so easy to get trapped into feeling that I have to be sacrificing all the time. And it's so easy to focus only on making sure my needs are being met. Lead me to a right perspective that is healthy and pleasing to You. Amen.

The Power of the Blood

All her household are doubly clothed in scarlet.... Her clothing is ... of purple [such as that of which the clothing of the priests and the hallowed cloths of the temple were made].

—PROVERBS 31:21–22

The woman in Proverbs was well aware of the power of blood within the Jewish sacrificial system. Under the law almost everything was purified by blood for the release of sin, guilt, and punishment due. Therefore she covered her family in scarlet garments that may have well represented the blood of the coming Messiah to her.

One of the things you can do as a confident woman is apply the blood of Jesus Christ by faith to your household. I do this regularly. I apply it to my own life, my mind, emotions, will, body, conscience, spirit, finances, relationships, my walk with God, my husband, children and their families, co-workers, and all the partners of our ministry.

Regularly repenting for sin in my life and keeping my conscience covered with the blood of Jesus helps me be more confident before God, in my prayers and daily life. Guilty people don't function well. You don't have to be guilty and condemned; you can admit your sins, and ask God to forgive you and to cleanse you in the blood of Jesus. As you place confidence in His Word, your own confidence will increase.

Lord, search my heart and show me any sins that I have not confessed to You. Cleanse me by Your blood and free me from guilt and condemnation. Amen.

Bless Others

Her husband is known in the [city's] gates, when he sits among the elders of the land. She makes fine linen garments and leads others to buy them; she delivers to the merchants girdles [or sashes that free one up for service].   —PROVERBS 31:23–24

Our woman has a famous husband, but it is because of his fine wife. What a huge compliment to her! Just imagine if your husband went to a party and everyone flocked around him, commenting about what a great wife he had. Make a decision to be the kind of wife that will cause others to believe your husband is blessed because he has you.

Our multi-talented woman even makes garments to sell in the marketplace. What a woman—she adds to the family income by using some of the same skills she needs at home to be a blessing to others. I like the fact that she makes sashes that free one up for service. The clothing style of the culture she lived in required people to gather up their skirts and tie them so they could work unhampered. She made sashes that would do this. It was also something everyone needed. She reminds us that if we are going to go into business, we need to make sure a lot of people will need what we are going to offer.

Lord, I want to be a blessing to all of my loved ones as well as to excel at the services I provide, whether at home or in the workplace. Help me to bless others today. Amen.

Be Prepared

Strength and dignity are her clothing and her position is strong and secure; she rejoices over the future [the latter day or time to come, knowing that she and her family are in readiness for it]!

—PROVERBS 31:25

This woman's strength and dignity are her clothing, and her position is strong and secure. This certainly must have increased her confidence. She isn't afraid of losing her position or something bad happening. She boldly faces the future because she knows she and her family are prepared for it.

Proverbs 27:23 tells us: "Be diligent to know the state of your flocks, and look well to your herds." Lack of preparation is one of the major causes for low confidence. Being prepared requires working ahead of time instead of putting things off until the last minute. Matthew 25 tells us of the five wise virgins who took extra oil with them as they waited for the bridegroom to come, but the five foolish virgins didn't do anything to prepare. When the bridegroom was delayed, the foolish lost their opportunity to meet the bridegroom.

This same scenario happens to many people in life. They procrastinate until it is too late to take advantage of an opportunity that could have been a tremendous blessing to them. Knowing you are prepared for whatever comes will increase your confidence in an amazing way.

Lord, help me to be diligent and prepared for the opportunities You will bring my way. I want to walk in the confidence that I am always ready to go. Amen.

Be Kind

She opens her mouth in skillful and godly Wisdom, and on her tongue is the law of kindness [giving counsel and instruction].
—PROVERBS 31:26

Our woman in Proverbs 31 knows the importance of words. She opens her mouth in skillful and godly wisdom. The law of kindness is in her tongue. Speaking kindly to other people is a tremendous attribute and one that certainly enhances a godly woman. She knows that "anxiety in a man's heart weighs it down, but an encouraging word makes it glad" (Proverbs 12:25). We all need kindness, and I believe we will reap what we sow. Proverbs 18:20–21 says that we will have to be satisfied with the consequences of our words and that the power of life and death are in the tongue. It goes on to say that we will eat the fruit of our words for life or death.

Not only do we have the capability of speaking life or death to other people, we have the same ability in our own lives. We can speak words that build confidence in ourselves and others or we can speak words that destroy confidence. Be especially careful about self-talk. This is the conversation that you have with yourself inside yourself. Be sure what you are saying is something you want to live with.

Lord, make my heart to be kind and compassionate, so that it overflows in kind words to others. May my words have the power of life in them, to build up others and encourage them. Amen.

Be Responsible

She looks well to how things go in her household, and the bread of idleness (gossip, discontent, and self-pity) she will not eat.
—PROVERBS 31:27

Our friend in Proverbs is a responsible woman. She stays alert to how things go in her household, she refuses to be idle, and she doesn't waste her time in things such as sitting around gossiping or wallowing in self-pity. She is not discontented. She appreciates life, and I believe she celebrates it fully each day. Idleness, waste, self-pity, gossip, and discontentment are thieves of the great life Jesus died to give you.

The apostle Paul gave this exhortation to some members in the church in Thessalonica, "Indeed, we hear that some among you are disorderly [that they are passing their lives in idleness, neglectful of duty], being busy with other people's affairs instead of their own and doing no work" (2 Thessalonians 3:11). Don't allow these sins to rule you. When you maintain a positive attitude, you will enjoy more confidence.

Doing what one believes to be right will always increase confidence. You can't go wrong when you keep God as the focus of your life. Follow the example of the Proverbs 31 woman. She gives us tremendous insight in how to be the best and most confident homemaker, wife, and mother we can be.

———————

Lord, I never want to waste my life and all the blessings You have given me. Help me to find my contentment in walking with You and following hard after You in service. Amen.

Be Blessed

Her children rise up and call her blessed (happy, fortunate, and to be envied); and her husband boasts of and praises her, [saying], Many daughters have done virtuously, nobly, and well [with the strength of character that is steadfast in goodness], but you excel them all. —PROVERBS 31:28–29

"A virtuous and worthy wife [earnest and strong in character] is a crowning joy to her husband" (Proverbs 12:4). She enjoys the praise of her children and husband. They rise up to call her blessed. Her husband says that many daughters have been virtuous and noble but that she exceeds them all. In other words, he says that she is the best wife anyone could ever have. He applauds and celebrates her strength of character and goodness.

One year my birthday happened to be during one of our conferences, and my husband, Dave, stood up and read Proverbs 31 to me in front of a room filled with people. Then my children one by one rose up to say kind and edifying things to me. There is no better feeling than to spend years raising your children, and then have them tell you that they honor you, love you, and don't believe they could have had a better mother. Or to have your husband say you are the best wife in the world. Those comments certainly were confidence boosters for me.

Lord, whether anyone ever gives me these commendations, I want to live my life in a way that brings joy and blessing to others. Build strength into my character. Amen.

Be Free

And Moses said to the Lord, O Lord, I am not eloquent or a man of words, neither before nor since You have spoken to Your servant; for I am slow of speech and have a heavy and awkward tongue. And the Lord said to him, Who has made man's mouth?...Now therefore go, and I will be with your mouth and will teach you what you shall say.

—EXODUS 4:10–12

Put on a coat or a jacket and have someone tie your wrists together. Then try and take off your jacket. It can't be done, can it? That's what happens when you struggle with believing in yourself, when you let fear and self-doubt tie you up in knots. It's pretty much impossible to succeed! Self-doubt and confidence don't work together; they work against each other. Confidence will destroy self-doubt, but self-doubt will destroy confidence.

Self-doubt is tormenting. The woman who doubts herself is unstable in everything she does, feels, and decides. She lives in confusion most of the time and wrestles with making decisions and sticking with them, because she is forever changing her mind just in case she might be wrong. A confident woman is not afraid of being wrong! She realizes she can recover from making a mistake and doesn't allow the fear of making one to imprison her or tie her up in self-doubt.

———————————

Lord, I can empathize with Moses' self-doubts. Help me to honestly face those areas of my life where I have not put my trust in You. Amen.

Beyond Our Feelings

*So we take comfort and are encouraged and confidently and boldly
say, The Lord is my Helper; I will not be seized with alarm [I will not
fear or dread or be terrified]. What can man do to me?*

—HEBREWS 13:6

In the Bible, James 1:5–8 teaches us that God cannot answer the
prayers of a double-minded person. God responds to our faith, not
our fears. Self-doubt is fear—fear that we will make mistakes or do the
wrong thing. It often goes beyond being afraid one will do the wrong
thing; more often it involves how people feel totally wrong about themselves. They carry a deep-rooted shame and just can't seem to accept
themselves or have confidence in their decision-making ability.

Probably right about now you may be thinking, "Well, Joyce, I really
can't help how I feel. I wish I felt confident, but I just don't." What I am
getting ready to say to you may be one of the most important things
you have ever heard in your life: YOU DON'T HAVE TO FEEL CON-
FIDENT TO BE CONFIDENT! To live in victory, each of us must learn
to go beyond our feelings. I have learned that I can feel wrong and still
choose to do what is right. I have also learned that I don't have to feel
confident to present myself in a confident manner.

———————————

**Lord, I am tired of allowing my feelings of a lack of confidence
to hold me back. I put my trust in You as my Helper. I will not
be afraid. Amen.**

Walk in Peace

And let peace from Christ rule in your hearts to which as one body you were also called. —COLOSSIANS 3:15

If I make a decision and believe it is right at the time I make it, I don't have to change my mind later just because I begin to think or feel I might have made a mistake. If God shows me I have made a mistake, I need to change my decision, but I don't have to bow down to every wild thought or feeling that I encounter. We have to live deeper than emotions. God's Word teaches us to pursue peace (Psalm 34:14; Hebrews 12:14; 1 Peter 3:11).

I have had times in life when I felt peace in my heart about a direction I was taking and yet my head argued with me. James 1:22 clearly teaches us that reasoning leads us into deception and betrayal. When we change our mind about a decision we have made, it should be because we have lost our peace about the direction we intended to take or have gained some wisdom or insight that we did not have previously.

———————

Lord, help me to be sensitive to the peace that You give me in my heart . . . and to not allow my head to talk me out of it. Amen.

Trust God, Trust Yourself

Oh, how great is Your goodness, which You have laid up for those who fear, revere, and worship You, goodness which You have wrought for those who trust and take refuge in You before the sons of men!
—PSALM 31:19

Self-doubt causes a person to shrink back in fear. Faith is being confident in God and His Word. Perhaps you have a good relationship with God and have no problem trusting Him, but when it comes to trusting yourself to do the right thing, you shrink—you allow fear to control you and pull you back.

God once revealed to me that if I didn't trust myself, I didn't trust Him. He said that He was living in me and directing, guiding, and controlling me because I asked Him to do so. I needed to believe God's promises, not my feelings or thoughts. Of course, any one of us can miss God and we can make mistakes. We can think we are going in the right direction and then discover we are wrong, but it's not the end of the world, nor is it anything to become excessively concerned about. If our hearts are sincere and we are honestly seeking God's will, even if we do make a mistake, He will intervene and get us back on track. Quite often, He does it without us even knowing.

Lord, help me to step forward and trust myself when it comes to following what I believe is Your will. If I make a mistake, I know You will redirect me. Amen.

Be a Risk Taker

He who had received the five talents went at once and traded with them, and he gained five talents more. And likewise he who had received the two talents—he also gained two talents more. But he who had received the one talent went and dug a hole in the ground and hid his master's money. —MATTHEW 25:16–18

When Jim Burke became the head of a new products division at Johnson & Johnson, one of his first projects was the development of a children's chest rub. The product failed miserably, and Burke expected that he would be fired. When he was called in to see the chairman of the board, however, he was met with a surprising reception.

"Are you the one who just cost us all that money?" asked Robert Wood Johnson. "Well, I just want to congratulate you. If you are making mistakes, that means you are taking risks, and we won't grow unless you take risks." Some years later, when Burke himself became chairman of Johnson & Johnson, he continued to spread that word.

Don't be afraid of making mistakes. You will never succeed without making mistakes and possibly many of them. Making mistakes is something we do as human beings, but we are still God's children, and He has a good plan for our lives. He is long-suffering, plenteous in mercy, and filled with loving kindness.

Lord, help me to use the talents You have given me and to not be afraid of making mistakes. Give me wisdom on how to be the best I can be for You. Amen.

Gain Confidence

For the Lord God helps Me; therefore have I not been ashamed or confounded. Therefore have I set My face like a flint, and I know that I shall not be put to shame. He is near Who declares Me in the right. Who will contend with Me? Let us stand forth together!

—ISAIAH 50:7–8

Eleanor Roosevelt (1884–1962) became the leading woman politician of her day. When her husband was struck with polio in 1921, she organized Democratic women to help Franklin be elected governor in 1928 and then president four years later. In 1945, President Truman appointed her as a delegate to the United Nations where she largely shaped the Universal Declaration of Human Rights. She said, "You gain strength, courage, and confidence by every experience in which you really stop to look fear in the face. You are able to say to yourself, 'I lived through this horror, I can take the next thing that comes along.' You must do the thing you think you cannot do." She learned that "No one can make you feel inferior without your consent."

We need to "know fear," not look for "no fear." So many times we want to dismiss fear and keep it away, but fear cannot stop faith and determination. When fear comes knocking on your door, let faith answer and perhaps someday you will be in the history books.

————————

Lord, I set my face like a flint toward You, and I know that I shall not be put to shame. With You standing at my side, what can fear do to me? Amen.

Learn from Mistakes

I will praise and give thanks to You with uprightness of heart when I learn [by sanctified experiences] Your righteous judgments [Your decisions against and punishments for particular lines of thought and conduct]. I will keep Your statutes.   —PSALM 119:7–8

I believe people give their mistakes more power than they need. We should admit them, repent, and ask God to forgive us for them. We should also learn from our mistakes because by doing so, they can add value to our lives. Instead of allowing mistakes to make you feel guilty and bad, let them be your teacher, and always remember that just because you make a mistake does not mean you are a mistake. Just as God has promised in His Word (John 16:13), trust Him to lead you by His Holy Spirit into all truth.

Dave and I have four grown children, and I can assure you that over the years they have made many mistakes, but I love them just as much as if they had never made the mistakes. Some parents never allow their children to make any of their own decisions or mistakes. This is the biggest mistake of all. To grow we must step out and try things. We learn what works and what doesn't. Learning from firsthand experience is a much better teacher than a textbook.

Lord, I've made my share of mistakes, but I refuse to let them rule over me. I take them as lessons that I am learning from, and I know You will lead me into all truth by Your Spirit. Amen.

Expect Good Things

He did this that He might clearly demonstrate through the ages to come the immeasurable (limitless, surpassing) riches of His free grace (His unmerited favor) in [His] kindness and goodness of heart toward us in Christ Jesus.   —EPHESIANS 2:7

Self-doubt is simply the fear of being wrong. The Spirit you have received is not a spirit of slavery to put you once more in bondage to fear (Romans 8:15). God does not want you to live in fear, doubting yourself or doubting Him.

If you think about it, doubt is actually sin, because in Romans 14:23 the Bible says that "whatever does not originate and proceed from faith is sin [whatever is done without a conviction of its approval by God is sinful]." When we allow doubt and despair and fear to take over, that's when the wall to God's blessings starts going up. Don't let that wall even begin to build in your life.

Doubt is a fear of negative things happening, but faith expects good things to take place. It actually takes less emotional energy to walk in faith than in doubt and fear. People who believe and are positive are much healthier than those who are filled with fear, doubt, and negativity. Positive people age slower than negative ones and in fact can live longer.

There's every reason to replace doubt with expectation.

———————————

Lord, You have shown me the surpassing riches of Your grace and kindness in Christ Jesus. I know that Your heart only wants what is best for me. I look to You and by faith I expect good things to come. Amen.

A Life Worth Living

I will extol You, O Lord, for You have lifted me up and have not let my foes rejoice over me. O Lord my God, I cried to You and You have healed me. O Lord, You have brought my life up from Sheol (the place of the dead). —PSALM 30:1–3

You may have developed negativity because of various disappointing events in your life, but you were never created by God to be negative, fearful, and doubtful.

I grew up in a very dysfunctional home. My father was an alcoholic with an explosive temper. He was almost impossible to please. He was physically abusive to my mother and sexually, mentally, emotionally, and physically abusive toward me. I experienced many disappointments and devastations by the age of eighteen. I expected bad things to happen, thinking it would protect me from being disappointed when they did.

I believed in God and prayed for His help, but I knew nothing about the laws of faith. Praying and being negative won't bring an answer. Praying and living in fear won't either. I had much to learn, but over the years God has been faithful, patient, and loving. He changed me, healed me, and gave me the opportunity to help other people who are hurting also. He lifted me out of the ash heap and gave me a life worth living. He will do the same for you.

———————————

Lord, I recognize that the areas of my life where I am fearful and negative are not a part of Your design for my life. I ask You to lift me up and bring Your healing touch. Amen.

Answer with Faith

Then said David to the Philistine, You come to me with a sword, a spear, and a javelin, but I come to you in the name of the Lord of hosts, the God of the ranks of Israel, Whom you have defied.

—1 SAMUEL 17:45

I left home when I was eighteen, got a job, and started trying to take care of myself. I thought I got away from my problems at home because I physically walked away from it; but I didn't realize I took it with me inside my soul. My mind and emotions were damaged and in need of healing. My will was rebellious and obstinate because I promised myself that nobody would ever hurt me again. My spirit was wounded. I was a broken-hearted person with a very negative attitude.

Today, by God's grace, I am free from fear, negativity, and self-doubt. This doesn't mean that these things never try to visit me, but I have learned that I can say "NO" to them just as easily as I can say "YES." When negative thoughts or conversations come up, I am reminded by the Holy Spirit (or sometimes my husband) that being negative will not help anything or anyone, and I decide to change.

When fear knocks on your door, answer with faith. When self-doubt knocks, answer with confidence!

———————————

Lord, I want to have the heart of David and speak words of faith to the giants of fear and doubt in my life. Help me to remember Your name in all I do today. Amen.

God Gives the Victory

You shall tread upon the lion and adder; the young lion and the serpent shall you trample underfoot. Because he has set his love upon Me, therefore will I deliver him; I will set him on high, because he knows and understands My name.   —PSALM 91:13–14

God created each of us with a free will. This gives us the ability to make our own decisions apart from outside influence. Satan tries to force us to do things by placing outside pressure on us, but God attempts to lead us by His Holy Spirit. Jesus is not demanding or harsh, hard, sharp, or pressing. He is humble, gentle, meek, and lowly (Matthew 11:29–30). We are indeed complex creatures. Our mind can think one thing, while our emotions want something else and our will certainly seems to have a mind of its own. Once a person's willpower is renewed by God's Word and she knows enough to choose good over evil, she becomes very dangerous to Satan and his kingdom of darkness. The renewed person can override all the negative things Satan has planned by exercising her willpower to agree with God and His Word.

I have discovered that doubt is a thought planted in our heads by the devil. He uses it to keep us from enjoying life and making progress in God's good plan for us.

Lord, thank You for the power of Your Word to renew my mind. I choose to stand with Your truth and overcome the darkness that surrounds me. Amen.

Go Forward in Faith

*I call heaven and earth to witness this day against you that I have
set before you life and death, the blessings and the curses; therefore
choose life, that you and your descendants may live.*
—DEUTERONOMY 30:19

I have discovered that no matter how doubtful I feel, I can decide to
go forward in faith. My feelings are not me. I am greater than my feelings and so are you. No matter how we feel, we can still choose to do
the right thing. Going against your feelings is not always easy because
feelings are frequently very strong, but standing against them until you
enjoy freedom is much better than continuing to let them run your life
and hold you in bondage.

In Joshua 24:15 we see Joshua make a decision. He says, "Choose for
yourselves this day whom you will serve, whether the gods which your
fathers served on the other side of the River, or the gods of the Amorites, in whose land you dwell; but as for me and my house, we will serve
the Lord." Joshua made his mind up, and nobody was going to change
it. He didn't make his decision based on what others did. He refused to
live under the fear of man. If you make a decision, don't allow yourself
to become doubtful just because someone else is not doing what you
are doing.

What will you serve? Faith or feelings?

**Lord, I choose to not live by my feelings today or let them hold
me in bondage. I put my faith in You and will serve You with
all my heart. Amen.**

Train Yourself

For as he thinks in his heart, so is he.   —PROVERBS 23:7

I encourage you to practice being a positive person. It's just a matter of breaking one bad habit and forming a new one. I was so negative at one time in my life that if I even tried to think two positive thoughts in a row my brain got into a cramp. But now I am very positive and actually don't enjoy being with people who are negative.

Discipline is required any time you are forming a new habit. You might consider putting some reminders around your house or in your car, like little signs that say "Be positive." Ask a good friend or spouse to remind you if they hear you slipping into negativism.

Practice trusting yourself rather than doubting yourself. If you are applying for a promotion at work, don't think to yourself or say, "I probably won't get it." Pray and ask God to give you favor with your employer and then say, "I believe I will get the job!" And if you try and the outcome isn't what you were hoping for, then tell yourself, "If the job was right for me, God would give it to me, and since He didn't, He must have something even better in mind for me." You can train yourself to be positive in what appears to be a negative situation.

Lord, show me where I am stuck in negativity and need to break through to trusting You. Help me to have the right thoughts and attitudes that move me forward. Amen.

Live in God's Favor

But the Lord was with Joseph, and showed him mercy and loving-kindness and gave him favor in the sight of the warden of the prison. . . . For the Lord was with him and made whatever he did to prosper.   —GENESIS 39:21, 23

God wants to give you favor—kindness that you don't deserve. We see mention of God's favor toward many in the Bible, and there's no reason to think He can't offer it to you as well. Learn to believe God for favor.

Living in God's favor is very exciting. When Joseph was cruelly mistreated by his brothers and they sold him into slavery, God gave him favor everywhere he went. He had favor with Potiphar and was placed in charge of his household. He had favor with the jailer during his imprisonment for a crime he did not commit. He had so much favor with Pharaoh that Joseph became second only to Pharaoh in power. Yes, God's favor is an exciting way to live. We see so many men and women that we admire in the Bible being given favor. There was Ruth, Esther, Daniel, and Abraham, just to name a few.

Confess several times a day that you have favor with God and man. You will be amazed at the exciting things that happen to you if you speak God's Word instead of how you feel.

———————

Lord, I ask You to be with me today and to give me favor with those in my life. I want to prosper and be successful in all that I do. Amen.

Enjoy God's Best

Constantly praising God and being in favor and goodwill with all the people; and the Lord kept adding [to their number] daily those who were being saved [from spiritual death].   —ACTS 2:47

If you have made your mind up that you intend to enjoy the best life God has for you, you must realize that it begins with you. You must believe what God's Word says about you more than you believe what others say or what your feelings or own mind says.

Maybe you had negative messages fed to you since you were a child. It could have been parents who had troubles themselves and took their frustrations out on you. It could have been a teacher who delighted in belittling you in front of the rest of the class. Perhaps your parents excessively compared you to another sibling, giving you the impression that you were flawed. You may have experienced one or more broken relationships and became convinced it was your fault. But whatever the reason for your self-doubt and negative attitude toward yourself, it has to change if you truly desire to enjoy God's best in your life.

Resist and refuse to let doubt convince you that good things won't happen to you and your family; aggressively expect good things! Ask God to give you divine supernatural favor and then expect to see it in your life daily.

———————————

Lord, I believe that Your favor supersedes anything that has happened in my life. I expect to see Your blessings poured out today. Amen.

Be Patient

Now Moses kept the flock of Jethro his father-in-law, the priest
of Midian; and he led the flock to the back or west side of the
wilderness and came to Horeb or Sinai, the mountain of God.
The Angel of the Lord appeared to him.

—EXODUS 3:1–2

Can you really think of anyone who is an expert at something who does not practice and prepare? I can't. A concert pianist practices, a world-class gymnast practices, a dancer practices. All of that practice and preparation builds confidence in the individual.

Moses had a call on his life to deliver the Israelites from bondage where they were being held captive in Egypt. He wanted to get started right away, but as he did, he killed an Egyptian and was forced to flee from Egypt for many years. Taking action without God's permission showed clearly that Moses was not ready yet. He had zeal but no knowledge. He was emotional but not prepared. God led him into the wilderness where he remained for forty years being prepared by God for the job ahead of him.

When God gives us a job to do, we often think it will be easy to accomplish. However, most things are harder than you ever thought they would be, they take longer than you ever thought you could endure, but they also pay greater dividends than you could ever imagine.

Lord, help me to persevere as You continue to prepare and equip me for the job You have for me. Lead me and shape my character to glorify You. Amen.

Be Prepared

Study and be eager and do your utmost to present yourself to
God approved (tested by trial), a workman who has no cause to
be ashamed, correctly analyzing and accurately dividing [rightly
handling and skillfully teaching] the Word of Truth.

—2 TIMOTHY 2:15

Preparation equips us to move confidently. Many women lack confidence because they are not properly prepared for what they attempt to do. There could be a variety of reasons for this lack of preparation. They don't realize the importance of preparation, they are lazy, or they are too busy doing things that don't help them accomplish their goals and then have no time to do what would help them. Imagine a doctor trying to be confident if he never had any training or preparation. Anyone who is serious about playing a sport always practices and gets prepared.

As a teacher of God's Word, I never go to the pulpit without being thoroughly prepared. I study, pray, and go over and over my notes. Quite often I don't even look at the notes while preaching, because by the time I stand up to teach, they have become such a part of me that they flow out with ease. Knowing I have done my best to be prepared helps me minister with confidence.

Take the time to prepare; you'll be amazed at the confidence *that will* follow.

Lord, whether or not anyone else notices, I will do everything
in my power to prepare myself for what You have called me
to do. I want to be confident that I am always being the best I
can be and that I'm ready for more. Amen.

Don't Wing It

Although He was a Son, He learned [active, special] obedience through what He suffered and, [His completed experience] making Him perfectly [equipped], He became the Author and Source of eternal salvation to all those who give heed and obey Him.

—HEBREWS 5:8–9

Ever found yourself in a situation where you did not take time to prepare for something at work or at church and you're expected to do something? Your heart starts hammering, the butterflies in your stomach start flittering, and you quietly think to yourself, *I'll just wing it.* You're not prepared, but you're hoping you can pull it off anyway and nobody will ever know. Even if you do manage to deceive other people, you will know the truth and you won't feel good about it. Down deep inside you will know that you did not do your best. You might feel relieved that you managed to get through it, but you did it in fear rather than confidence.

Even Jesus was trained and prepared by the suffering He went through. He was equipped for His office as High Priest through His times of preparation. If Jesus needed preparation in order to be equipped for His job, there is no doubt that we need the same thing. Sometimes the bitter experiences we endure are the best teachers we have in life.

Lord, I ask You to use all of my life experiences to shape me as they shaped You. I want to be a person of substance and godliness with something to give to others. Amen.

God Always Provides

And the word of the Lord came to him, saying, Go from here and turn east and hide yourself by the brook Cherith, east of the Jordan. You shall drink of the brook, and I have commanded the ravens to feed you there.   —1 KINGS 17:2–4

When God called me into the ministry, I spent every free hour I could find studying God's Word and reading books that taught me biblical doctrine and principles. Many of my friends did not understand my new zeal, and some got angry and rejected me when I said no to their invitations to do things. It was hard for me emotionally to be so misunderstood. I later learned that God was calling me to separate myself as part of my preparation.

I taught home Bible studies for five years to groups that consisted of twenty-five or thirty people. I was faithful and received no financial benefits during that time. As part of my preparation, God led me to quit my job so I would have some time to prepare. It involved sacrificing the salary I made and being willing to trust God for our needs to be met. Learning to trust God in this way was part of my preparation for the ministry we now have, where we must trust God for literally everything. Trust doesn't just appear in our lives, but it grows as we take steps of faith and experience God's faithfulness.

Lord, guide me to take steps of genuine faith in You today. I rest in Your faithfulness and abundance of provision. Amen.

Be Trainable

For you see your calling, brethren, that not many wise according to the flesh, not many mighty, not many noble, are called. But God has chosen the foolish things of the world to put to shame the wise, and God has chosen the weak things of the world to put to shame the things which are mighty . . . to bring to nothing the things that are, that no flesh should glory in His presence.

—1 CORINTHIANS 1:26–29 NKJV

All we need to do is look at some of the disciples Jesus chose and we quickly see that God does not always or even usually call those who seem to be qualified. I can say for sure that God will prepare you in whatever way He chooses. It may be formal training and it may not, but God will use everything in your life to train you if you are willing to be trained. It's sad to say that many people have a great calling on their life but they are too impatient to go through the preparation that is necessary to equip them for the job.

Esther had to have a year of preparation before she was allowed to go before the king. For twelve months, she went through the purifying process, but even more than her physical beauty, her inner beauty showed through, and God used her to save her people from wicked Haman's evil plot.

If you're feeling unqualified for something you believe God is calling you to do, don't let that stop you. He will be your trainer.

Lord, thank You for calling me to follow You. I am delighted to be one of Your disciples. Equip me for the service You have for me. Amen.

Be Humble

Therefore humble yourselves [demote, lower yourselves in your own estimation] under the mighty hand of God, that in due time He may exalt you.   —1 PETER 5:6

Joseph dreamed of having authority and being a great man. However, he was young and impetuous. Joseph's brothers hated him and sold him into slavery. God used the situation as an opportunity to test and train Joseph. He even spent thirteen years in prison for something he didn't do, but whatever happened to Joseph during those years definitely equipped him for his God-ordained role in history. Joseph rose to power with only Pharaoh himself being greater. He was placed in a position to feed multitudes of people, including his father and brothers during seven years of famine.

Peter had to be prepared by going through some very humbling experiences; he was a powerful man but a proud man as well. The Lord had to humble him before He could use him. Most strong leaders have a lot of natural talent, but they are also full of themselves (pride) and have to learn how to depend on God. They have to trade in their self-confidence for God-confidence.

Your pain can become someone else's gain. Your mess can become your ministry if you will have a positive attitude and decide to let everything you go through prepare you for what is ahead.

———————————

Lord, I humble myself before You and recognize I can do nothing of lasting value apart from You. Work through all that's going on in my life to prepare me for what is ahead. Amen.

The Trap of Pride

Pride goes before destruction, and a haughty spirit before a fall.
—PROVERBS 16:18

A fear of being prideful may keep a person trapped in an attitude of self-abasement. The Bible does teach us not to have an exaggerated opinion of our own importance (Romans 12:3). We are to estimate ourselves according to the grace of God, knowing that our strengths come from Him and make us no better than others. We all have strengths and weaknesses!

Knowing our gifts come from God, we are not to critically appraise or look down on someone who is unable to excel at the same things we do. We definitely need to avoid pride. Pride is very dangerous. Many great men and women of God have fallen into sin due to pride.

Don't fall into the trap of pride, but don't go to the other extreme and think that self-rejection, self-hatred, and self-abasement is the answer. Jesus Himself said, "Apart from Me . . . you can do nothing" (John 15:5). Be confident, but remember the strength that comes from confidence can quickly be lost in conceit. It is vital to remain humble. I know I can do nothing of any real value unless Christ is flowing through me.

Seek to be what I call an "everything nothing" person—everything in Christ and nothing without Him.

———————————

Lord, keep me from the extremes of self-rejection and pride. The gifts and strengths I have come from You, and my weaknesses don't make me worse than others. By Your grace I am what I am. Amen.

At the Right Time

For the vision is yet for an appointed time and it hastens to the end [fulfillment]; it will not deceive or disappoint. Though it tarry, wait [earnestly] for it, because it will surely come; it will not be behindhand on its appointed day.   —HABAKKUK 2:3

As I have already stated, the kind of preparation you need depends on what you are being called to do and your season in life at that time. For many people, schooling is the first type of preparation they get, but for others that isn't possible. A married woman with three small children and a part-time job probably could not leave for two years to go to Bible college or to get a degree in business administration. If you do desire schooling and cannot get it full-time, you might consider taking some evening classes or even Internet classes. Follow your heart and God will lead you to the right destination at the right time.

If you have something in your heart that you believe you are supposed to do but are unable to do now, don't let that discourage you. We hold some things in our hearts for years before we see them manifest. Let your dream incubate in your heart. Pray about it and do whatever you can to be ready when the time is right.

––––––––––––––

Lord, You see the dreams in my heart . . . even the ones I've given up on and the ones that seem so distant. Breathe life into me by Your Spirit and fulfill the vision You have for me. Amen.

Keep Learning

The wise also will hear and increase in learning, and the person of understanding will acquire skill and attain to sound counsel [so that he may be able to steer his course rightly].   —PROVERBS 1:5

It is important that you understand the idea that preparation for what God wants you to do does not have to be formal or conventional training. It is also important that you understand that God does not call everyone into full-time ministry. He may call you into business, government, or some other thing, but if you want to do it with confidence, you will need preparation.

Even the people who are able to get formal training still need to have some experience. Knowing something in our head and knowing how to apply it practically can be two different things. God is looking for people with experience in life, so ask Him to begin your training and preparation today and you can learn anything you will need for your future. We need to be lifetime learners, and we can all learn something every day if we let all of life be a school we attend.

In my case, I was not able to go to college when I got out of high school, but God taught me everywhere I was.

Wherever you are, you're in God's classroom.

Lord, what are You trying to teach me today? I open my heart to the lessons that will come my way. Give me the experiences that will make me a woman after Your heart. Amen.

Don't Be Boxed In

At Joppa there was a certain disciple named...Dorcas. This woman
was full of good works and charitable deeds which she did....
And all the widows stood by him weeping, showing the tunics and
garments which Dorcas had made while she was with them.

—ACTS 9:36, 39 NKJV

Don't try to put God in a box by thinking that everyone has to do the same thing. Not everyone who serves God in ministry went to seminary or Bible school. Not everyone who is the president or CEO of a major corporation went to college. Some people get on-the-job training. They are simply not book people and learn much more quickly by the hands-on method. However we learn, we can be assured that God will prepare us in His own way.

Microsoft czar Bill Gates dropped out of Harvard in his junior year. Instead of going to college, Truett Cathy started a chicken restaurant with strong biblically-based business principles and Chick-fil-A is now the second largest quick service chicken restaurant chain in the country. Our youngest son did not go to college; he is the CEO of our USA office and does a fantastic job. God equips some people with very strong natural skills and a lot of common sense. It is amazing what we learn in life that we don't even realize we are learning until we need to put it into practice.

Lord, I don't want to copy others because I'm unsure of
myself. I want to follow You and be trained and used by You in
the way You have for me. Amen.

Small Things

Who [with reason] despises the day of small things?
—ZECHARIAH 4:10

I encourage you to let everything in life be preparation for the things you have in your future. Don't despise the days of small beginnings. Those small beginnings are usually all we can handle at the time. God will give more when He knows we are ready. Enjoy every step of your journey. Don't be in such a hurry to rush through things that you miss the lessons you can draw from each day.

If you do what you can do, God will do what you cannot do. Do your best to be prepared for the job in front of you and God will come through with some supernatural abilities that will amaze you. I study diligently for my sermons and quite often I hear myself say things when I am teaching that I did not even know that I knew. I did my part, and God came through supernaturally with some things to make my message even better.

To be prepared for whatever God's calling is for you, you don't have to worry about the part you don't know how to do, just do the part you know. Your faith-filled actions are seeds you sow. Sow your seed in faith and God will bring a harvest at just the right time.

Lord, I don't want to be rushing so fast that I miss the small things in life. I will give You my best, and I trust You to do what I cannot do. Amen.

God's Gifts

Therefore it is said, When He ascended on high, He led captivity captive [He led a train of vanquished foes] and He bestowed gifts on men. —EPHESIANS 4:8

I am gifted in communication. My worship leader is gifted musically. My two sons are gifted in business administration. My husband is gifted in wisdom and financial management. We make a good team because we have different abilities. We complement and complete each other. A lot of people never do anything because they cannot do everything. They are negative people who concentrate on what they cannot do instead of seeing what they can do and then do it.

If you confidently step out and do your part, God will surround you with people who have the gifts and abilities that you don't have. However, when a person lacks confidence, quite often they cannot receive help from other people. They are too busy making comparisons to receive the help God has sent them. Insecurity and a lack of confidence will steal the wonderful life that God has planned for you. It causes us to be jealous of and resent those whom we should appreciate.

You don't have to be prepared to do the entire job by yourself, just prepare yourself to do the best that you can do and remember that God will add what you don't have.

———————————

Lord, You have designed me with gifts and abilities to develop and use in service with others. Keep me from being jealous of others, and help me to enjoy the journey. Amen.

Know Your Weaknesses

However, when Simon saw that the [Holy] Spirit was imparted
through the laying on of the apostles' hands, he brought money and
offered it to them, saying, Grant me also this power and authority.
—ACTS 8:18–19

Make sure that whatever you are trying to do is something you are really meant to do and not just something you want to do to impress people. How do you know what you can do and what you cannot do? It's important to understand this if you are to be well prepared. This will prevent you from wasting your time on something you won't succeed at anyway. I am a good public speaker, but I quickly discovered that I had zero ability as a musician. Had I continued to insist on learning to be a musician, I would have felt like a failure. As hard as you may try, you cannot be properly prepared and feel confident to do something you are not meant to do.

I cannot play musical instruments, but God has always provided me musicians for my ministry. I am not afraid to say that I'm not good at something, and I don't waste my time trying to develop my weaknesses.

Don't be afraid to admit what you cannot do. Know your weaknesses and pray for God to send people into your life to do what you cannot do.

Lord, it's easy to be jealous of other people's gifts. Help me to focus on what I was meant to do and keep me from wasting time on my weaknesses. Amen.

Be a Lifetime Learner

Whatever your hand finds to do, do it with all your might.
—ECCLESIASTES 9:10

Over the years we have released several great people from the ministry because they did not continue with their training, even when we offered it to them, so they could go into the future with us. It has always amazed me how some people will be aggressive and obtain whatever training they need to be all they can be in life, while others do nothing but complain because nobody is dropping opportunities in their lap. We don't deserve a promotion and pay raise just because we sit in a company chair for another year. We must be willing to be more valuable to our employer, and the only way we can do that is by taking more responsibility or doing the job we do better than we have done it in the past.

Be a lifetime learner. Read, listen, and learn. Go to school or take special classes to keep up with advancing technology in your field. If you make an investment, you will reap a reward. The more you know about what you are doing, the more confidence you will have. The more confidence you have, the more confidence others will be able to place in you. If you get prepared now, you will be promoted later.

———————

Lord, I don't want to be left behind in my life because I was too lazy or inattentive to get the training I need to stay current and relevant. Help me to invest in the right things that will reap a reward. Amen.

Brag about God

I will confess and praise You for You are fearful and wonderful and for the awful wonder of my birth! Wonderful are Your works, and that my inner self knows right well. —PSALM 139:14

When David describes how God creates us in our mother's womb with His very own hand, he is basically saying, "I am wonderful, and I know that in my heart." He is not bragging on himself, but on God who created him. You can build confidence by being bold enough to realize that you are a great person with wonderful abilities.

For instance, if you are a good mother and homemaker, then say so. I believe I am a good wife and mother—not a normal one, but a good one. It took me a long time to be willing to say that. For many years the devil convinced me that I was not a good wife and mother, because I was not able to do all the things other wives and mothers did. I finally realized that I did not call myself into the ministry; God did. He also gave a grace (special ability) to my family for me to be in ministry. Yes, there were sacrifices that had to be made, but God has provided benefits far greater. Each time in life you sacrifice, you will eventually reap the seed you have sown.

Lord, I affirm that You have made me "very good," because You are a wonderful Creator. Give me the grace and wisdom to develop my abilities into the full person You want me to be. Amen.

Pray First

Keep awake and watch and pray [constantly], that you may not enter into temptation; the spirit indeed is willing, but the flesh is weak.   —MARK 14:38

Praying is probably the most important part of life preparation, yet so many people today ignore or forget this vital part of the process. I suggest you don't do anything without first praying. The Bible says that we should acknowledge God in all our ways and He will direct our steps and make them sure (Proverbs 3:6). It's not enough to know that He's there. We must call on Him daily for His guidance and His strength.

I have been walking with God most of my life, and I am still learning the importance of not trying to do anything without praying. The Bible says we are to pray without ceasing. This does not mean that we do nothing all day except pray, but it does make the point that prayer is one of the most important things we can ever do. We need to pray our way through the day. Prayer opens the door for God to work in our lives, situations, and the lives of our loved ones. God will enable you to do things that will frequently surprise you if you take Him as your partner in life. But you must start with prayer.

————————

Lord, teach me to pray. Help me to bring You into every moment of my day and life. I need Your guidance and strength in all that I do. Amen.

Get Help

But the Helper, the Holy Spirit, whom the Father will send in My name, He will teach you all things, and bring to your remembrance all things that I said to you. —JOHN 14:26 NKJV

I once heard of a region in Africa where the first converts to Christianity were very diligent about praying. In fact, the believers each had their own special place outside the village where they went on private footpaths through the brush to pray in solitude. When grass began to grow over one of these trails, signaling that the person to whom it belonged was not praying very much, other new believers would go to the person and lovingly warn, "Friend, there's grass on your path!"

Prayer makes tremendous power available (James 5:16). Don't let your prayer life reflect weeds of inconsistency or neglect. New confidence can quickly form when you have the power of God's Holy Spirit working in your life. Jesus sent the Holy Spirit to be our Helper in life. He is always ready to get involved, but we must ask for His help. It's like preparing to cook dinner and a world-renowned gourmet chef walks in and tells you he's available to assist you. The Holy Spirit offers world-renowned supernatural service. Don't live in weakness when power is just a prayer away.

Make sure there's no grass in your path.

Lord, I ask You to send the Holy Spirit into my heart and work to empower me to serve You. Spirit of God, breathe upon my prayer life and help me to pray with both my spirit and my mind. Amen.

The Fear of Man

The fear of man brings a snare, but whoever leans on, trusts in, and puts his confidence in the Lord is safe and set on high.

—PROVERBS 29:25

The apostle Paul made it clear that if he had tried to be popular with people he would not have been an apostle of Jesus Christ (Galatians 1:10). God uses men and women who are set on obeying and pleasing Him, not those who are controlled by the fear of man. We all want to be liked and accepted, but we cannot let that desire control us. If it does, we are guaranteed to reap Henry Swope's formula for failure, which is "try to please everybody."

King Saul lost the kingdom because he allowed his fear of man to cause him to disobey God (1 Samuel 13:8–14). God took the kingdom away from Saul and gave it to David, a man after His own heart. David did not let people control him as Saul did. David's own brother Eliab showed disapproval of him, but the Bible says that David turned away from Eliab and continued on with what he was supposed to do (1 Samuel 17:28–30). We should turn away from the people who try to discourage or accuse us instead of allowing what they say or think to affect us adversely.

Lord, the fear of what others think about me is always in front of me, calling out for my servitude. Help me to be true to Your call and pleasing in Your sight alone. Amen.

Press On

I have strength for all things in Christ who empowers me [I am
ready for anything through Him who infuses inner strength in me;
I am self-sufficient in Christ's sufficiency.   —PHILLIPIANS 4:13

History is filled with people who accomplished great things even though they had to persevere past the criticism and judgment of others. Some of the world's greatest inventors were persecuted by their family or friends, but they pressed on because they believed in what they were doing.

Benjamin Franklin longed to write for his older brother's newspaper where he worked as a printing apprentice, but his brother refused to let him. Ben wrote stories anyway, under a pen name, Silence Dogood. Every letter was snuck under the printing shop's door at night to avoid discovery, and "Silence Dogood" became wildly popular. When Ben finally admitted that he was the writer who was getting so much attention, his brother only grew angrier and more jealous. This resulted in Ben receiving beatings and finally running away. Among the many inventions and improvements he created in his lifetime, Ben eventually started his own printing shop and took over a newspaper, the *Pennsylvania Gazette*, which under his supervision became the most successful in the colonies.

You can accomplish great things if you'll listen to God instead of others.

———————————

Lord, strengthen me in my inner being to be able to persevere against adversity. I can move forward confidently if I know it is Your way. Amen.

Expect a Battle

Then [the guiding angel] showed me Joshua the high priest standing before the Angel of the Lord, and Satan standing at Joshua's right hand to be his adversary and to accuse him.   —ZECHARIAH 3:1

Expect that the world might say, "No! You can't do that, you're a woman." That is what I heard when God called me into the ministry. Most of my family and almost all of my friends turned against me. At that time I didn't really understand the Scriptures that people tried to use against me, but I'm not the first woman to be told that I should ignore God's leading on my life or was offered suggestions that conflicted with my primary purpose or desire of serving God. As I mentioned earlier, the war between women and Satan got its start in the Garden of Eden and has not stopped. Satan hates women because it was a woman who gave birth to Jesus, and it is Jesus who has defeated Satan.

However, don't think that just because the devil is against you that success is out of your reach. Even though most of the world told me I could not do it, I have been doing it for over thirty years and intend to continue until Jesus calls me out of this world. God has done it in spite of what everyone thought. People and the devil cannot stop God!

Lord, I'm so glad that You have defeated Satan on the cross. I feel the accusations of the adversary, but I will triumph in Jesus' name. Amen.

Know Your Heart

If anyone serves Me, he must continue to follow Me [to cleave steadfastly to Me, conform wholly to My example in living and, if need be, in dying] and wherever I am, there will My servant be also. If anyone serves Me, the Father will honor him.

—JOHN 12:26

Anyone who tries to keep all the people happy all the time will never fulfill their destiny. Consider the story of the woman from California who kept two bottled water coolers in her kitchen. It wasn't because she was extra thirsty or on a health kick; it was because she couldn't say no to either water company when they called! She was afraid that the salesmen would say bad things about her if she said no.

Maybe you don't have problems saying no to telemarketers, but maybe you do struggle with saying no to your friends, or your family, or your church family, even at the detriment of what you feel God is calling you to do. People are not always happy for your success, and even well-meaning people will try to stop you from making progress. You must know your own heart and what you believe you are supposed to be doing and do it. If you make a mistake, you will know it soon enough; when you do, don't be too proud to say, "I was wrong."

Lord, I want to be where You are leading, whether other people agree with it or not. I cleave to You in love and will serve You all of my days. Amen.

Step Out

Arise [from the depression and prostration in which circumstances have kept you—rise to a new life]! Shine (be radiant with the glory of the Lord), for your light has come, and the glory of the Lord has risen upon you!
—ISAIAH 60:1

"Step out and find out" is my slogan. I hate to see people shrink back in fear and be so afraid of making a mistake that they never try to do anything. I know a young man who quit a good job to go into music ministry. It was a bold step, and he did everything he could to make it work, but it just didn't (at least not at this time). However, I am proud of him that he was bold enough to try. At least now he won't spend the rest of his life wondering what could have been if only he had tried.

Unless you listen to God and follow your own heart, you will live an unfulfilled and frustrated life. Anyone who allows other people to control her and guide her destiny will eventually become bitter and feel used and taken advantage of. I think it is better to try and fail than never to try at all. Sometimes the only way we can discover what we are supposed to do with our lives is to try different things until we see what works and what fits right in our heart.

Don't let fear of making a wrong choice stop you from stepping out.

———————

Lord, I don't want to live with regrets. Help me to be bold and step out and follow what I believe You've put in my heart to do. Amen.

Enjoy Life

But we all, with unveiled face, beholding as in a mirror the glory of the Lord, are being transformed into the same image from glory to glory, just as by the Spirit of the Lord.

—2 CORINTHIANS 3:18 NKJV

I think the greatest tragedy in life is to live and not enjoy life. If you are warring with yourself all the time, you are not enjoying your life. God changes us from one degree of glory to another, but don't forget to enjoy the glory you are in right now while you are headed for the next one. Don't compare the glory you are in with the glory of some friend or family member who appears to be in a greater degree of glory. Each of us is an individual, and God deals with us differently, according to what He knows we need and can handle.

You may not notice changes on a daily basis, but as you look back over time you will see very definite changes in yourself. Believe that God is working, just as He said He would. Remember, we see *after* we believe, not *before*. We wrestle and struggle with ourselves because of all that we are not, when we should be praising and worshipping God for all that we are. As we worship Him for Who He is, God's character is released into our lives and begins to manifest.

Lord, I will be glad today because You are changing me from glory to glory. Thank You for working in my life. Amen.

Use Your Sword

For the word of God is living and powerful, and sharper than any two-edged sword, piercing even to the division of soul and spirit, and of joints and marrow, and is a discerner of the thoughts and intents of the heart.   —HEBREWS 4:12 NKJV

The Word of God is a key weapon in the bringing down of mental strongholds that keep us from confidence. In my life, for years I thought that because I was sexually abused in my childhood that I could never be any good, that nobody would ever want me. Eventually I began to get some truth down inside me. Now when those negative thoughts arise, the Spirit rises within me and wields the two-edge sword of the Word against the lies of the enemy.

I use my mouth to speak forth that truth: "No, Satan, I am good in God. I am not good in myself, but His goodness dwells in me, and He has a good plan for my life. I have overcome my past because I have let go of what lies behind and am pressing on to the good things that lie ahead." Speaking the truth of God's Word to the devil is the only way to see a mind-set change. Bring your thoughts into line with the Word and press on toward the good things He has in store for you. The choice is yours!

Lord, help me to get Your truth down inside of me and make me strong to apply it in my thought life. I choose Your Word to defeat the enemy. Amen.

Be Unstoppable

Go, gather together all the Jews that are present in Shushan, and fast for me; and neither eat nor drink for three days, night or day. I also and my maids will fast as you do. Then I will go to the king, though it is against the law; and if I perish, I perish.

—ESTHER 4:16

Hedy Lamarr, a popular movie star from the 1930s and 1940s, was extremely creative and intelligent. She earnestly wanted to help with the war effort during World War II and considered leaving acting to join the National Inventors Council but was told her pretty face and star status could do more for the war by encouraging people to buy war bonds. But Hedy never gave up on her dream and helped invent a remote-controlled radio communications system that was patented during World War II. In addition to her invention that has contributed to multiple technologies used today, she raised millions of dollars to help the war effort.

It is amazing that those who have contributed so much to the progress of society have often had to endure tremendous criticism, judgment, and persecution in order to make something in the world better. This clearly shows how Satan fights progress of any kind. He uses all kinds of fears to try and stop people, but the confident woman will keep pressing on and say "Yes" even when the world screams "No."

Lord, I will use my gifts to make my small part of the world a better place today. I ask for your help and strength to do this. Amen.

It's Not about Age

Let no one despise or think less of you because of your youth, but be an example (pattern) for the believers in speech, in conduct, in love, in faith, and in purity.　　　—1 TIMOTHY 4:12

Timothy, Paul's "spiritual" son in the ministry, was very young, and he was fearful and worried about what people thought of his youth. Paul told him to let no man despise his youth. It really does not matter how old or young a person is. If God calls someone to do something, and they have the confidence to go forward, nothing can stop them.

How you respond to your age and, for that matter, how others respond is really up to you. We all age in years, but we don't have to get an "I'm too old" mind-set. Moses was eighty years old when he left Egypt to lead the Israelites to the Promised Land. Confident people don't think about how old they are; they think about what they can accomplish with the time they have left. Remember, confident people are positive and look at what they have, not what they have lost.

Even if you are reading this book and let's say you're sixty-five years old and feel you have wasted most of your life doing nothing—you can still start today and do something amazing and great with your life.

Lord, You used people of all ages throughout the Bible, and You can use me. Today is a new day, and I am excited about what You have for me to accomplish. Amen.

Confront Injustice

Then Pharaoh charged all his people, saying, Every son born [to the Hebrews] you shall cast into the river [Nile]. . . . Then Pharaoh's daughter said to her, Take this child away and nurse it for me . . . And the child grew, and she brought him to Pharaoh's daughter and he became her son. And she called him Moses.

—EXODUS 1:22; 2:9–10

Dorothea Lynde Dix (1802–1887) initiated the most widespread reform for the mentally ill that occurred during the nineteenth century. Her first experience in mental health reform came about as a result of an opportunity to conduct a Sunday school class in a jail where she found mentally ill people kept in unheated cells because "the insane do not feel heat or cold." One of the conclusions of her research was that by merely improving the living conditions of the mentally ill, their illness could be greatly alleviated. Dix played a major role in founding thirty-two mental hospitals, fifteen schools for the feebleminded, a school for the blind, and numerous training facilities for nurses.

All that must happen in order for a tragic injustice to crumble is for someone to confront it. That person must have perseverance and must not be easily defeated by opposition. It is totally amazing what one woman can accomplish if she will press forward confidently rather than shrink back in fear.

———————————

Lord, help me to reach out to those who are in need around me and do what I can do for them. Help me to confront what's wrong and have the perseverance to overcome it. Amen.

Not the Weaker Sex

In the same way you married men should live considerately with [your wives], with an intelligent recognition [of the marriage relation], honoring the woman as [physically] the weaker, but [realizing that you] are joint heirs of the grace (God's unmerited favor) of life, in order that your prayers may not be hindered and cut off. [Otherwise you cannot pray effectively.]

—1 PETER 3:7

One of the misguided ideas about women is that they are weaker than men. The Bible says that they are physically weaker, but it never indicates they are weaker in any other way. Women have the babies and believe me when I say that you cannot be weak and do that. I am not weak, and I am not a quitter. As a woman, refuse to see yourself as the "weaker sex." Don't let that wrong mind-set take hold of you. You can do whatever you need to do in life.

Some men think that if a woman is a stay-at-home mom and homemaker that she does nothing all day. He may say things like, "I worked all day. What did you do?" These types of comments can make a woman feel devalued. Raising a family, taking care of a man, and being a good homemaker is a full-time job that requires overtime with no overtime pay. I applaud the stay-at-home moms, especially those who do their job with joy. You are my heroes!

———————————

Lord, I reject the idea that I am weak because I am a woman. By Your grace I will be strong in all I do. Amen.

True Strength

Sing to God, sing praises to His name, cast up a highway for Him Who rides through the deserts—His name is the Lord—be in high spirits and glory before Him! A father of the fatherless and a judge and protector of the widows is God in His holy habitation. God places the solitary in families and gives the desolate a home in which to dwell.
　　　　　　　　　　　　　　　　　　　　　—PSALM 68:4–6

The world is filled with single mothers whose husbands walked out on them and refuse to support their children financially. Men who merely walk away need to remember that strength does not walk away, but it works through situations and takes responsibility.

More than ten million single mothers today are raising children under the age of eighteen. That number is up drastically from the three million reported in 1970, and it's estimated that 34 percent of families headed by single mothers fall under the poverty line (making less than $15,670 annually). Their biggest concerns are much more basic than many two-parent homes—they worry about quality child care for their children, keeping a car running, and living in a safe house or apartment, all within a restricted budget. They work hard and try to be both mom and dad to their children. They sacrifice time, personal pleasures, and everything else imaginable because they love their children fiercely. They are certainly not weak.

These moms are giants in my eyes.

———————————

Lord, I pray for the single moms whom I know. Give them the strength and protection and fullness of Your blessings. Champion their cause and provide for them in abundance. Amen.

Freedom of a Child

Then little children were brought to Jesus, that He might put His hands on them and pray; but the disciples rebuked those who brought them. But He said, Leave the children alone! Allow the little ones to come to Me, and do not forbid or restrain or hinder them, for of such [as these] is the kingdom of heaven composed.

—MATTHEW 19:13–14

Children seem to be able to make a game out of anything. They quickly adjust, don't have a problem letting other children be different than they are, and are always exploring something new. They are amazed by everything!

Oswald Chambers wrote in *My Utmost for His Highest*: "The freedom after sanctification is the freedom of a child, the things that used to keep the life pinned down are gone." We definitely need to watch and study children and obey the command of Jesus to be more like them (Matthew 18:3). It is something we have to do on purpose as we get older. We all have to grow up and be responsible, but we don't have to stop enjoying ourselves and life.

Don't let the world steal your confidence. Remember that you have been created on purpose by the hand of God. He has a special, unique, wonderful plan for you. Go for it! Don't shrink back, conform, or live in fear.

———————————

Lord, I can't be a child again, but I can have the freedom and the wonder of a child. I come to You as a child now, and I ask You to renew a childlike faith in me. Amen.

Get Understanding

My people are destroyed for lack of knowledge. —HOSEA 4:6

I believe marriages, friendships, and business relationships are destroyed due to men and women not understanding the differences that make us unique. In our pride we usually think that we are a shining example of what is right, and we expect everyone to act as we do and like what we like, but that is fantasy, not fact.

In his best-selling book *Love and Respect*, Dr. Emerson Eggerichs points out that the obvious differences found in men and women can be seen in something as simple as looking into a closet. Eggerichs writes about a couple getting dressed for the day: *She says, "I have nothing to wear." (She means, she has nothing new.) He says, "I have nothing to wear." (He means, he has nothing clean.)*

God made men and women to be different in many different ways. Whether you are married or single, you will encounter and need to deal with men throughout your life. I believe it is important for our confidence level as women to understand ourselves and the differences between us and men. We need to remember that those differences aren't better or worse, they're just different. Once we accept those differences, we can understand and appreciate what each gender offers.

———————

Lord, I ask You to help me understand myself as well as to understand men in general. Then help me apply that understanding in practical, helpful ways in my relationships. Amen.

Stop Competing

Some trust in and boast of chariots and some of horses, but we will trust in and boast of the name of the Lord our God.

—PSALM 20:7

Perhaps you've heard the saying, "It's a man's world, and if you want anything in this world, you have to fight for it." I choose to believe it is my world also, and I don't fight—I trust God that He will help me be all I can be. I don't have to compete with a man for his position; I have my own position, and I am comfortable with it. I like being a woman, and I don't want to be a man. But I must admit there are mornings when I wish all I had to do was comb my hair and shave instead of doing my skin care routine, putting on makeup, curling my hair, arching my eyebrows, and trying on three outfits before I finally feel it is safe to go outside.

Some women have such a competitive spirit with men that they forget to be women. Recently a minister whom I greatly respect said, "Joyce, you are a woman in ministry who still knows how to be a woman. You are not trying to act like a man or preach like one." If you try to act like men, it will lead to failure and rejection. Remember: you can be strong but feminine.

Lord, the competition factor has been drilled into me since childhood. I choose to trust in You and to be content in the position You have for me. Amen.

What's the Difference?

The beginning of Wisdom is: get Wisdom (skillful and godly Wisdom)! [For skillful and godly Wisdom is the principal thing.] And with all you have gotten, get understanding (discernment, comprehension, and interpretation).   —PROVERBS 4:7

The Bible encourages us to seek understanding. Read a couple of good books on the differences between men and women and also one on the differences in personalities. If you do, it may prevent thousands of arguments or misunderstandings.

Women offer unsolicited advice and give direction, and men usually don't take advice very well. The woman thinks she is just trying to help, but the man thinks she doesn't trust him to make the right decision.

When a woman disagrees with a man, he takes it as disapproval, and it ignites his defenses. Men only want advice after they have done everything they can do. Advice given too soon or too often causes him to lose his sense of power. He may become lazy or insecure.

Men are motivated and empowered when they feel needed. Women are motivated when they feel cherished.

Men are visual creatures; once an image is in their head, it's hard to get it out. Women are more inclined to remember emotions or how something made them feel.

Seek understanding first, then speak.

———————————

Lord, I want to be a woman of wisdom and understanding. Help me comprehend why men are the way they are and how I can improve in my communications and friendships. Amen.

Deal with It

Become useful and helpful and kind to one another, tenderhearted (compassionate, understanding, loving-hearted), forgiving one another [readily and freely], as God in Christ forgave you.

—EPHESIANS 4:32

Communication experts say that the average woman speaks more than twenty-five thousand words a day while the average man speaks only a little over ten thousand. One business executive said, "The problem is that by the time I get home from work I have already spoken my ten thousand, and my wife hasn't even gotten started."

Men tend to go into their cave and want to think about what is bothering them, but women want to talk about what's bothering them. Men don't feel like they have to share everything, while women usually share everything and more.

In one survey, more than 80 percent of men said that in a conflict they were likely to feel disrespected. Women, on the other hand, would feel unloved.

When a man and woman have had a problem and the man is ready to reconnect, he doesn't need to talk about his upset feelings because he is no longer upset. He wants to forget it and move on. She wants to talk about it and make a list of ways they can avoid having it happen again. Before I learned better, I always wanted to try to figure out why we had the argument to begin with, and Dave simply said, "It is part of life."

Understanding our differences helps us understand each other.

Lord, I want to come to grips with how to become a better communicator. Give me the grace to stop and think before I speak. Amen.

Revise Your Expectations

Say to skillful and godly Wisdom, You are my sister, and regard
understanding or insight as your intimate friend.

—PROVERBS 7:4

Understanding does make all the difference in the world. My husband, for example, is very protective of me and is constantly telling me how to do things to prevent me from getting hurt. I thought that he thought I was dumb. I often said, "You don't need to tell me that. I am not stupid." He would look hurt and say, "I'm just trying to help you." Now that I understand, his actions make me feel cherished.

Women want to be loved, respected, valued, complimented, listened to, trusted, and, sometimes, just to be held. Men want tickets for the World Series.

Women want affection. Men want sex.

Most women cry an average of five times per month. I haven't seen my husband cry five times in forty years. Women are simply more emotional than men. Men are very logical.

Men are simple, whereas women are not simple, and they always assume that men are just as complicated and intricate as they are. The whole point is that guys don't think deeply all the time like women do. They are just what they appear to be. I recall once getting irritated with Dave and telling him that we needed to have deeper conversation. He said, "This is as deep as I get."

Lord, help me to be balanced in my thinking when it comes to men. Help me to revise my expectations and not bring frustration or hurt to those whom I love. Amen.

Being Dependent

For from Him and through Him and to Him are all things. [For all things originate with Him and come from Him; all things live through Him, and all things center in and tend to consummate and to end in Him.] To Him be glory forever! Amen (so be it).

—ROMANS 11:36

Several studies show that women are more likely to be dependent on others than men are and often have more difficulty establishing their independence. These facts help form the way we cope with issues when we grow up. Males are often known to be good at independence but not good at relationships. Females are usually better at relationships but not so good with independence.

Let me establish what I mean by independence. We are never to be independent from God. As I have said repeatedly, we cannot do anything properly without Him and should be dependent on God at all times for all things (John 15:5).

Needing God and needing people is not a sign of weakness. We can be dependent and independent at the same time. Bruce Wilkinson once said, "God's power under us, in us, surging through us, is exactly what turns dependence into unforgettable experiences of completeness." We can feel complete when we acknowledge our dependence on our heavenly Father.

———

Lord, I confess my utter dependency upon You for all things, and I recognize how dependent I am upon others as well. But help me to also establish my independence of others. My only ultimate dependence is upon You. Amen.

Unbalanced Dependence

Yet the Lord is faithful, and He will strengthen [you] and set you on a firm foundation and guard you from the evil [one].
—2 THESSALONIANS 3:3

When a boy is growing up, he begins to realize that he is not like his mother, and he differentiates himself from her. His masculinity is defined by separation. He will normally seek his own identity and individuality. A girl does not feel this need and usually remains close to and dependent upon her mother.

About twice as many women as men experience depression, and about 70 percent of the mood-altering or anxiety-relieving drugs are taken by women. In her book *Unfinished Business: Pressure Points in the Lives of Women,* Maggie Scarf has suggested this reason:

> Women are statistically more depressed because they have been taught to be more dependent and affection-seeking, and thus they rarely achieve an independent sense of self. A woman gives her highest priorities to pleasing others, being attractive to others, being cared for, and caring for others. Women receive ferocious training in a direction that leads away from thinking "What do I want?" and toward "What do they want?" They may be in danger of merely melting into the people around them and fail to realize they are an individual with rights and needs, and they need to establish independence.

Ask yourself today, "What do I want?"

Lord, it is so easy to lose my sense of independence and get caught in totally depending upon others. Strengthen me and set me on Your firm foundation of freedom. Amen.

Balanced Independence

And you are in Him, made full and having come to fullness of life
[in Christ you too are filled with the Godhead—Father, Son and
Holy Spirit—and reach full spiritual stature]. And He is the Head
of all rule and authority [of every angelic principality and power].
—COLOSSIANS 2:10

I believe that women have a need to feel safe and cared for, and I don't believe that is wrong. My husband takes very good care of me and I like it. He is protective and always wants to make sure that I am safe. The difference in me and perhaps someone who has an out-of-balance attitude in this area is that, even though I thoroughly enjoy Dave taking care of me, I also know that I could take care of myself if I needed to. Even though I am dependent upon him and rightfully so, I am not so dependent that I am handicapped by it.

A balanced independence is what we should seek, and to me that is being able to trust and depend on God and other people and yet establish my individual identity. The Bible teaches that we are not to be conformed to the pattern of this world (Romans 12:2). Everyone has his or her own idea of what we should be. To establish a balanced independence in our lives must become our high priority.

———————————

Lord, I cannot change myself, but I can be transformed by the renewing of my mind according to Your Word. Bring balance to my relationships that leads to inner harmony. Amen.

Do What God Expects

*Thus says the Lord of hosts: Do not listen to the words of the [false]
prophets who prophesy to you. They teach you vanity (emptiness,
falsity, and futility) and fill you with vain hopes; they speak a vision
of their own minds and not from the mouth of the Lord.*

—JEREMIAH 23:16

Don't let the people around you determine your values or behavior
patterns. It seems that everyone expects something a little different,
but one thing for sure is that all these people expect us to keep them
happy and give them what they want.

Many times the expectations people put on us and we accept are
unrealistic. If you want to have confidence, you must stop trying to be
"superwoman." Realize you have limitations and that you cannot keep
all the people happy all the time.

This is one of the amazing traits we see in Jesus. He was the same all
the time. He changed people; they did not change Him.

When unhappy people are unsuccessful in making you unhappy,
they begin to respect and admire you. They see that your Christianity
is something real. Even people who seek to control you will disrespect
you if you allow them to have power over you. I encourage you to be
your own person. Do what God expects you to do, and don't live under
the tyranny of other people's expectations.

———————————

Lord, I can't possibly fulfill everyone else's expectations and
demands. Help me to clearly see Your values and live according to them. Keep me free from others who want control.
Amen.

Guard Your Reactions

He who rebukes a scorner heaps upon himself abuse, and he who reproves a wicked man gets for himself bruises. Reprove not a scorner, lest he hate you; reprove a wise man, and he will love you. Give instruction to a wise man and he will be yet wiser.

—PROVERBS 9:7–9

It has been statistically proven that 10 percent of people will never like you, so stop trying to have a perfect record with everyone and start celebrating who you are. A person who knows how to live independently does not allow the moods of other people to alter hers.

A story is told of a Quaker man who knew how to live independently as the valued person God had created Him to be. One night as he was walking down the street with a friend, he stopped at a newsstand to purchase an evening paper. The storekeeper was very sour, rude, and unfriendly. The Quaker man treated him with respect and was quite kind in his dealing with him. He paid for his paper, and he and his friend continued to walk down the street. The friend said to the Quaker, "How could you be so cordial to him with the terrible way he was treating you?" The Quaker man replied, "Oh, he is always that way. Why should I let him determine how I am going to act?"

Who are you letting determine how you act?

————————

Lord, help me to not allow others to steal my joy and peace by the things they say and do. I want to be kind and cordial, but I won't let my mood be determined by others. Amen.

When Criticism Comes

But [as for me personally] it matters very little to me that I should be put on trial by you [on this point], and that you or any other human tribunal should investigate and question and cross-question me. I do not even put myself on trial and judge myself.... It is the Lord [Himself] Who examines and judges me.

—1 CORINTHIANS 4:3–4

No matter what you do in life you will be criticized by someone, so you must learn to cope with it and not let it bother you. Criticism is very difficult for most of us, and a person's self-image can be damaged by one critical remark. But it is possible to learn how not to be affected at all by criticism. Every great man or woman has had to learn how to cope with criticism. We must know our own hearts and not allow others to judge us.

The apostle Paul experienced criticism about many things. People love you when you are doing everything they want you to do and are quick to criticize when just one little thing goes wrong. Paul said that he was not in the least bit concerned about the judgments of others. He said that he did not even judge himself. He knew he was in God's hands and that in the end he would stand before God and give an account of himself and his life.

We should only be concerned with God's judgment, not others'.

———————————

Lord, when criticism comes, help me to remember that You are my only true judge. Rather than let it hurt me, I bring it to You and leave it in Your hands. Amen.

The Secret Place

In the secret place of Your presence You hide them from the plots of men; You keep them secretly in Your pavilion from the strife of tongues.   —PSALM 31:20

One of the ways that the enemy attacks us is through other people talking about us, judging us, or criticizing us. But when we spend time with the Lord in prayer and in His Word, we are in the secret place of God's presence. The secret place is a place of peace and security, a place where we can give Him our cares and trust Him to take care of us. When we spend time in God's presence, He becomes our protection, our stability, our place of refuge. He becomes the source of our help, not only when others want to hurt us and speak evil against us, but in every situation and circumstance.

Dedicate a portion of time daily for this purpose. Try not to be legalistic about it, but try to be as regular with it as you can. During that time, read the Bible and any other Christian books that minister to you. Talk to God. Sometimes you may want to listen to Christian music and worship; other times you may just want to sit there and enjoy the silence. If you do, you will begin to sense and know the presence of the Lord.

Lord, I ask You to draw me into the secret place of Your presence and be my refuge. Protect me from the enemy's attacks in all that I do. Amen.

Keep Life Interesting

*The Lord our God said to us in Horeb, You have dwelt long enough
on this mountain. . . . Behold, I have set the land before you; go in
and take possession of the land which the Lord swore to your fathers.*
—DEUTERONOMY 1:6, 8

I think it may be good to occasionally (or perhaps frequently) do something that seems outrageous to people and perhaps even to you. Do
something that people won't expect. It will keep your life interesting
and keep other people from thinking they have you tucked away nicely
in a little box of their own design.

One great woman who was seventy-six years of age said that her
goal was to do at least one outrageous thing every week. People become
bored because their lives become predictable. A recent Gallup Poll said
that 55 percent of workers "are not engaged" in their workplace. In
other words, they show up but have no real interest in being there.

We are not created by God to merely do the same thing over and
over until it has no meaning left at all. God is creative. If you don't
think so, just look around you. All the animals, bugs, plants, birds,
trees, and other living things are totally amazing. The sun, moon, stars,
planets, space, and gravity—all of which God has created—can boggle
our minds.

What outrageous thing will you do?

**Lord, I refuse to be bored and just limp along through my life.
Help me to not be predictable but to be creative and add fun to
whatever is done. Amen.**

Personal Integrity

*When pride comes, then comes shame; but with the humble is
wisdom. The integrity of the upright will guide them, but the
perversity of the unfaithful will destroy them.*

—PROVERBS 11:2–3 NKJV

We live in a society that has so lost its sense of moral values that common decency is often not even practiced. Our world no longer honors
God and is not concerned about integrity. Whether it involves cheating or committing fraud or speaking half-truths and exaggerations that
lead others to believe something that is not true, our culture is satu-
rated with the lies of the enemy.

As believers, we live *in* the world but are not to be *of* the world (John
17:11, 14). If we want to walk in confidence, we cannot compromise
our integrity and act as the world does. *Integrity* is "a firm adherence to
a code or standard of values." Our code is the Word of God. There are
certain things we wouldn't even think of doing, but there are too many
compromises, even in the lives of God's people. There are things we do
that Jesus would not do, and He is our standard of integrity.

Integrity is being committed to a life of excellence, as our God
is excellent. It is doing the right thing every time, no matter what it
costs us. *That* is a recipe for confidence.

**Lord, cause Your Word to come alive inside of me that I may
conform my life to it. Make me a person of integrity who will
not compromise the truth. Amen.**

Know What You Believe

*Elijah came near to all the people and said, How long will you halt
and limp between two opinions? If the Lord is God, follow Him! But
if Baal, then follow him. And the people did not answer him a word.*
—1 KINGS 18:21

Opinions are very interesting because we all have different ones. You
are entitled to your opinion, but that does not mean you should always
give it to others. Most of the time people don't want our opinions, and
even if they do ask for it, they hope we agree with them. Wisdom knows
when to keep quiet and when to talk.

Although we should be wise about how freely we give our opinion,
we should resist letting popular opinion become ours just because it is
popular. Know what you believe and why you believe it!

Our youngest son, Danny, said one day to his father and me, "I
don't know if I believe what I believe because I believe it or because you
believe it." As a child growing up in a Christian home, it is easy to sort
of be grafted into the faith. What Danny was going through was not
only normal but healthy. I don't want my children to merely have my
faith; I want them to have their own.

Do you know when to keep quiet and when to talk?

**Lord, I pray for wisdom and discretion. Help me to know
when to speak and when to be quiet. Amen.**

Break the Mediocre Mold

This is a trustworthy saying, and I want you to insist on these teachings so that all who trust in God will devote themselves to doing good. These teachings are good and beneficial for everyone.
—TITUS 3:8 NLT

The world is not hungry for mediocrity, when we are merely doing an average job in life. This world needs tens. I believe everyone can be a ten at something, but we often work so hard on trying to overcome our weaknesses that we never develop our strengths. Whatever we focus on grows larger in our eyes—too large, in fact. We can turn something into a huge problem when, in reality, it would be a minor nuisance if only we viewed it in perspective with our strengths.

For example, let's say you are not a "numbers" kind of person. You could obsess about your inability to "do the math" and maybe even take a class at the community college. But that obsession could eat up time that could be devoted to stuff you're great at—like teaching Sunday school, creative writing, or raising funds for charity. You rob time and effort from the tens in your life just to bring a lowly three up to a mediocre five.

———————

Lord, I dedicate myself to developing and using my strengths for Your honor and glory. I want to excel at what I am gifted to do. Help me to know my strengths and to handle my weaknesses in a way that does not distract me from being effective for You. Amen.

Don't Fake It

Now when Peter had come to Antioch...before certain men came from James, he would eat with the Gentiles; but when they came, he withdrew and separated himself, fearing those who were of the circumcision. And the rest of the Jews also played the hypocrite with him, so that even Barnabas was carried away with their hypocrisy.
—GALATIANS 2:11–13 NKJV

Wanting to please people is not necessarily an abnormal trait, but many times we find that we cannot be what others want us to be. However, the mistake that many people make is that they decide to pretend. As one person said to me one day, "I'll just fake it until I make it." That is being untrue to yourself and something you should never do. Jesus did not appreciate the hypocrites, pretenders, and phonies.

The world is full of pretenders. People pretend to be happy when they are miserable. They try to do jobs that are way over their head just because they feel they "should" in order to be admired or to maintain a certain reputation with people. People have many masks and can become quite adept at changing them as needed. I believe that not being true to one's own self is one of the biggest joy thieves that exists. Always remember that to establish independence you must not be a pretender. Be yourself!

————————

Lord, I know that You have no time for pretenders and hypocrites. Help me to stop pretending and to be free to be myself. Amen.

In the Beginning

Now the Lord God said, It is not good (sufficient, satisfactory) that the man should be alone; I will make him a helper meet (suitable, adapted, complementary) for him. . . . And the rib or part of his side which the Lord God had taken from the man He built up and made into a woman, and He brought her to the man.

—GENESIS 2:18, 22

God created man first—but quickly discovered he needed a helper. Not a slave, but a helper. He created a woman from one of Adam's ribs—from something close to his heart, not the bottom of his feet. Women were never intended to be walked on, disrespected, bullied, or belittled. Eve was created because Adam needed her. God said Adam was not complete without her. It's the same today; men need women, and they need them to be more than a cook, housekeeper, sex partner, or baby-making machine.

Please don't misunderstand my point. Everyone does not have to be married to be complete. While most people desire to get married and have a partner for life, God calls and especially enables many men and women to remain single all of their lives. You do not have to be married to enjoy your life and do great things. Just because most women get married, that does not mean something is wrong with you or is missing in your life if you don't.

Lord, teach me what it means to be complete and whole. Help me to find contentment and joy in the role You have for me to live in this world. Amen.

Open the Way

And when she [Lydia] *was baptized along with her household, she earnestly entreated us, saying, If in your opinion I am one really convinced [that Jesus is the Messiah and the Author of salvation] and that I will be faithful to the Lord, come to my house and stay. And she induced us [to do it].*   —ACTS 16:15

Mary McLeod Bethune (1875–1955) was one of the most remarkable black women of her time. A graduate of Moody Bible Institute, she opened a school for black girls in Daytona Beach, Florida. From 1935–1944 she was a special advisor on minority affairs to President Franklin Roosevelt. She was the first black woman to head a federal agency and worked to see that blacks were integrated into the military. She also served as a consultant on interracial affairs at the charter conference of the United Nations. Bethune founded the National Council of Negro Women and was director of Negro Affairs for the National Youth Administration. The fifteenth of seventeen children born to slave parents, she came to have unrestricted access to the White House during Roosevelt's life.

I admire those who are the first to do anything because the one who goes first endures more opposition than those who follow later. They are pioneers, and they open the way and pay the price for future generations.

———————————

Lord, Lydia opened her door to help Paul and those traveling with him, and I can open the way for others as well. Help me to be practical and take advantage of every opportunity to make a difference. Amen.

When Mistreatment Comes

You shall not hate your brother in your heart; but you shall surely rebuke your neighbor, lest you incur sin because of him. You shall not take revenge or bear any grudge against the sons of your people, but you shall love your neighbor as yourself. I am the Lord.
—LEVITICUS 19:17–18

Western misogyny—the hatred of women—has roots that go back to ancient Greek mythology and literature. The philosopher Plato taught that the true punishment of men was to endure women. The poet Hesiod contended that Zeus, the supreme god in Greek mythology, hated women, and he painted women as the source of all temptation and evil. Satan has methodically taken centuries to build wrong thinking about women into the minds of society, causing women to be mistreated and, in turn, to lack confidence. It seems that women either have no confidence or they are radical feminists trying to correct a real problem in an extremist way that creates more problems than it solves.

Here's the bottom line: God created men and women to need each other—not to hate each other and feel they can get by without the other just fine. Certainly, women have been abused, maligned, and treated with contempt and disrespect throughout history. But a bitter, vengeful attitude is not the way to correct this wrong.

Ask God today to remove any bitterness from your heart.

———————————

Lord, no one ever faced more contempt and bitterness and suffering on the earth than You. As You forgave others freely, help me to forgive rather than to harbor bitterness. Help me to love as You love. Amen.

Keep Your Peace

And let the peace (soul harmony which comes) from Christ rule
(act as umpire continually) in your hearts [deciding and settling with
finality all questions that arise in your minds, in that peaceful state]
to which as [members of Christ's] one body you were also called [to
live]. And be thankful (appreciative), [giving praise to God always].
—COLOSSIANS 3:15

When you do feel you need to say no, you don't have to give a reason why. So often people want us to justify our decisions, and we really don't need to do that. I try to be led by God's Spirit—or another way of saying it is I try to be led by my heart—and sometimes I don't even fully understand why I don't feel something isn't right for me. But I have learned if I do feel that way, I am not going to go against my own conscience in order to have everyone be happy with me. I often say, "I just don't have peace about it," or "I don't feel right about it," or even a plain old "I don't want to" is sufficient.

There is nothing wrong with giving a reason if you have one, but I think we go overboard trying to explain ourselves sometimes. Follow your heart and keep your peace. Say no when you need to and yes when you should.

———————

Lord, make me more sensitive to the peace that comes when You are ruling in my heart. May I be quick to follow Your peace and leading in everything I do. Amen.

Avoid Burnout

But he [Elijah] *went a day's journey into the wilderness and came and sat down under a lone broom or juniper tree and asked that he might die. He said, It is enough; now, O Lord, take away my life; for I am no better than my fathers.* —1 KINGS 19:4

Those who are addicted to approval frequently get "burned out." For them there always exists the danger of attempting too much. They so desperately want to please that they do everything they feel is expected of them and then some. Sometimes they say yes just because they cannot say no, not because they think their actions are the will of God. They burn out for lack of discernment or because of unwarranted guilt. And then, their anger builds.

We become angry when we feel all used up and pulled in every direction. Burnout makes us angry, because we recognize deep down inside that it is not normal. We become angry with the people pressuring us, when in reality we are allowing ourselves to be pressured. To avoid pressure from others and from ourselves, we must take control of our lives under the guidance of the Holy Spirit.

Once when I was complaining about my heavy schedule, I heard the Holy Spirit say, "Joyce, you are the one who makes your schedule. If you don't like it, then do something about it."

What in your life do you need to "do something about"?

———————————

Lord, pressure comes from every side, and it seems impossible to keep up. Help me to take control of my commitments and eliminate what is not of You. Amen.

Time for Renewal

And He said to them, [As for you] come away by yourselves to a deserted place, and rest a while—for many were [continually] coming and going, and they had not even leisure enough to eat.
—MARK 6:31

Frequently we complain and live silently angry lives while at the same time we continue to do the very things that make us angry. We cannot blame others for what is ultimately our own responsibility. A normal Christian life should be lived within the boundaries of balanced living. Once a person has a serious case of burnout, it is not easy to fix. None of us, not even those of us "called by God," can break His natural laws without paying the penalty. Even though we may work for God, we cannot live without limits. Jesus rested. He walked away from the demands of the crowds and took time for renewal.

Many of God's most precious and well-known saints have suffered from weariness and burnout with a tendency toward depression. We must learn that not all of our problems are spiritual; some of them are physical. We often blame the devil for things that are our own fault. We must learn to say no and not fear the loss of relationships. I have come to the conclusion that if I lose a relationship because I tell someone no, I really never had a true relationship at all.

———————

Lord, give me wisdom to know when I must rest and be renewed. Help me to adjust my schedule when I need to be refueled. Amen.

Healthy Relationships

Do not be unequally yoked with unbelievers [do not make mismated alliances with them or come under a different yoke with them, inconsistent with your faith]. For what partnership have right living and right standing with God with iniquity and lawlessness? Or how can light have fellowship with darkness?

—2 CORINTHIANS 6:14

Relationships are an important part of life. God desires that we have enjoyable, healthy ones. A relationship is not healthy if one person is in control while the other struggles for approval, gaining it by being ready to do anything the other party wants, no matter what it is or how that individual feels about it personally. If we have to sin against our own consciences in order to have someone's approval, we are out of the will of God. You can buy friends by letting them control you, but you will have to keep them the same way you obtained them. Eventually you will get tired of having no freedom. It is actually better to be lonely than to be manipulated and controlled.

Sometimes people compromise in the early stages of a relationship in order to get something or someone they want. They think they can change the person later. I know many women who have married unbelievers thinking they could convince them to love Jesus later. Most of them ended up spending their lives being miserable.

Sometimes a "no" is much better than a "yes."

Lord, show me if I am compromising and allowing myself to be controlled in any of my relationships. I want to be free to enjoy and bless others. Amen.

Divine Connections

But the Lord said to Samuel, Look not on his appearance or at the height of his stature, for I have rejected him. For the Lord sees not as man sees; for man looks on the outward appearance, but the Lord looks on the heart.   —1 SAMUEL 16:7

When we choose the people with whom we think we want to be in relationship—whether work-related or personal—we often find later that our choices were not very wise. Ask God to give you "divine connections." He may choose relationships for you that you would never have chosen because you have preconceived ideas about what you want. Learn to look beyond the exterior of people and see their heart. Someone may look good outwardly and be a nightmare to be in relationship with. Another person may not appeal to you at first glance, and yet when you get to know that individual, he or she may turn out to be the best friend you ever had.

I was insecure and always wanted to be friends with the "popular people," but quite often I ended up getting hurt. I sought the approval of such people because I was filled with insecurity.

Wisdom always chooses now what it will be happy with later on. Don't live like there is no tomorrow, because tomorrow always comes.

———————————

Lord, only You can see people's hearts and give me the wisdom to know the best relationships for me. I ask You to connect me with the right friends and associates. Amen.

According to Your Gift

Having gifts (faculties, talents, qualities) that differ according to the grace given us, let us use them: [He whose gift is] prophecy, [let him prophesy] according to the proportion of his faith; [He whose gift is] practical service, let him give himself to serving; he who teaches, to his teaching. —ROMANS 12:6–7

It's a time-tested truth: most people who criticize others for what they are doing are usually doing nothing themselves. It is sad when people have nothing better to do than criticize those who are trying to do something to make the world a better place.

I recall being a member of one church in which the pastor felt that any woman who wanted to do anything other than pray, clean, or work in the nursery had to present her case to him and the elders for their approval. I was teaching a very successful home Bible study, and the pastor told my husband he should be teaching the meeting rather than me. The pastor had his rules, but God had called me to teach, and He had not called Dave in that way. Dave has other wonderful, valuable gifts, but he is not called to teach. Surely if God had not wanted me to teach, He would not have gifted me to do it—and given me a desire to do it. As far as I can discern from Scripture, God is not in the business of frustrating and confusing people.

What is your gift and your calling? Are you using it?

Lord, thank You for the spiritual gift You've given me. Direct me in how to use it to glorify Your name. Amen.

Break the Cycle

"Did we not strictly command you not to teach in this name? And look, you have filled Jerusalem with your doctrine, and intend to bring this Man's blood on us!" But Peter and the other apostles answered and said: "We ought to obey God rather than men."

—ACTS 5:28–29 NKJV

If people are not accustomed to being confronted, they may react very aggressively until they become accustomed to the change. You may even need to explain that you realize you have allowed them to have their way in everything in the past, but that you have been wrong. Explain that you have been insecure and have needed their approval, but that now you have to make a change. It will be hard for you and them, but in order to have a healthy relationship, you must do it.

Spend some time praying about it before confronting them. Ask God to give you courage. Ask Him to help the other person be willing to change. What is impossible with man is possible with God (Mark 10:27).

The important thing is to make a decision right now that with God's help you will break the cycle of approval addiction. Initially you may feel very uncomfortable with the thought that someone is not happy with you, but you must remember your only other choice is spending your life being unhappy. Breaking any addiction will produce suffering, but it leads to victory.

———————————

Lord, with Your help I know it is possible to break the cycle of needing another's approval. Give me the courage to stand my ground. Amen.

Give Space and Freedom

Two are better than one, because they have a good [more satisfying]
reward for their labor; For if they fall, the one will lift up his fellow.
But woe to him who is alone when he falls and has not another to lift
him up!   —ECCLESIASTES 4:9–10

Some people are always trying to get us to conform to preset patterns, but there are those rare individuals who actually encourage individuality and nonconformity. We must spend time with people who accept and affirm us. One of the many things I have appreciated about my husband over the years is that he gives me space and even encourages me to be me. For example, I am a person who likes to spend time alone. When I need a few hours or even a few days to have my space, I can simply tell Dave that and he does not feel as though I am rejecting him. He understands that is just the way I am.

I recently counseled a woman who said her husband was driving her crazy because he would never give her even one hour alone. He wanted to be with her constantly. When she tried to explain that she needed space, he got offended and took her need as a personal rejection. To nurture healthy relationships, we must give people space and freedom.

———————————

Lord, help me to be able to communicate my personal needs to those I love without making them feel rejected. Give them understanding hearts that accept me for who I am and encourage me. Amen.

Nurture

Now therefore, do not be afraid. I will provide for and support you and your little ones. And he comforted them [imparting cheer, hope, strength] and spoke to their hearts [kindly].   —GENESIS 50:21

Dave and I work together, see each other more than most average married couples, and we enjoy it. But there are times when we need to get away from each other. Dave plays golf or goes to baseball or football games and that gives him his space. There are evenings when I say to Dave, "Why don't you go out and hit some golf balls? I need an evening alone," and he says, "Okay, see you later."

A few times each year I try to get away by myself to reflect, read, pray, and just be quiet for several days at a time, and Dave is always understanding of my need. It is wonderful to be married to someone who is secure enough to encourage you to be who you are and help you celebrate your uniqueness and individual needs. Nobody wants to be made to feel as if there is something wrong with them because they want to do something a little out of the ordinary.

Be sure to spend time with people who encourage you in your quest to be an individual. Find friends who give you space to be yourself, space to make mistakes, and who respect your boundaries.

Lord, just as I need space to be myself, help me to see how to give space and encouragement to others. Help me to be a nurturer of others. Amen.

Venture off the Path

Now you [collectively] are Christ's body and [individually] you are
members of it, each part severally and distinct [each with his own
place and function].   —1 CORINTHIANS 12:27

If we want to be encouraged in our own individuality and independence, we must sow the same type of freedom and respect into other people's lives. "Live and let live" should be our motto. There was a time in my life when I was rather narrow-minded, and I well remember judging and rejecting one woman in particular who was a rather unique nonconformist. She dressed eclectically long before it became stylish. She was not rebellious against authority, but she was unpredictable and determined to live her own life. She was sort of like the wind—you never knew exactly what to expect. That bothered me, because in those days I was more of a legalist. Everything had to be one way—usually my way.

I look back now and think I probably missed out on a great relationship with someone who could have nurtured freedom in me. But, like many people, I was fearful of living outside the norm.

If you are tired of living on the beaten path that everyone else walks, venture into the woods. Some people would be afraid they would get lost, but a confident woman expects to have a new experience that might be outrageously wonderful.

Lord, help me to see beyond my narrow limitations for people.
I want to see what You see in them, but I'll never see it without
Your touch. Amen.

Like a Child

And He called a little child to Himself and put him in the midst of them, and said, Truly I say to you, unless you repent (change, turn about) and become like little children [trusting, lowly, loving, forgiving], you can never enter the kingdom of heaven [at all].

—MATTHEW 18:2–3

When Jesus said we should become like little children, I believe that one of the things He was telling us is to study the freedom that children enjoy. They are unpretentious and straightforward; they laugh a lot, and they're forgiving and trusting. Children are definitely confident, at least until the world teaches them to be insecure and fearful.

I remember letting our five-year-old grandson Austin come on the platform at a partners conference once and sing a song he'd learned. The next day I was going to sign books and have pictures made with some of the partners. A large crowd was lining up, and his mother, our daughter Laura, found Austin hiding behind a curtain. When she asked him what he was doing, he said, "I am trying to get some rest from all these people." She said, "Austin, why do you think these people are here?" He said, "Well, to take my picture of course!" Because of his simple, childlike confidence, Austin automatically assumed all the people were there to see him.

What areas of your life would be improved if you were more childlike?

———————————

Lord, I ask You to restore the wonderful qualities of a child to my life. Give me the freedom and confidence that comes from simply trusting You to be my Father. Amen.

Refuse to Live in Fear

*For God did not give us a spirit of timidity (of cowardice, of craven
and cringing and fawning fear), but [He has given us a spirit]
of power and of love and of calm and well-balanced mind and
discipline and self-control.*   —2 TIMOTHY 1:7

Back when I married my husband, Dave, in 1967, I constantly deflected
his love rather than receive it, because of the way I felt about myself
down deep inside. Fear causes a person to run, retreat, or shrink back.

A confident woman refuses to live in fear. "I will not fear" is the only
acceptable attitude we can have toward fear. That does not mean that
we will never feel fear, but it does mean that we will not allow it to rule
our decisions and actions. Fear is not from God; it is the devil's tool to
keep people from enjoying their lives and making progress. The Bible
says in Hebrews 10:38 that we are to live by faith and not draw back in
fear—and if we do draw back in fear, God's soul has no delight in us.
That does not mean that God does not love us; it means that He is disappointed because He wants us to experience all of the good things He
has in His plan for us. We can receive from God only by faith.

Lord, I put my faith in You, and I refuse to live my life in fear. I
will not run and hide when I feel afraid, but I will draw closer
to You and triumph over it. Amen.

Don't Stagnate

But those who wait on the LORD shall renew their strength; they
shall mount up with wings like eagles, they shall run and not be
weary, they shall walk and not faint.   —ISAIAH 40:31 NKJV

Have you ever seen a puddle of water that is stagnant? There's no cir-
culation, no fresh water source, and the water just sits there. If left over
time and the sun doesn't evaporate it first, bacteria can form and the
water can turn green. There's little life left.

We can slide into stagnation. It happens a little bit at a time and
often so slowly that it is almost imperceptible. Once life was exciting
and then it seems that suddenly we find ourselves with what the world
calls a "midlife crisis." We stop being daring, doing outrageous things,
and being creative. We settle in and conform to what people expect.

I believe everyone will stagnate if they don't fight back. It is easy
to just float along with everyone else doing the same thing every day.
Only rare individuals are willing to swim upstream when it would be
so easy to float downstream with everyone else. One of the most valuable things I have learned is that there are many things I must do "on
purpose." I can't wait to feel like doing them.

Swim upstream when necessary.

———————————

Lord, I don't want to become like the Dead Sea, taking in but
never giving out. Cause me to rise up today with wings like an
eagle and to walk with the vibrancy of new life that is of Your
Spirit. Amen.

Fear Not

The Lord is my Light and my Salvation—whom shall I fear or dread? The Lord is the Refuge and Stronghold of my life—of whom shall I be afraid? When the wicked, even my enemies and my foes, came upon me to eat up my flesh, they stumbled and fell.

—PSALM 27:1–2

Satan is a liar. He lies to people and places images on the picture screen of their minds that show defeat and embarrassment. For this reason, we need to know God's promises (His Word) so we can cast down the lies of the enemy and refuse to listen to him.

Fear seems to be an epidemic in our society. Are you afraid of anything? Is it rejection, failure, the past, the future, loneliness, driving, aging, the dark, heights, life, or death? The list of fears that people experience can be endless. Satan never runs out of new fears to place in any individual's life. At least not until she firmly makes her mind up that she will not live in fear. You can trade in pain and paralysis for power and excitement. Don't allow feelings of any kind to dominate you, but instead remember that God says, "Fear not." We must be determined that we will obey Him in this area. Fear may present itself as a feeling, but if we refuse to bow down to it, that is all it is...a feeling!

Lord, I make You my refuge and strength today, my present help in whatever trouble I will face. With You by my side, I will not fear. Amen.

God and God Alone

Yes, though I walk through the [deep, sunless] valley of the shadow of death, I will fear or dread no evil, for You are with me; Your rod [to protect] and Your staff [to guide], they comfort me.

—PSALM 23:4

Once I found myself worried about what I would do if Dave died. How could I run the ministry on my own? After several days of this mental attack, the Lord spoke to my heart and said, "If Dave died, you would keep doing exactly what you are doing, because I am the One holding you up, not Dave." I obviously needed Dave and was dependent on him for many things, but God wanted to establish in my heart from the beginning of our ministry that with or without Dave or anyone else for that matter, I could do what God had asked me do to as long as I had Him.

Every individual needs to believe this same thing. God is all you have to have. Many other things are nice and comforting, but God is the only presence we can never do without. The Bible says that Joseph's brothers hated him, but God gave him favor everywhere he went (Genesis 39:21). It just doesn't matter who is against you as long as God is for you.

Lord, it is an amazing comfort to know that there's nothing I can go through where You won't be with me. I ask You to imprint this truth deep into my heart and soul and mind. Amen.

In Times of Change

Be strong and courageous. Be not afraid or dismayed before the king of Assyria and all the horde that is with him, for there is Another with us greater than [all those] with him. With him is an arm of flesh, but with us is the Lord our God to help us and to fight our battles.   —2 CHRONICLES 32:7–8

When Peter, Judas, and others disappointed Jesus, He was not devastated, because His confidence was not misplaced. He was dependent and yet independent at the same time. I depend on many people in my ministry to help me accomplish what I am called to do. However, we see constant change. People who we thought would be with us forever leave, and God sends new ones who have amazing gifts. We quickly learned that if we don't become overly confident in any one person, we can avoid a lot of worry and concern.

I appreciate all the wonderful people God has placed in my life. My husband and children are amazing. Our ministry staff is top-notch, and the wonderful ministry partners God has given us are awesome. I need all of them, but if for any reason God ever decided to remove any of them from my life, I want to be a confident woman who knows that with God alone, all things are possible.

Lord, You are the One who helps me and who fights my battles today. I am so glad for all the people in my life, but You alone are the One who makes all things possible. Amen.

Stand with God

And God is able to make all grace (every favor and earthly blessing) come to you in abundance, so that you may always and under all circumstances and whatever the need be self-sufficient [possessing enough to require no aid or support and furnished in abundance for every good work and charitable donation].

—2 CORINTHIANS 9:8

When Mother Teresa (1910–1997) left for India to begin her mission work there, she was told she could not do it because she had no money and no one to help her. I was told she said she had three pennies and God, and that was all she needed.

All of us are familiar with the amazing work she did to help the poor in India. Her willingness to stand with God alone, having all her confidence in Him, allowed God to work through her in a remarkable way. She was a rare individual who knew how to work with people, but who believed that with or without people, she could do all God was asking her to do.

That is the kind of attitude I want to maintain. We need people, but we know it is God working through people to help us. We look to God to meet our needs, not people. If He decides to change who He works through, that should be no concern of ours. Our confidence must be in Him more than it is in anything or anyone else.

Lord, I am not Mother Teresa, but I want to learn to stand with You, and look to You to meet my every need. Amen.

Give Fear No Place

Peace I leave with you, My peace I give to you; not as the world gives do I give to you. Let not your heart be troubled, neither let it be afraid.   —JOHN 14:27 NKJV

Fear. We've all experienced it. It's that unsettled feeling you get in your stomach; it's the panic that can overtake you with no notice. Everyone is inevitably afraid of something. If we ever truly want to become confident women, it's vital that we understand the nature of fear.

I believe that fear is the master spirit that the devil uses against people. Think about the problems you currently have. How many of those are tied to fear? I bet if you think about it, you will say most have something to do with being afraid. Our worries come from fear. We try to control people and circumstances due to fear. We let people control us because of fear. People who are afraid of being poor become greedy and stingy. Someone who is afraid of not having friends pretends to be someone they're not. We get into wrong and harmful relationships due to the fear of being lonely, and the list goes on and on. However, I believe we can conquer fear if we make time to understand it and see fear for what it really is—a spirit that has no place in a life turned over to Christ.

Lord, I thank You for the peace that You offer. Help me to walk in the peace that knows You are with me today and to rebuke fear. Amen.

God Is for Us

What then shall we say to [all] this? If God is for us, who [can be]
against us? [Who can be our foe, if God is on our side?]
                                                    —ROMANS 8:31

God is for us. We also know that Satan is against us. The question we must ask is are we going to get into agreement with God or with the devil? You know the answer. Stop being against yourself just because Satan is against you!

Sad to say, sometimes we discover people are also against us. Satan works through people as well as independently. He attacks our confidence through the things people say or don't say. How important are people's opinions of us? Are we thinking for ourselves, or are we always taking everyone else's opinion? If people's opinions, judgments, and attitudes toward us are sometimes inspired by the devil, instead of agreeing with what they think and say, we must resist it.

If we know God is for us, then it shouldn't matter how we feel or what other people think of us. As the Bible says, "So we take comfort and are encouraged and confidently and boldly say, The Lord is my Helper; I will not be seized with alarm [I will not fear or dread or be terrified]. What can man do to me?" (Hebrews 13:6).

Lord, I often find I'm my worst enemy, especially when I allow what others say and do to affect my confidence in You. I need to know in my heart that You truly are on my side. I need Your constant love. Amen.

Extraordinary Things

Now the Angel of the Lord came and sat under the oak (terebinth) at Ophrah, which belonged to Joash the Abiezrite, and his son Gideon was beating wheat in the winepress to hide it from the Midianites. And the Angel of the Lord appeared to him and said to him, The Lord is with you, you mighty man of [fearless] courage.

—JUDGES 6:11–12

Throughout history, God has used ordinary people to do amazing, extraordinary things. Yet all of them had to take a step of faith first. They had to confidently press forward into the unknown or unfamiliar before making any progress. They had to believe they could do what they were attempting to do. "Achieve" comes before "believe" in the dictionary, but the order is switched in real life.

It's important to note that, in many cases, successful people have tried many times and failed before they ultimately succeeded. They not only had to begin with confidence, they had to remain confident when every circumstance seemed to shout at them, "Failure! Failure! Failure!"

Consider inventor Thomas Edison. He once said, "I speak without exaggeration when I say that I have constructed three thousand different theories in connection with the electric light, each one of them reasonable and apparently likely to be true. Yet only in two cases did my experiments prove the truth of my theory."

Lord, I want to achieve extraordinary things for You. Help me to believe, to really believe in You and what You're calling me to, and to take that first step of faith. Amen.

Master It

David . . . was much afraid of Achish king of Gath. And he changed his behavior before them, and pretended to be insane in their [Philistine] hands, and scribbled on the gate doors, and drooled on his beard. —1 SAMUEL 21:12–13

Fear torments and prevents progress and can develop from seemingly endless sources. It causes people who should be bold and aggressive to shrink back, to hide and be cowardly and timid. Fear is a thief. It steals our destinies. What we run from or hide from has power over us. The only acceptable attitude we should have toward fear is "I WILL NOT FEAR!" Each of us must be firm in our resolve that we will not allow fear to rule in our lives. There is far too much at stake to take a light attitude toward this huge problem.

Confrontation is extremely difficult for many people, but it must be done unless we want other people and other things to control our lives. The best way to overcome anything is to expose it. Anything hidden has power over us, but once it is brought into the light it can be dealt with and overcome. Always remember what Franklin Roosevelt once pointed out: The one thing we must fear is fear itself; for if we allow it to, it will control us. If we confront it, we will master it.

Say it out loud: "I WILL NOT FEAR!"

Lord, I hate what fear does to me. I am sick of how it steals from my potential and torments me into shrinking back. I will not allow it to control me any longer. Amen.

In the "Deep End"

Now to Him Who is able to keep you without stumbling or slipping or falling, and to present [you] unblemished (blameless and faultless) before the presence of His glory in triumphant joy and exultation [with unspeakable, ecstatic delight]—to the one only God, our Savior through Jesus Christ our Lord, be glory (splendor), majesty, might and dominion, and power and authority, before all time and now and forever (unto all the ages of eternity).

—JUDE 24–25

Just as a little three-year-old girl in the middle of a swimming pool can feel in over her head, at various points in our lives, all of us feel we're getting "out of our depth" or "in over our heads." But the reality is that without God we're always in over our heads.

There are problems all around in this life: a job is lost, someone dies, there is strife in the family, or a bad report comes from the doctor. When these things happen, our temptation is to panic, because we feel we've lost control. But think about it—just like the child in the pool, the truth is we've never been in control when it comes to life's most crucial elements. We've always been held up by the grace of God, our Father, and that won't change. God is never out of His depth, and therefore we're as safe when we're in life's "deep end" as we were in the kiddie pool.

Lord, I'm glad that I am safe in Your arms, even when I feel I'm in over my head. Hold me by Your grace. Amen.

The Real Culprit

And the dragon stood before the woman who was ready to give birth, to devour her Child as soon as it was born. She bore a male Child who was to rule all nations with a rod of iron. . . . Then the woman fled into the wilderness. —REVELATION 12:4–6 NKJV

It is time for the truth to be told and for people to realize the attack on women is actually from Satan himself. He works through people, but he is the source of the problem. And his handiwork litters our history. Women have been habitually discriminated against, contrary to God's will. In Genesis, the Bible simply states, "So God created man in His own image, in the image and likeness of God He created him; male and female He created them. And God blessed them and said to them, Be fruitful, multiply, and fill the earth, and subdue it [using all its vast resources in the service of God and man]; and have dominion over the fish of the sea, the birds of the air, and over every living creature that moves upon the earth" (Genesis 1:27–28).

God spoke to the man and woman equally, giving them both rights and authority and telling both of them to live fruitful lives. Any message that diminishes a woman's position and value as established in creation must be rejected as a satanic lie.

Lord, I bless You that You have given me dominion and authority to exercise in my life, and I reject every lie that says otherwise. I will be fruitful for Your glory. Amen.

Confrontation

Then Peter replied, we must obey God rather than men.
—ACTS 5:29

Maintaining healthy relationships occasionally requires confrontation. That means you must say no even when the other party wants to hear yes. It means you may have to choose to do something you know the other party won't approve of, if you know it is the right choice for you. You must follow God, not man.

If you have not been confrontational, making a change will not be easy. Once you develop a pattern of pleasing people out of fear, it takes a genuine step of faith to break the pattern.

I was very afraid of my father, and telling him no just didn't seem to be an option. When I left home, I fell into the same habit with other people who had personalities similar to his. I had difficulty maintaining my freedom, especially with strong-willed people. If the other person had a domineering personality, I always ended up being controlled. True freedom was something foreign to me. I did not know how to give other people freedom, and I did not know how to stand up for my own right to be free.

Seek and practice truth, even if it's the harder route.

———————————

Lord, help me to not run and hide if there is someone whom
I need to confront about our relationship. I don't want to control others or to be controlled by others. Amen.

The "S" Word

In like manner, you married women, be submissive to your own husbands [subordinate yourselves as being secondary to and dependent on them, and adapt yourselves to them], so that even if any do not obey the Word [of God], they may be won over not by discussion but by the [godly] lives of their wives.

—1 PETER 3:1

For the sake of order, God instructed that wives be submissive to their husbands. Many women don't like that particular "s" word, but think of it this way: you can't have two people driving a car at the same time. However, it was never God's intention that women be dominated and made to feel as if their opinions were of no value.

Sad to say, many women perform the role of the spiritual head of the home. Some women need their men to rise up and be real men, and I believe that means to be a man who seeks God regularly and leads his family in righteousness and godliness. Many fine men are doing that, but many need to make progress in this area. I encourage you to pray for your husband, that he will indeed take his place as the spiritual head of your home. I also encourage you to let him do that without opposing him. Some women say they want their husbands to be the head of the home, but resist them when they try.

Who is behind the wheel in your marriage?

———————

Lord, Your counsel to me is always good. I embrace it, and I ask You to bring clarity as to how I live this out today. Amen.

Whose Perspective Is It?

But [now] I am fearful, lest that even as the serpent beguiled Eve
by his cunning, so your minds may be corrupted and seduced from
wholehearted and sincere and pure devotion to Christ.
—2 CORINTHIANS 11:3

When encouraged to think positively, people often retort, "That is not reality." But the truth is that positive thinking can change your current reality. God is positive, and that is His reality. It is the way He is, the way He thinks, and the way He encourages us to be. He says that all things can work out for good if we love Him and want His will in our lives (Romans 8:28). He says we should always believe the best of every person (1 Corinthians 13:7).

It has been said that 90 percent of what we worry about never happens. Why do people assume that being negative is more realistic than being positive? It is a simple matter of whether we want to look at things from God's perspective or Satan's. Are you doing your own thinking, choosing your thoughts carefully, or are you passively thinking about whatever happens to just come to your mind? What is the origin of your thoughts? Are they agreeing with Scripture? If they are not, they didn't originate with God.

Thinking negatively makes you miserable. Why be miserable when you can be happy?

_____

Lord, I ask You to make Your Word come alive to me so that I can see life issues from Your perspective. I want my thoughts to be in line with Yours. Amen.

Do It Afraid!

And a woman who had suffered from a flow of blood for twelve years and had spent all her living upon physicians, and could not be healed by anyone, came up behind Him and touched the fringe of His garment, and immediately her flow of blood ceased. . . . And He said to her, Daughter, your faith (your confidence and trust in Me) has made you well!   —LUKE 8:43–44, 48

There was a woman we will call Joy who literally lived her entire life as far as she could remember in fear. It controlled her. She would not drive a car or go out at night. She was afraid of meeting new people. She was afraid of crowds, new things, airplanes, failure, and just about anything else one could imagine. Her name was Joy, but she certainly never experienced any, because her fears entrapped and tormented her. She so desperately wanted to be brave and courageous. She wanted to have an exciting life and be adventurous, but her dreams were constantly squelched by her fears.

Joy was a Christian. One day she was lamenting her woes once again to her longtime Christian friend Debbie, who looked her friend right in the eyes and said forcefully, "Well, why don't you just do it afraid?" What a powerful truth! This was the beginning of a new life for Joy, because for the first time she saw fear for what it was.

Lord, I know that the only way to be truly free is to simply trust in You. I will do it, no matter how I feel about it. Amen.

Facing Others

Then David's anger was greatly kindled against the man...Then Nathan said to David, You are the man!   —2 SAMUEL 12:5, 7

Fear means running away from or taking flight, but confrontation means facing something head-on. Sometimes those confrontations require us to face ourselves—maybe we're fearful of failure or fearful of success. Sometimes the fears or concerns you have will require confronting someone else, maybe a parent or a husband, even a child.

David Augsburger, in his book *Caring Enough to Confront*, suggests ways you can express your thoughts while at the same time showing that you care about the other person: "I feel deeply about the issue at stake." "I want respect for my view." "I want you to trust me with your honest feelings." "I want your unpressured, clear, honest view of our differences." "I want your caring-confronting response." "I care about our relationship." "I want to hear your view and respect your insights." "I trust you to be able to handle my honest feelings." "I will not trick, pressure, manipulate, or distort the differences between us."

We may think that there is less risk of us being hurt or someone else being hurt if we don't deal with something. Just remember, though, if you run, you will have to keep running.

Lord, give me wisdom for any issue of fear regarding another person. Help me to be honest and to show that I care, and give me the courage to take a stand and deal with it. Amen.

God's Creation

Know (perceive, recognize, and understand with approval) that the
Lord is God! It is He Who has made us, not we ourselves [and we
are His]! We are His people and the sheep of His pasture.
—PSALM 100:3

Like most people, I struggled for years always comparing myself with others, and in the process rejecting and disapproving of the person God created me to be. After years of misery, I finally understood that God does not make mistakes. He purposely makes all of us different, and different is not bad; it is God showing His creative variety. Psalm 139 teaches us that God intricately formed each of us in our mothers' wombs with His own hand and that He wrote all of our days in His book before any of them took shape. We should accept ourselves as God's creation and let Him help us be the unique, precious individual that He intended us to be.

Confidence begins with self-acceptance—which is made possible through a strong faith in God's love and plan for our lives. I believe it is insulting to our Maker (God) when we compare ourselves with others and desire to be what they are. Make a decision that you will never again compare yourself with someone else. Appreciate others for what they are and enjoy the wonderful person you are.

Lord, I confess that You did not make a mistake when You made me. You formed me to be unique because You wanted me to be unique. I celebrate how You formed me to express You to the world. Amen.

Higher Things

If then you have been raised with Christ [to a new life, thus sharing His resurrection from the dead], aim at and seek the [rich, eternal treasures] that are above, where Christ is, seated at the right hand of God. And set your minds and keep them set on what is above (the higher things), not on the things that are on the earth.

—COLOSSIANS 3:1–2

A confident woman does not live in "if only" and "what if." The world is filled with people who feel empty and unfulfilled because they have spent their lives bemoaning what they did not have, instead of using what they do have. Don't live in the tyranny of "if only." If only I had more education, more money, more opportunity or someone to help me. If only I had a better start in life; if only I had not been abused; if only I were taller. If only I weren't so tall. If only, if only, if only…

Where the mind goes, the man follows. Pay more attention to your thoughts and choose to think on things that will help you instead of hinder you, and God's power will be released to help you be the confident woman God wants you to be. Think confident and you will be confident!

Lord, make me aware of where I am hanging on to old thoughts of "if only" or "what if." Help me to focus on what will propel me forward and release Your power in me rather than what will hinder me. Amen.

Stop Pretending

So Abram said to Lot, Let there be no strife, I beg of you, between you and me, or between your herdsmen and my herdsmen, for we are relatives. Is not the whole land before you? Separate yourself, I beg of you, from me. If you take the left hand, then I will go to the right.   —GENESIS 13:8–9

Don't spend your life pretending that you like things you despise or being with people all the time whom you don't enjoy. I called a pastor one day to ask his advice about letting an employee go. I wanted to do the right thing, but after several years of trying, I just could not be with this particular person and enjoy her. We just didn't adapt well to each other. My pastor friend said something that was very freeing to me. He said, "Joyce, I have finally decided that I am too old and have been doing this too long to spend the rest of my life working with people I don't like and pretending that I do."

To some people this type of thinking might sound very "un-Christian," but it really isn't. Jesus told us to love everyone, but He did not say we had to love being with everyone. There are people in life with whom we simply don't fit. I made a change, and we were both better off for it.

If something in your life is pretense, get honest.

———————————

Lord, free me from the feeling that every relationship has to be perfect. If there's someone I don't fit with, help me to be honest about it. Amen.

Still Running?

I had a dream which made me afraid, and the thoughts and
imaginations and the visions of my head as I was lying upon my
bed troubled and agitated me.   —DANIEL 4:5

In April 2005, many Americans and the world heard the story of the "runaway bride," Jennifer Wilbanks. The thirty-two-year-old Duluth, Georgia, resident disappeared just days before her six-hundred-guest wedding was to take place. Her family and fiancé, certain she had been kidnapped, pleaded for her safe return, and the missing bride became a national story for the major news media. When she turned up alive, the truth was revealed that the bride-to-be ran because of "certain fears" that controlled her life.

Most of us would say, "Well, she should have talked to her fiancé or her pastor instead of running away." But how many of us easily confront our fears? You may not have ever physically run away as did Wilbanks, but I bet emotionally there are things you're running from. You're constantly looking over your shoulder trying to keep whatever you're afraid of from catching up with you.

Satan loves causing people to dread and avoid confronting unpleasant issues, because he knows that he loses power when his lies are confronted. Even though a lie is not true, it becomes reality for the person who believes it. Don't believe the lies Satan tries to deceive you with.

———————

Lord, expose the lies that I've believed and that give strength to the fears that harass me. Shine Your light of truth on them and break their deceptive power. Amen.

Time for a Change

And the man said, The woman whom You gave to be with me—she gave me [fruit] from the tree, and I ate. And the Lord God said to the woman, What is this you have done? And the woman said, The serpent beguiled (cheated, outwitted, and deceived) me, and I ate.

—GENESIS 3:12–13

Satan tempted Eve initially and then used her to tempt Adam, and women have gotten a bad rap ever since. I believe Adam should have stepped up to the plate and refused to do what Eve was tempting him to do—instead of doing it and then blaming her for the mess they were in. After all, God did create Adam first, and it was to Adam that He gave the command not to eat of the fruit.

I am sure Adam told Eve about God's command, but it certainly was not her fault that he didn't use discipline when temptation came. Actually, the Bible states that sin came into the world through one man, Adam (Romans 5:12; 1 Corinthians 15:21–22). I am not making excuses for Eve here. She made a bad choice and needed to take responsibility for her part, but she was not the sole cause of a great sin. Unfortunately, men and women have blamed each other for creating problems since the Garden of Eden. It is time for a change.

What would your life look like if it didn't include blame?

———————

Lord, I'm sick of the blame game in relationships, and I know the solution starts with my taking responsibility for what I do. I can't change others, but I can change me. Amen.

Both Men and Women

I will pour out my Spirit upon all people.... In those days I will pour out my Spirit even on servants—men and women alike.

—JOEL 2:28–29 NLT

I believe that most women possess a sixth sense that God did not give to men. It's often called women's intuition, and it's the real deal. Men are usually very logical, while women tend to be more "feeling" orientated. For example, a male manager might look at a job candidate's résumé, job application, college GPA, and work history and be ready to hire him, based on the "facts." However, this male manager's female counterpart might evaluate the same candidate and intuitively pick up on personality quirks or subtle-but-destructive attitudes that don't show up on paper. This does not mean that women are innately better leaders than men or that their instincts are based on a special God-to-woman frequency to which men aren't attuned. In fact, a woman's emotions can also get her in trouble, and she frequently needs the left-brain logic of a man to help her see things clearly.

The point is that women and men need one another; they can complement one another. That's why men and women should work together, side by side in harmony, respecting one another as equals.

———————————

Lord, I thank You for making me the way You have. Help me to use my intuition and other gifts to be a blessing, and surround me with those who will help me see clearly. Amen.

Power from on High

But you shall receive power (ability, efficiency, and might) when the Holy Spirit has come upon you, and you shall be My witnesses in Jerusalem and all Judea and Samaria and to the ends (the very bounds) of the earth. —ACTS 1:8

Boom!

When the 120 people gathered in the upper room on the day of Pentecost, the count included women (Acts 1:14–15). If women did not need power to spread the Gospel, why were they included in the outpouring of the Holy Spirit?

When Joel prophesied about the future outpouring of the Holy Spirit, he said that God would pour His Spirit out upon all flesh. Upon his menservants and his maidservants He would pour His Spirit out (Joel 2:28–29). He said that "they" would prophesy. He did not say that just men would prophesy. To prophesy can mean the same thing as teaching and preaching. It means to speak forth the inspired Word of God.

Of the thirty-nine co-workers that Paul mentions throughout his writings, at least one-fourth are women. In Philippians 4, Paul encourages Euodia and Syntyche to keep cooperating and states that they had toiled along with him in spreading the good news of the Gospel. Beyond that, I could create a very long list of women who have been successfully used throughout church history to do major things in God's kingdom.

Lord, I ask You to send the Holy Spirit with power to make me a witness for Your name. Help me to spread Your name throughout the world. Amen.

Strength for Today

[Most] blessed is the man who believes in, trusts in, and relies on the Lord, and whose hope and confidence the Lord is. For he shall be like a tree planted by the waters that spreads out its roots by the river; and it shall not see and fear when heat comes; but its leaf shall be green. It shall not be anxious and full of care in the year of drought, nor shall it cease yielding fruit. —JEREMIAH 17:7–8

When Jesus instructed us not to worry about tomorrow, He was saying that we should deal with life one day at a time. He gives us the strength we need as we need it. When we take that strength He gives us and apply it to worry instead of action, we rob ourselves of the blessings God intended for us to have today—not tomorrow or the next, but today. We miss out on good things because we worry about bad things that may not even come to be!

For several years a woman had trouble getting to sleep at night because she feared burglars. One night her husband heard a noise in the house, so he went downstairs to investigate. When he got there, he did find a burglar. "Good evening," said the man of the house. "I am pleased to see you. Come upstairs and meet my wife. She has been waiting ten years to meet you."

Don't waste precious time with worry.

_____

Lord, I want to be like that tree planted by the waters. My hope and confidence are in You alone. Amen.

Get a Life!

If the Lord delights in us, then He will bring us into this land and give it to us, a land flowing with milk and honey. Only do not rebel against the Lord, neither fear the people of the land, for they are bread for us. Their defense and the shadow [of protection] is removed from over them, but the Lord is with us. Fear them not.

—NUMBERS 14:8–9

A shy person shrinks back from many things that she should confront. There are many things she would like to say or do, but she's paralyzed by fear. I believe we must learn to step out into things and find out what God has for us in life. A more timid approach may protect individuals from making mistakes, but the result is that they spend their lives wondering "what could have been." Bold people, on the other hand, make more mistakes, but they recover and eventually find what is right and fulfilling for them.

Making mistakes is not the end of the world. We can recover from most mistakes. But one of the few mistakes we cannot recover from is the mistake of never being willing to make one in the first place! God works through our faith, not our fear. Don't sit on the sidelines of life wishing you were doing the things you see other people doing. Take action and make the most of life!

———————

Lord, I put my trust in You and look forward to moving into new areas of life. I will not sit on the sidelines any longer. Amen.

In His Hands

And the vessel that he was making from clay was spoiled in the hand
of the potter; so he made it over, reworking it into another vessel as
it seemed good to the potter to make it.   —JEREMIAH 18:4

It is useless to worry about anything and doubly useless to worry about
something that is over and done with and that nothing can be done
about. If you made a mistake in the past that can be rectified, go ahead
and take action to correct it. But if you cannot do anything about it
except be sorry, then ask for forgiveness from God and anyone you may
have hurt, and don't worry about it any longer.

Let me remind you that worry is useless…so why do it? God has
given us wisdom, and a wise person will not spend her time doing
something that produces nothing of any value.

The Bible teaches us in Ephesians 2:10 that we are re-created in
Christ Jesus so we might do the good works He planned beforehand for
us and live the good life He made ready for us. The word *re-created* indicates we were created, messed up, and in need of repair. In Jeremiah
18:1–4 we read of the potter who had to remake his vessel because it
had been marred. That is a picture of us in the hands of the Lord, the
Master Potter.

Lord, I'm glad to be in Your hands and that You've forgiven
my past. Remake me in Your image that I may live the life to
which You are calling me. Amen.

Let Go of the Past

It is because of the Lord's mercy and loving-kindness that we are not consumed, because His [tender] compassions fail not. They are new every morning; great and abundant is Your stability and faithfulness.   —LAMENTATIONS 3:22–23

We can find peace in the knowledge that God's compassion and kindness is new every morning and that His faithfulness is abundant. God has provided a way for your past to have zero power over you, but it is up to you to receive His gracious gift of forgiveness, mercy, and a new beginning. Also, we must never forget that He is able to overcome and do far more than we could ever imagine that He could do for us (Ephesians 3:20).

When you ask God to forgive you for something that you have done wrong, He is faithful and just to do it. He continuously cleanses us from all unrighteousness (1 John 1:9). We are said to be new creatures when we enter into a relationship with Christ. Old things pass away. We have an opportunity for a new beginning. We become new spiritual clay for the Holy Spirit to work with. God makes arrangements for each of us to have a fresh start, but we must be willing to let go of the past and go on.

Don't allow mistakes in your past to fester and threaten your future.

———————————

Lord, I want to be a new creature in Your Spirit today. Thank You for Your abundant mercy and faithfulness to me. I want to be faithful to You as well. Amen.

Enmity

And I will put enmity between you and the woman, and between
your offspring and her Offspring; He will bruise and tread your
head underfoot, and you will lie in wait and bruise His heel.
—GENESIS 3:15

It may have been that Satan thought he could play on Eve's emotions more easily than Adam's. In any case, Satan was successful in getting Eve to do what she knew she was not supposed to do. He lured her into sin through deception, and he's still doing the same thing today to anyone who will listen to him.

When God dealt with what Adam and Eve had done, He dealt not only with them but with Satan also. Loren Cunningham and David Joel Hamilton make an interesting observation in their book *Why Not Women?*: "Ever since the Garden of Eden when God told Satan that the Seed of the woman would bruise his head, the devil has been ferociously attacking women all over the world."

Genesis 3 makes it clear that Satan and the woman are at odds with one another. Why? Satan has hated women almost from the beginning, because it was a woman who would ultimately give birth to Jesus Christ, the defeater of Satan and all of his evil works. Just as God said, her offspring bruised his head (his authority).

Lord, I am aware of the enemy's enmity and hatred every day.
I know the spiritual warfare that is set against me. I confess
the blood of Jesus as my protection this day, and I declare
victory in Jesus' name. Amen.

Believe Something Good

Now the mind of the flesh [which is sense and reason without the
Holy Spirit] is death [death that comprises all the miseries arising
from sin, both here and hereafter]. But the mind of the [Holy] Spirit
is life and [soul] peace [both now and forever].

—ROMANS 8:6

People don't enjoy being around an individual who is negative, so I often felt rejected—which added to my fears and lack of confidence. Being negative opened the door for a lot of problems and disappointments, which in turn fueled my negativity. It took time for me to change, but I am convinced that if I can change, anybody can. Fear is the darkroom where all of your negatives are developed, so why not look at the brighter side of life? Why not believe something good is going to happen to you? If you think you are protecting yourself from being disappointed by not expecting anything good, you are mistaken. You are living in disappointment if you are doing that. Every day is filled with disappointment if all your thoughts and expectations are negative. What is wrong with looking at the sun instead of the clouds? What is wrong with seeing the glass half full instead of half empty?

Thinking negatively prevents you from being aggressive, bold, and confident. Why not think positively and walk with confidence?

Lord, give me eyes of faith to see You through the darkness
that surrounds me. I expect good things to happen in my life
because You are my God. Amen.

Transformation

So that they [even] kept carrying out the sick into the streets and placing them on couches and sleeping pads, [in the hope] that as Peter passed by, at least his shadow might fall on some of them. And the people gathered also from the towns and hamlets around Jerusalem, bringing the sick and those troubled with foul spirits, and they were all cured.   —ACTS 5:15–16

Peter was a man with a past. He was bold and not afraid of change, but he also had many faults. In Matthew 16:22–23, we see Peter trying to correct Jesus. In Matthew 26:31–35, we see that Peter thought more highly of himself than he should have. In Matthew 26:69–75, it is recorded that Peter denied even knowing Jesus.

Once Peter realized the depth of his sin, he wept bitterly, which showed that he had a repentant heart (v. 75). God is merciful and understands our weaknesses. In John 21, we see Jesus lovingly restore Peter. Peter had been included in God's plans for the future even though he had a past record of foolishness and failure. Peter had denied Christ, and yet he became one of the best-known apostles. Peter could have spent his entire life feeling bad about his denial of Jesus, but he pressed past that failure and became valuable to God's kingdom. You can, too.

———————————

Lord, You are a God of transformation. Help me to press past my failures and become a valuable servant of Yours today. Thank You for including me in Your plans for the future. Amen.

Receive God's Blessing

And Jacob called the name of the place Peniel [the face of God],
saying, For I have seen God face to face, and my life is spared and
not snatched away.   —GENESIS 32:30

Jacob was a man with a past. He had been a schemer, a trickster, and a swindler (read Genesis 25–32). He was a liar. He was also selfish and sometimes downright cruel to others. He took advantage of people in order to get what he wanted. Jacob took advantage of his brother Esau's weak state and stole his birthright. He lied to his father, pretending to be Esau in order to receive the prayer of blessing that belonged to the firstborn.

Eventually, Jacob experienced a change of heart. He became tired of running and hiding. Jacob finally left everything he had and turned toward his homeland. On the way, he began to wrestle with God. He was determined to receive a blessing from God no matter what it cost him. God changed Jacob's name, which meant trickster, schemer, and swindler, to Israel, which meant contender with God. Jacob went on to become a great leader and man of God. He had a past that could have easily labeled him a failure, but once he faced it and repented of it, he also had a future.

Lord, I look into Your face today and know that I am being changed to be more like You. All the labels of the past have fallen off, and I am living in Your blessings for my life. Amen.

Healing in His Wings

But unto you who revere and worshipfully fear My name shall
the Sun of Righteousness arise with healing in His wings and His
beams, and you shall go forth and gambol like calves [released] from
the stall and leap for joy.   —MALACHI 4:2

Around our world, horrible crimes and unspeakable acts happen every day to women and children who are powerless to stop them. Every act affects the life of a precious person, created in God's image. Many women are hurt, wounded little girls trapped inside adult bodies, afraid to come out for fear of being hurt more.

I understand the feelings of these women. As I noted in the Introduction, I was sexually abused by my father for many years. I also suffered abuse at the hands of other men throughout the first twenty-five years of my life. I developed a hardened attitude toward all men and adopted a harsh, hard manner.

But I want everyone to know that, through God's Word and the help of the Holy Spirit, I was healed in my spirit, emotions, mind, will, and personality. It was a process that unfolded over several years, and I have enough firsthand experience to highly recommend God's ways of restoration and healing rather than the world's ways. It is much better to let God heal you than to spend your life being bitter about the past.

Lord, I rejoice today that You did not leave me to heal myself.
I worship You alone, and I receive from You all the healing
and grace that I need for this day. Amen.

Oneness in Christ

There is [now no distinction] neither Jew nor Greek, there is neither slave nor free, there is not male and female; for you are all one in Christ Jesus.   —GALATIANS 3:28

The battle for women's rights was long and grueling, and I personally appreciate those who fought the good fight and paved the way for the freedom I enjoy today. Sad to say, though, discrimination against women is still apparent in many areas. I recently read that in the United States, women still earn only 77 percent of the salary a man does for doing the same job.

As a woman in ministry, I have dealt with my share of criticism and judgment for no reason other than because I am a woman. Because of the lingering discrimination, many women still lack confidence. They live in fear of stepping beyond what they feel is acceptable "female" behavior. I can remember feeling that I wasn't "normal" because I was aggressive, had dreams and goals, and wanted to do great things. I kept trying to settle down and be a "normal" woman, but it just never worked for me. I am glad now that I found courage to do something radical and chase my dreams.

Bottom line: Our gender does not determine our value; our God does. We are all one in Christ Jesus, and we should treat one another accordingly.

———————————

Lord, I thank You that my worth or value is not based on men or women, just on You. Help me to experience what it means to be one in Christ. Amen.

Give What You Have

They said to Him, We have nothing here but five loaves and two
fish. He said, Bring them here to Me. Then He ordered the crowds
to recline on the grass; and He took the five loaves and the two fish,
and, looking up to heaven, He gave thanks and blessed and broke
the loaves and handed the pieces to the disciples, and the disciples
gave them to the people.   —MATTHEW 14:17–19

One of the biggest mistakes we can make in life is to focus on what
we don't have or have lost and fail to take an inventory of what we do
have. When Jesus desired to feed five thousand men—plus women and
children—the disciples said all they had was a little boy's lunch, which
consisted of five small loaves of bread and two fish. They assured Him
it was not enough for a crowd the size they had. However, Jesus took
the lunch and multiplied it. He fed thousands of men, women, and
children and had twelve baskets of leftovers (Matthew 14:15–21).

If we will just give God what we have, He will use it and give us back
more than we had to begin with. The Bible says that God created everything we see out of "things that are unseen," so I have decided that if
He can do that, surely He can do something with my little bit—no matter how unimpressive it is.

What do you have to give God? It is enough!

———————————

Lord, thank You for all You have given me. I ask You to use it
for Your glory and to provide all that I need. Amen.

The Prayer of Agreement

Again I tell you, if two of you on earth agree (harmonize together, make a symphony together) about whatever [anything and everything] they may ask, it will come to pass and be done for them by My Father in heaven.   —MATTHEW 18:19

Because our prayer power multiplies when we are in agreement with those around us (1 Peter 3:7), we need to be in agreement all the time, not just when we face a crisis situation. There will be times in our lives when what we are up against is something that is bigger than we are by ourselves. At such times, we will be wise to pray together with someone who is in agreement with us in that situation.

Dave and I often pray in agreement while driving down the highway. We are trying to break ourselves of the bad habit of "talking about praying later" and to develop a new habit of "praying right away." When possible, we hold hands as we pray in agreement.

If you feel you have nobody in your life with whom you can agree in prayer, don't despair. You and the Holy Spirit can agree. He is here on the earth, with you and in you as a child of God.

Many people will never succeed at being themselves because they cannot even get into agreement with God.

———————————

Lord, I ask You to bring the right people into my life with whom I can pray, especially on big matters. Give us a spirit of agreement that our prayers might be effective. Amen.

Deal with the Little Things

And [the Lord] said to me, You are My servant, Israel [you who strive with God and with men and prevail], in whom I will be glorified. Then I said, I have labored in vain, I have spent my strength for nothing and in empty futility; yet surely my right is with the Lord, and my recompense is with my God.   —ISAIAH 49:3–4

It is highly probable that you dread more little things than you do major things. First of all, we have a lot of little things we deal with all the time, but the major things come fewer and farther in between. As I began to examine this area of dread in my own life, I realized it operated in little daily areas, such as going to the grocery store, doing laundry, running an errand, or looking for a parking place in a crowded shopping mall. I dreaded waiting because, historically, I have not been an extremely patient person. Waiting in lines, traffic, or for slow people to get a job done were things I dreaded and I allowed those things to frustrate me.

I have learned it does no good at all to dread something I have to do anyway. It steals my current joy, and I am not willing to give up any-more joy. I hope you feel that way too. Make the Lord your recompense and deal with the little things.

———————

Lord, Solomon said it is the little foxes that spoil the vine-yards. Help me to deal with the little things in my day that sap my joy. Amen.

Up with Joy

Many say, Oh, that we might see some good! Lift up the light of Your countenance upon us, O Lord. You have put more joy and rejoicing in my heart than [they know] when their wheat and new wine have yielded abundantly. In peace I will both lie down and sleep, for You, Lord, alone make me dwell in safety and confident trust.

—PSALM 4:6–8

Have you wasted a lot of your life in fear, worry, or dread because you did not have enough knowledge to know how to deal with it? If so, I believe those days are coming to an end for you. Don't let the things that defeat other people defeat you. Don't faint in your mind when you look at a job that needs to be done and give up before you ever get started. I have faith that the knowledge you are receiving will enable you to enjoy a different quality of life than you previously did—a confidence no one can steal.

A conference was being held where those in attendance were given helium-filled balloons and told to release them at some point in the service when they felt like expressing the joy in their hearts. All through the service balloons ascended, but when it was over, one-third of the balloons were still unreleased. Let your balloon go. Let your joy be known, even in the little things.

Lord, I receive Your joy for this day. Help me to walk in the Spirit through everything I face. May others experience You through touching my life. Amen.

Take Your Rightful Place

Now Sarah saw the son of Hagar the Egyptian, whom she had borne to Abraham, mocking [Isaac]. Therefore she said to Abraham, Cast out this bondwoman and her son, for the son of this bondwoman shall not be an heir with my son Isaac.   —GENESIS 21:9–10

If a person with authority administers it in a godly way, it becomes a protection and safety net for those under it. However, it's clear today that a lot of people don't know how to use their authority with responsibility and love. For instance, the statistics regarding child abuse of every kind are staggering—and increasing at an alarming rate. Some parents take their frustrations out on their children, verbally and physically, depriving them of the emotional nurturing they need.

My purpose is to encourage you, to tell you that it is time for you to take your rightful place in the family and society and not allow this to happen. It is time for you to have a healthy self-respect, balanced self-love, and a firm, unshakable confidence in God and the gifts, talents, and abilities that He has placed on the inside of you. You are woman! God loves you, you are equal to men, and you have a destiny. It is high time you realize who you really are and that you act accordingly!

Lord, Sarah refused to fear and did not back down when she saw wrong happening within her family. Help me to rise up and take my place as the woman You have made me to be. Amen.

A God-Ordained Destiny

I commend to you our sister Phoebe, who is a deacon in the church in Cenchrea. Welcome her in the Lord as one who is worthy of honor among God's people. Help her in whatever she needs, for she has been helpful to many, and especially to me.

—ROMANS 16:1–2 NLT

Historically, women have often been allowed to do a lot, if not most, of the praying and servant-type work in the church. The debate of whether or not it is proper for women to be used in ministry still rages today, at least in some circles. I am grateful for the men who actually fight for women's rights and those who have tried to bring a balanced understanding of women's roles in the church. Nevertheless, there are entire denominations that are very much against women holding key positions in church leadership, or doing anything that would be defined as preaching or teaching anything more than a children's Sunday school class.

No wonder most of the women I talk to about this subject are confused about the whole thing. Especially the ones who believe God is calling them to do something for Him, but are being told to do so would be against Scripture. Why should women be prevented from fulfilling their God-ordained destiny by those who refuse to look at everything God has to say about women?

———

Lord, I want to walk boldly in the destiny that You have ordained for me. Help me to honor You in all that You call me to do. Amen.

Exercise Self-Control

*Adding your diligence [to the divine promises], employ every effort
in exercising your faith to develop virtue (excellence, resolution,
Christian energy), and in [exercising] virtue [develop] knowledge
(intelligence), and in [exercising] knowledge [develop] self-control,
and in [exercising] self-control [develop] steadfastness (patience,
endurance), and in [exercising] steadfastness [develop] godliness
(piety), and in [exercising] godliness [develop] brotherly affection,
and in [exercising] brotherly affection [develop] Christian love.*

—2 PETER 1:5–7

Does the thought of mowing the lawn get you discouraged? Do you
think, "Oh man, I wish I didn't have to mow the lawn today. I really
dread it. I wish I could just go shopping or do something fun." If so,
you're not abnormal. We are all tempted to think like that, but the good
news is God has given you the spirit of self-control and you can choose
what you will think about any situation (2 Timothy 1:7). You can also
choose to do what you know is right no matter how you feel at the
moment.

Dale Carnegie said, "You can conquer almost any fear if you will
only make up your mind to do so. For remember, fear doesn't exist any-
where except in the mind."

We can conquer worry and fear, and we can also conquer dread.
God has given us a spirit of self-control; all we have to do is exercise it
and we will experience freedom from fear and dread.

**Lord, I thank You that I don't have to live bound by what I feel
about situations. Strengthen my mind and thoughts with the
power of Your Word. Amen.**

God Will Fight for You

Then I said to you, Dread not, neither be afraid of them. The Lord your God Who goes before you, He will fight for you just as He did for you in Egypt before your eyes, and in the wilderness, where you have seen how the Lord your God bore you, as a man carries his son, in all the way that you went until you came to this place.
—DEUTERONOMY 1:29–31

Dread is expecting something unpleasant to happen, and it has nothing to do with faith. Faith looks forward to something good. I believe dread is very deceptive. Because sometimes it is so subtle that it is imperceptible, it becomes a significant problem that people really need to consider in their lives and see just how it afflicts them. The instant you begin to dread something, your joy starts to go and a "down feeling" sets in. Everything about the devil is down. It is all doom and gloom, depressing and discouraging, negative and yucky. Don't dread anything, but instead face everything with courage and believe you can do anything you need to do and do it with a good attitude.

We know that lack of confidence, worry, dread, and other tormenting emotions are rooted in fear. Fear is the source of these problems, but you can stop fear. Listen and obey the word of the Lord, and He will fight for you.

———————

Lord, all the dreads that come my way today are no match for You. I thank You that I can face them with boldness and overcome them with joy. Amen.

God Has the Answer

Of whom have you been so afraid and in dread that you lied and were treacherous and did not [seriously] remember Me, did not even give Me a thought? Have I not been silent, even for a long time, and so you do not fear Me?   —ISAIAH 57:11

Babies don't worry, and they don't dread things, so why do adults? As babies, we are not responsible for anything, and everything is taken care of for us. As we mature and begin to take on responsibility, we either learn to be confident, placing our trust in God, or we live in fear, worry, and dread. If we don't look to God and place our trust in Him, we carry a burden that we were never meant to bear alone. We also fall prey to compromising our values.

Worry is simply fear that things won't work out the way we want them to. But the person who trusts in God has confidence that even if things don't work out the way she desires, God will have a better plan than she had anyway. Confidence believes that all things work together for good for those who love God and are called according to His purpose (Romans 8:28). Confidence in God is absolutely wonderful, because it gives you the confidence that God has answers even when you don't.

Lord, You have called me according to Your purpose. I believe You have the answers for me in life, and I trust You to reveal them at just the right time. Amen.

Our Vindicator

For I know that my Redeemer and Vindicator lives, and at last He [the Last One] will stand upon the earth. And after my skin, even this body, has been destroyed, then from my flesh or without it I shall see God, whom I, even I, shall see for myself and on my side! And my eyes shall behold Him, and not as a stranger!

—JOB 19:25–27

I often say that Psalms are right after Job, because after getting beat up in Job, you need some psalms. God only knows what this man was going through, how hard it must have been. He lost his whole family, had boils all over his body, and all of his friends turned against him. Yet what does Job say? God is a God of justice.

Job knew who he was. He knew his own heart. He knew what he was doing. He knew his motives for doing what he was doing. He didn't really care what others thought about him. He knew that his Vindicator was God. He didn't have to defend himself, because if he needed to be vindicated, God would do it. It might take a year or five years or ten years, but sooner or later God would come around and vindicate him. If he didn't know that God was his Vindicator, he would have had to try to vindicate himself.

Lord, You are my Redeemer and Vindicator. You know my heart, and Your approval of my life is all that I need. Help me to not listen to others' judgments. Amen.

Knowledge and Confidence

To you it was shown, that you might realize and have personal knowledge that the Lord is God; there is no other besides Him. Out of heaven He made you hear His voice, that He might correct, discipline, and admonish you; and on earth He made you see His great fire, and you heard His words out of the midst of the fire.

—DEUTERONOMY 4:35–36

One night I was lying in bed and heard a noise upstairs. The longer I listened to it the more frightened I became. Finally, shaking from fear, I went upstairs to see what it was. I had to laugh when I discovered it was ice cubes falling in the ice tray from the ice maker. It just happened that the way they were falling was making a noise they did not normally make.

Lack of knowledge causes fear, and knowledge removes it. Knowledge will help you have confidence. If you are going for a job interview, make sure you are prepared and have all the knowledge you will need with you to answer questions the interviewer may ask you. We live in a world today where knowledge is as close as your computer. Not only can you do online research about the company you're applying to, but you can find tips on how to have a successful interview.

Replace fear with knowledge.

Lord, equip me with the knowledge I need to be confident and that leads to success. Point me to what I need to know to be effective for You. Amen.

Know What You're Facing

Caleb quieted the people before Moses, and said, Let us go up at once and possess it; we are well able to conquer it. But his fellow scouts said, We are not able to go up against the people [of Canaan], for they are stronger than we are....And we were in our own sight as grasshoppers, and so we were in their sight.

—NUMBERS 13:30–31, 33

A woman was once walking along a riverbank with her child. Suddenly the child slipped into the river. The mother screamed in terror! She couldn't swim, and, besides, she was in the latter stages of pregnancy. Finally, somebody heard her screaming and rushed down to the riverbank. The utter tragedy was, when they stepped into those murky waters to retrieve the child, now dead, they found that the water was only waist deep!

The mother must have felt terrible, because she could have easily saved her child but didn't because of a lack of knowledge. But fear makes us behave irrationally. Between fear of the child drowning and fear of the water, she was paralyzed and did nothing. Knowledge could have changed this entire tragic story.

Instead of being afraid of something you are not familiar with, familiarize yourself with it. Do some research or ask some questions. It might take a little effort to do so, but it is better than being tormented by fear.

Lord, help me to dispel any irrational fears that I have by learning the truth about them. I will not let fear keep me back from where You are leading me. Amen.

Light the Shadows

After this, there arose war at Gezer with the Philistines; then Sibbecai the Hushathite slew Sippai, of the sons of the giant, and they were subdued. There was war again with the Philistines, and Elhanan son of Jair slew Lahmi the brother of Goliath the Gittite, the staff of whose spear was like a weaver's beam.

—1 CHRONICLES 20:4–5

You can move from pain to power by reeducating your mind. The Bible refers to this process as renewing the mind. Simply put, we must learn how to think differently. If you have been taught to fear, you can be taught to be bold, courageous, and confident.

Rather than allowing fear to prevent your success and joy in life, you can accept that it is a fact of life. Fear has a large shadow, but fear itself is actually very small. When we fear we will suffer, we already suffer the things we fear. Fear brings torment!

Instead of thinking that you cannot do things if you are afraid, make up your mind that you will do whatever you need to do even if you are afraid. Change your thinking about fear. We allow fear to become a monster in our thinking, but it is one that will back down quickly when confronted. Fear is like the school bully. It pushes everyone around until someone finally challenges it.

Lord, so much of what troubles me in life is merely shadows that disappear when the light of truth shines upon them. Help me to aggressively stand up to these lies and fears with the authority of Your Word. Amen.

Times and Places

The women should keep quiet in the churches, for they are not authorized to speak, but should take a secondary and subordinate place, just as the Law also says. But if there is anything they want to learn, they should ask their own husbands at home, for it is disgraceful for a woman to talk in church [for her to usurp and exercise authority over men in the church].

—1 CORINTHIANS 14:34–35

What did Paul mean in these verses? First, realize that there are absolute truths in Scripture, and there are truths that are relative to the times in which they were written. When Paul told the women to be silent, he had already told two other groups to be silent. It appears that those who spoke in tongues, those who prophesied, and some of the women were all disrupting the service (vv. 28, 32, 34). They were not using wisdom to know when to speak out. The women were uneducated and may have been asking questions at inappropriate times. It is possible that some of the women who had converted from noisy pagan worship may have reverted to some of their pagan ways in their excitement and enthusiasm. All of these instructions were intended to bring order to the service—not to silence the people forever or prevent them from teaching and preaching the Gospel of Jesus Christ.

Lord, help me to study and understand Your Word and ways. I want to be able to share Your Gospel and truth effectively, with power and authority that impacts other lives. Amen.

Restoration Is a Process

For we do not have a High Priest Who is unable to understand and sympathize and have a shared feeling with our weaknesses and infirmities and liability to the assaults of temptation, but One Who has been tempted in every respect as we are, yet without sinning.

—HEBREWS 4:15

Jesus understands us when nobody else does. He even understands us when we don't understand ourselves. He knows "the why behind the what."

People only see what we do, and they want to know why we are not doing it better or more. Jesus knows why we behave the way we do. He sees and remembers all the emotional wounds and bruises in our past. He knows what we were created for. He knows the temperament that was given to us in our mother's womb. He understands our weaknesses—every fear, every insecurity, every doubt, all our wrong thinking.

Once we put our faith in Jesus, He begins a process of restoration in our lives that will not be entirely finished until we leave the earth. One by one He restores to us everything Satan has stolen from us. We must aggressively resist the legalistic attitudes that condemn us for not doing enough. Jesus understands us, He loves us unconditionally, and He is committed to working with us through the Holy Spirit—and He does not condemn us while He is at it.

Lord, who You are making me into is so much more important than the doing that others expect from me. Help me to trust Your hand and the shaping You are doing in my life. Amen.

Get Revelation

But when He, the Spirit of Truth (the Truth-giving Spirit) comes, He will guide you into all the Truth (the whole, full Truth). For He will not speak His own message [on His own authority]; but He will tell whatever He hears [from the Father; He will give the message that has been given to Him].   —JOHN 16:13

Instead of fighting a fear or merely putting up with it, start praying about how it gained entrance into your life. I always became fearful when Dave corrected our children, and it was because I was corrected in an abusive way when I was a child. I didn't understand the reason for my fear until God revealed it to me through prayer. You might even need to get some counseling to find the root of your fears, but whatever you do, don't just put up with them.

John Ortberg tells the story of a snow skier who, after pointing his ski tips down the barrel of a black-rated slope, quickly entered the land of no control and instinctively leaned backward in hope of reversing sure disaster. "We all do that," says Ortberg. "But in life, as in snow skiing, the answer is not to react in fear and lean back and away from the experience, but rather lean into it. When we lean into the dilemma and trust the hand of God—we gain control. Fear is a snare!"

———————————

Lord, I want to lean in and trust Your almighty hand with all of my heart and soul. Show me anything that is holding me back. Amen.

Stepping into the Unknown

*And I said to you, You have come to the hill country of the Amorites,
which the Lord our God gives us. Behold, the Lord your God has set
the land before you; go up and possess it, as the Lord, the God of
your fathers, has said to you. Fear not, neither be dismayed.*
—DEUTERONOMY 1:20–21

Parents, teachers, and other role models can teach children how to
fear or they can teach them to be bold. A mother who is fearful herself
will transmit that fear to her children. She will be overly cautious about
many things, and a silent fear sinks into the heart of her children. We
should not teach our children to live recklessly, but we should teach
them to be bold, take action, and to never be so afraid of making mistakes that they won't try things. I believe we should teach our children
and those under our authority to take chances in life. If we never take a
chance, we will never make progress. Progress always requires stepping
into the unknown. Experience gives us confidence, but we never get
experience unless we step out and try things we have not tried before.

I encourage you to teach others by word and example how to be
bold and courageous. Tell people to try things, reminding them that
making a mistake is not the worst thing that can happen.

**Lord, help me both in word and deed to show others to
be bold and courageous. I will gladly follow You into the
unknown. Amen.**

God Holds the Future

Who of you by worrying and being anxious can add one unit of measure (cubit) to his stature or to the span of his life? And why should you be anxious about clothes? Consider the lilies of the field and learn thoroughly how they grow; they neither toil nor spin. Yet I tell you, even Solomon in all his magnificence (excellence, dignity, and grace) was not arrayed like one of these. But if God so clothes the grass of the field, which today is alive and green and tomorrow is tossed into the furnace, will He not much more surely clothe you, O you of little faith?   —MATTHEW 6:27–30

None of us knows for sure what the future holds. This lack of knowledge often opens the door to fear. What if I become disabled? What if my spouse dies? What if my child dies? What if we have another war? What about terrorism? What kind of world will I be living in twenty-five years from now?

Wondering about things we don't have answers to opens the door to fear. Instead of wondering about what you have absolutely no control over, trust God that whatever your future holds He will enable you to handle it when the time comes. Wherever you are going, God has already been there and paved the way for you.

Lord, despite my wondering about the future, I recognize that my anxiety over it only damages me. I release to You the future and today, knowing that I am safe in Your hands. Amen.

God Enables

God is our Refuge and Strength [mighty and impenetrable to temptation], a very present and well-proved help in trouble. Therefore we will not fear, though the earth should change and though the mountains be shaken into the midst of the seas, though its waters roar and foam, though the mountains tremble at its swelling and tumult. —PSALM 46:1–3

I look at some of the things people go through and I think to myself, *I am afraid I could never go through that with the graciousness and courage I have seen them display.* Then I remind myself that when we must go through something, God gives us the strength to do so. When we fear going through something, we do it without any help from God at all.

When I look back over my life and remember some of the things God has brought me through, I think, *How did I do that?* It was because of God's grace and power. He enabled me to do what I needed to do at the time, and He will always do the same thing for you if you ask Him to. We may not know the future, but if we know the One who holds the future in His hands, we can look forward to it expectantly and without fear. If God brings you to it, He will bring you through it.

Lord, thank You that I can trust You for the strength to go through whatever life brings my way. I take You as my Refuge and Strength for any troubles today. Amen.

Stress Relief

Be anxious for nothing, but in everything by prayer and
supplication, with thanksgiving, let your requests be made known to
God; and the peace of God, which surpasses all understanding, will
guard your hearts and minds through Christ Jesus.
—PHILIPPIANS 4:6–7 NKJV

Stress is one of the biggest problems we face in our society today. Everything is so fast-paced, loud, and excessive that our mental, emotional, and physical systems stay on overload. We are inundated with information. We have newspapers, magazines, and twenty-four-hour news networks that don't just reach us through our television but through our cell phones and other mobile devices. At one time, a popular Web search engine indexed more than 3,307,998,701 Web pages! It's hard enough to think about that number, let alone the content that goes with it. We have information overload, and it is no wonder we have trouble calming our minds down so we can rest.

In addition to what the world throws at us, we have schedules that are insane. There are never enough hours in any day to get everything done we are trying to do. We hurry and rush, we feel frustrated and tired, and we're the first to say, "I'm under so much stress that I feel I am going to explode." And stress takes its toll on our confidence.

Where can you cut back stress inducers in your life?

———————————

Lord, I can't change the world around me, but I can bring my life and requests to You. May Your peace guard my heart and mind today. Thank You that I can rest in You. Amen.

Your Heart Desires

*Delight yourself also in the Lord, and He will give you the desires
and secret petitions of your heart. Commit your way to the Lord
[roll and repose each care of your load on Him]; trust (lean on, rely
on, and be confident) also in Him and He will bring it to pass. And
He will make your uprightness and right standing with God go forth
as the light.*   —PSALM 37:4–6

If you have been under a lot of stress lately, I encourage you to take an
honest inventory of not only what you are doing, but why you are doing
it. If fear is the reason you're involved, eliminate some stress by getting
your priorities straight. Your priority is not to keep everyone else in
your life happy by doing all the things they expect; it is to live a life that
is pleasing to God and one that you can enjoy.

Too many people are not living their dreams because they are living
their fears. In other words, instead of doing things out of their heart,
they do them because they are afraid of what will happen if they don't.
"Someone will get angry! I will get left out! People will talk about me!"
It is time that you started being the person you really want to be. It is
time to reach for your dreams.

———————————

**Lord, I will delight myself in You today. You know the desires
of my heart, and I entrust my dreams to You. Help me to be
the person You created me to be. Amen.**

Being Spirit Led

And when he was about to enter into Egypt, he said to Sarai his
wife, . . . when the Egyptians see you, they will say, This is his wife;
and they will kill me, but they will let you live. Say, I beg of you, that
you are my sister, so that it may go well with me for your sake and
my life will be spared because of you.   —GENESIS 12:11–13

Are you so afraid of displeasing people that you say yes to a lot of
things you know you should be saying no to? If so, your stress is not
caused by all the things you have to do, it is because you are afraid of
disapproval.

We are afraid to be different, so we desperately try to keep up with
all the other people in our lives, and it wears us out. The truth is we just
want to go home and sit in a chair, but we don't want people to think
we are a dud, so we keep pushing ourselves to do things we don't want
to do.

Take a minute to stop and look closely at the reasons you are doing
the things you currently do. If any of them are being done out of fear,
then eliminate them. You will be amazed at how much time you may
have if you have a Spirit-led schedule rather than a people-driven one.

Lord, it's so easy to succumb to the intimidation we feel from
others. Help me to be true to myself and live for Your approval
alone. Amen.

Faith Energizes

Trust in, lean on, rely on, and have confidence in Him at all times, you people; pour out your hearts before Him. God is a refuge for us (a fortress and a high tower). Selah [pause, and calmly think of that]!
—PSALM 62:8

You might ask, "Doesn't a really confident person get involved in a lot of things?" Yes, she probably does, but it isn't because of fear. Whatever she is involved in, she is confident about being involved in. When we do things out of desire and confidence, they affect us in a totally different way than when we do them out of wrong motives and fear. God will not energize our fears, but He does energize us if we have faith that we are doing the right thing and approach a project with confidence in Him.

Fear drains you of whatever energy you might have had and leaves you feeling stressed to the max, but confidence and faith actually energize you. A confident person can do more with less stress because they live with an ease that fearful people never experience.

I don't believe that what we do creates stress nearly as much as how we do it. If we do something fearfully and under pressure with no real desire to do it, then stress and no joy is the result. Fortunately, just the opposite can be true.

———————

Lord, help me to do what I'm doing with desire and confidence. I pour out my heart to You and ask You to energize my faith. Amen.

Take Action

Blessed above women shall Jael, the wife of Heber the Kenite, be....
[Sisera] asked for water, and she gave [him] milk.... She put her
[left] hand to the tent pin, and her right hand to the workmen's
hammer. And with the wooden hammer she smote Sisera, she smote
his head.   —JUDGES 5:24–26

Margaret Thatcher (born 1925) became Britain's first woman prime minister in 1979 and continued until 1990 when she voluntarily stepped down. She was the first prime minister to be elected three times to office in the twentieth century. Thatcher came up the political ladder with little encouragement. She was the daughter of a grocery owner and Methodist lay preacher and won distinction at Oxford earning degrees in chemistry and law. When she became active in Tory politics, she served as Secretary of State for Education and Science. She expressed her philosophy of leadership this way: "There can be no liberty unless there is economic liberty.... Extinguish free enterprise and you extinguish liberty." She also said, "In politics, if you want anything said, ask a man. If you want anything done, ask a woman."

A confident woman will also be an activist. She will take action when it is needed. Don't be the kind of woman who thinks something to death. There is a time to think and a time to act, so make sure you know the difference.

———————

Lord, make me a woman of action, one who's fearless and quick to stand up for what's right. May I value what You value and be unafraid to fight for causes in Your heart. Amen.

Why Wait?

And God blessed them and said to them, Be fruitful, multiply, and fill the earth, and subdue it [using all its vast resources in the service of God and man]; and have dominion over the fish of the sea, the birds of the air, and over every living creature that moves upon the earth.   —GENESIS 1:28

What has God placed in your heart? Is there something you want to do that you have been waiting on? I believe God's timing is very important, and I certainly don't think we should take action foolishly, but some people never do anything but "wait" all of their lives. They wait for something to happen when they should be making something happen.

When people are frustrated and feel unfulfilled, it creates stress. There is nothing more stressful than going through the motions every day and still feeling at the end of each day, week, month, and year that you are no closer than you ever were to reaching your dream or goal. God has created us to bear good fruit. He said, "Be fruitful and multiply." If we are not doing that, we will feel frustrated.

I have a feeling that some of my readers have not even begun to live yet, and NOW is the time for you to stop "playing it safe" and start being bold and courageous.

Lord, take my talents and life and help me to be fruitful and multiply what You've given me. Give me a nudge forward if I'm waiting when You're saying to make it happen. Amen.

Develop Your Potential

*Through skillful and godly Wisdom is a house (a life, a home,
a family) built, and by understanding it is established [on a sound
and good foundation], and by knowledge shall its chambers
[of every area] be filled with all precious and pleasant riches.*
—PROVERBS 24:3–4

I hope you have a dream or a vision in your heart for something greater than what you have now. Ephesians 3:20 tells us that God is able to do exceedingly abundantly above and beyond all that we can hope or ask or think. If we are not thinking, hoping, or asking for anything, we are cheating ourselves. We need to think big thoughts, hope for big things, and ask for big things.

I always say I would rather ask God for a lot and get half of it, than to ask Him for a little and get all of it. However, it is an unwise person who only thinks, dreams, and asks big but fails to realize that an enterprise is built by wise planning.

Dreams for the future are possibilities, but not what I call "positivelies." In other words, they are possible, but they will not positively occur unless we do our part. All of us have potential, and many of us want a manifestation of it, but too often we are not willing to wait, be determined, and work hard at developing that potential.

Ask God for a lot today!

———————

Lord, I need to think and hope and ask for bigger things from You. Help me to develop my potential to accomplish great things for Your glory. Amen.

Empowered through Christ

Be strong in the Lord [be empowered through your union with Him];
draw your strength from Him [that strength which His boundless
might provides].   —EPHESIANS 6:10

Most of the things that are truly worth doing are never easy—we are not filled with the Spirit of God to do easy things. He fills us with His Spirit so we can do impossible things!

If you want to develop your potential and succeed at being all you can be, keep your eyes on the prize and press on! It won't all be easy, but it will all be worthwhile.

Most of those who blame everyone and everything for their failures had potential, but either did not know how to develop it or were unwilling to meet its requirements. When things don't work out in our lives, it is not God's fault. It isn't really circumstances or other people who are to blame, because if God is on our side, they are not mightier than He is (Romans 8:31).

The truth is, when things don't work out for us, it is because we have not obeyed God, not pressed on and been willing to take giant steps of faith. The world wants us to conform, but the Lord wants to transform us, if we will do things His way.

———————

Lord, I ask You to fill me with Your Spirit right now so that I am fully equipped to do Your will in this world. I will press on and fight my way through all the fear and doubts that stand in my way. Amen.

Be Excellent

Let us strip off and throw aside every encumbrance (unnecessary weight) and that sin which so readily (deftly and cleverly) clings to and entangles us, and let us run with patient endurance and steady and active persistence the appointed course of the race that is set before us. —HEBREWS 12:1

To develop our potential and succeed at becoming what God intended us to be, we will have to lay aside other things. To be a winner in life we must do those things that support our goals and help us fulfill our purpose. We must learn to say no to well-meaning people who want us to get involved in endless things that ultimately steal our time and produce no fruit.

The apostle Paul was intent on developing his potential. He pictured himself in a race, straining every nerve and muscle and exerting every ounce of strength lest he come short of the goal.

We must make up our mind and get into agreement with God that we are going to be excellent, not mediocre. We must take an inventory of our life and prune off anything in it that entangles us or steals our time. We must be determined, work hard, and refuse to quit or give up—drawing strength from God and not depending on ourselves. If we will do these things persistently, we will eventually have victory.

———————————

Lord, show me the things in my life that are keeping me back from fulfilling my purpose. I depend upon You for the strength to run the race before me. Amen.

In Due Season

And let us not grow weary while doing good, for in due season we shall reap if we do not lose heart. —GALATIANS 6:9 NKJV

"Due season" is God's season, not ours. We are in a hurry, God isn't. He takes time to do things right—He lays a solid foundation before He attempts to build a building. We are God's building under construction. He is the Master Builder, and He knows what He is doing. We may not know what He is doing, but He does, and that will have to be good enough. We may not always know, but we can be satisfied to know the One who knows.

God's timing seems to be His own little secret. The Bible promises us that He will never be late, but I have also discovered that He is usually not early. It seems that He takes every available opportunity to develop the fruit of patience in us. Patience is a fruit of the Spirit that grows under trial.

Developed potential without character does not glorify God. If we were to become a huge success and yet be harsh with people—that would not be pleasing to the Lord. Therefore, if we get ahead of ourselves in one area, He gently but firmly blocks our progress in that area until the other ones catch up.

Remember: God is never late.

Lord, thank You for Your patience with me. I want everything now, but You are building my life with eternity in mind. I don't understand everything You're doing, but I trust You. Amen.

Make a Difference

And David said to Abigail, . . . blessed be your discretion and advice,
and blessed be you who have kept me today from bloodguiltiness and
from avenging myself with my own hand. For as the Lord, the God
of Israel, lives, . . . if you had not hurried and come to meet me, surely
by morning there would not have been left so much as one male to
Nabal.   —1 SAMUEL 25:32–34

Theodora, Empress of Byzantium (c. 497–548), married Justinian, who ruled from 527–565, but it was Theodora, a former actress, who saw to it that important legislation was passed and demonstrated the initiative to save her husband's rule by resisting a revolt in 532. Justinian was ready to flee when Theodora persuaded him to defend the capital. In the end he won power for thirty more years, during which time Theodora's name appeared in almost all important laws, including prohibitions against white slavery and the altering of divorce laws to make them more humane to women. When it came to religion, she strongly supported expressions of the Christian faith upholding the divinity of Christ. After her death in 548, her husband passed practically no important legislation.

They say that behind every great man there is a great woman. I wonder just how many men have gotten credit for the accomplishments of the great women standing behind them?

Lord, help me to never shrink back in fear when someone
needs to step forward and make a difference. I need the power
of Your Holy Spirit within me to be that person. Amen.

Light Up the Darkness

Fear not [there is nothing to fear], for I am with you; do not look around you in terror and be dismayed, for I am your God.
—ISAIAH 41:10

God's Word is clear on this point: We are not to fear. Notice that He doesn't say that we are never to feel fear, but He does say we shouldn't allow fear to control us and steal our destiny.

It's important to remember that what we hide in the darkness has to be brought into the light if we're going to get rid of it. Go into a completely dark room and switch on the light. What happens? The darkness is swallowed up. That is the way God and His Word work in our lives. When we do what God's Word tells us to do, those fears that try to torment us are swallowed up. They're gone, and they have no power over you.

How I wish I had a magic wand I could wave or a prayer I could say that would end fear in your life once and for all. Unfortunately, that's not going to happen. Prayer does give us the strength to stand against fear, but for us to overcome and be conquerors as God intends us to be, we must realize that we can "feel the fear and do it anyway," and then we'll be free.

———————

Lord, may the power of Your Word be effective in dealing with the fears I bring to You now. Show me the truths that set my soul free. Amen.

Move It!

I went by the field of the lazy man, and by the vineyard of the man
void of understanding; and, behold, it was all grown over with
thorns, and nettles were covering its face, and its stone wall was
broken down.... A little sleep, a little slumber, a little folding of the
hands to sleep—so shall your poverty come as a robber.
—PROVERBS 24:30–34

Too much activity and no rest definitely is the culprit behind most
stress, but no activity is also a problem. I am sure you have heard that
exercise is a great stress reliever, and it is very true. I would rather be
physically tired from exercise and movement than tired in my soul from
doing nothing and being bored. God gave us all the joints in our body
because He expected us to move!

The Bible clearly warns against the dangers of laziness (Proverbs
12:27; 2 Thessalonians 3:6–10). The lazy man has nothing, and he gets
exactly what he deserves, which is nothing. If you give things to a lazy
man or woman, they won't take care of them, and you'll notice that
everything around them is in shambles. People who are lazy spend
their lives "wishing" that something good would happen to them. They
want others to do for them what they should be doing for themselves.
They are miserable human beings, and their lives bear no good fruit.

Which joints and muscles do you need to use?

————————

Lord, I will not sit back and wait for something good to happen. Help me to break free from all passivity and rise up and
conquer. Amen.

Created to Work

When Jesus noticed him lying there [helpless], knowing that he had already been a long time in that condition, He said to him, Do you want to become well? [Are you really in earnest about getting well?] The invalid answered, Sir, I have nobody.   —JOHN 5:6–7

Work is good for all of us. As a matter of fact, God said we should work six days and rest one. That shows how important work and activity are in God's eyes. God has created us to work, not to sit idly by and do nothing. Perhaps some of you are at a place in life where you simply need to "get up and get going."

In the fifth chapter of John we see one example. A man was crippled, and he lay by the pool of Bethesda for thirty-eight years waiting for his miracle. When Jesus came to the man and asked him how long he had been in that condition, the man gave the length of time and told Jesus how he had nobody to put him into the pool at the right time. Jesus told the man to "Get up! Pick up your bed (sleeping pad) and walk!" (John 5:8). The man felt sorry for himself, so he just lay there and did nothing. The answer to his problem surfaced when he made an effort to move.

Lord, thank You that we can respond to Your voice, and thank You for miracles. Help me to do all I can to work Your will out in my life. Amen.

It's Your Time

But when he perceived and felt the strong wind, he was frightened,
and as he began to sink, he cried out, Lord, save me [from death]!
—MATTHEW 14:30

The boat of my past that I needed to step out of was the childhood sexual abuse I suffered. I felt as though my dad stole my childhood, and I was so mistreated. I was bitter about the people who should have helped me and didn't, and then there were the "could haves" and "would haves" and "wish I hads." In my thirties, I was still taking it out on everybody who had anything to do with it. I didn't trust men and had a chip on my shoulder. I was miserable, but I sat in the boat.

I remember how afraid I was when God told me that I was going to have to confront my dad about the sexual abuse of my childhood, because I was petrified of my father. The fear was rooted so deeply in me, even after I had been away from it for years. Whenever I would be around him or anyone who had a personality like his, I would feel the knot of fear come up in my gut. Finally, God got in my face and said, "Look, you can be pitiful or you can be powerful." Jesus was walking by my boat, and it was time to walk on water.

Lord, thank You that You won't let me sink when I step out in obedience and deal with issues in my life. Help me to keep my eyes fixed on You. Amen.

Change Ingredients

To everything there is a season, and a time for every matter or purpose under heaven:...a time to break down and a time to build up,...a time to cast away stones and a time to gather stones together,...a time to get and a time to lose, a time to keep and a time to cast away.   —ECCLESIASTES 3:1–6

If you are stressed out all the time, something will have to change in order for the stress to be relieved. It will not just go away as long as you keep doing the same thing. If you want different results, you have to change the ingredients.

Now, as soon as I mentioned the word *change*, perhaps you tensed up because you are afraid of change. Almost one hundred years ago, the clerk of Abbington Presbytery came up with percentages for the kinds of attitudes people have about change, and I think they still apply today:

Early innovators (2.6 percent) run with new ideas; Early adaptors (13.4 percent) are influenced by innovators but are not initiators; Slow majority (34 percent) are the herd-followers; Reluctant majority (34 percent); Antagonistic (16 percent) will never change.

If you're like the bottom 84 percent of people in the above list, you want the safety of sameness. It is amazing to me how some people spend their lives resisting change while others thrive on it. Change keeps life fresh and adventurous.

Lord, my time is in Your hands. Help me to be fearless as I face change and embrace change. I want to be vibrant and fully alive. Amen.

Make the Change

Work out (cultivate, carry out to the goal, and fully complete) your own salvation with reverence and awe and trembling (self-distrust, with serious caution, tenderness of conscience, watchfulness against temptation, timidly shrinking from whatever might offend God and discredit the name of Christ). —PHILIPPIANS 2:12

Take some bold steps of faith and change anything the Lord leads you to change. If what you are doing with your time is not bearing good fruit, make a change. If you are not getting enough rest, make a change. If you are not disciplining your children and their behavior is causing you a lot of stress, make a change. If you are bored, make a change. If your friends are taking advantage of you, make a change!

Stress can be relieved if you're not afraid to make changes. You may be afraid of change, and even if you find the courage to make the necessary changes it is possible that other people in your life won't like the changes you make. Don't be afraid of them either. You will get used to the changes, and so will they. If you don't take action now, you will still be complaining about the same things a year from now, and ten years after that. The time is NOW! Boldness takes action, but fear breeds inactivity and procrastination. The choice is yours!

Lord, I know that I am far from perfection and need to keep changing into Your image. Regardless of what others think, I will be bold to take action. Amen.

Brighter and Clearer

But the path of the [uncompromisingly] just and righteous is like the light of dawn, that shines more and more (brighter and clearer) until [it reaches its full strength and glory in] the perfect day [to be prepared]. The way of the wicked is like deep darkness; they do not know over what they stumble.   —PROVERBS 4:18–19

Maybe you're still thinking to yourself, *Joyce, I'm a timid and shy person, that's just my nature. I don't think I can change.* You may feel timid and shy, but you can choose to walk boldly through life. The main thing I want you to remember is that you can feel afraid, you can feel timid, you can feel downright cowardly, and yet you can make the choice to walk boldly and as if fear did not exist! Your free will is stronger than your feelings if you will exercise it.

You may be like thousands of others who have catered to their fearful feelings for so long that the fear has taken control. Your will, like a muscle, becomes weak if not exercised. As you begin to ask God to help you and exercise your willpower against your feelings, it will get easier and easier to be the person you truly want to be, the person God has designed you to be.

———————

Lord, there are certain feelings that control my life and tear down my confidence. I trust that as I exercise my willpower, You will strengthen me and make my path brighter and clearer and easier to walk. Amen.

Seek Wisdom

A fool's wrath is quickly and openly known, but a prudent man ignores an insult.... There are those who speak rashly, like the piercing of a sword, but the tongue of the wise brings healing.
—PROVERBS 12:16, 18

When I think of what boldness looks like on someone, I think of someone who is daring, courageous, brave, and fearless. Some people think they are bold but they are merely rude, forward, and impudent. That's how I was for many years of my life. I thought I was a bold woman, but the truth is I was very fearful. I was not facing my fears, and I was pretending to myself and the rest of the world that I was not afraid of anything. There is a difference between truly facing fear and just ignoring it and pretending you are not afraid and covering your fear with a phony boldness that is rude and impudent.

I was quick to speak my mind, but what I said was often foolish and inappropriate. I took control of situations thinking I would step out in boldness and do something since nobody else seemed to be doing anything, only to later realize that I had taken authority that was not mine to take. I made many mistakes and hurt a lot of people because I did not take time to seek wisdom.

Be bold—and seek wisdom.

Lord, I want to be confident and bold, but give me the wisdom that insures it is genuine. The last thing I want to be is rude and pushy. Amen.

God's Timing

Except the Lord builds the house, they labor in vain who build it;
except the Lord keeps the city, the watchman wakes but in vain.
—PSALM 127:1

During the three years of Jesus' earthly ministry, people thought He was crazy. His own brothers were embarrassed by Him, and in an effort to save their reputation they told Him He needed to go somewhere else and do His works. If He was unwilling to do that, they told Him to take action and stop doing His works in secret. They tried to convince Him it was time to show Himself and His works to the world. They wanted Jesus to impress the people with what He could do.

He responded to them by saying, "My time (opportunity) has not come yet" (John 7:6).

How many of us could show that type of self-control? If you could do the miracles that He could do and were being made fun of and challenged to show your stuff, what would you do? Would you wait until you absolutely knew that it was the right time sanctioned by God?

It is good to have plans, and I believe we should plan boldly and aggressively, but we must be wise enough to know that our plans will ultimately fail without God. We must learn to wait for God's plans to develop. True boldness moves in God's timing.

Lord, I want to have a plan for my life that is worthy of Your name. But teach me to wait upon You and to move at the right times. Amen.

God-Confidence

These are all warning markers—danger!—in our history books,
written down so that we don't repeat their mistakes. Our positions
in the story are parallel—they at the beginning, we at the end—and
we are just as capable of messing it up as they were. Don't be so
naive and self-confident. You're not exempt. You could fall flat on
your face as easily as anyone else. Forget about self-confidence;
it's useless. Cultivate God-confidence.

—1 CORINTHIANS 10:11–12 THE MESSAGE

When I am teaching on confidence, people often express concerns about the difference between self-confidence and conceit. They say that they have been taught not to say (or even think) positive things about themselves. If they did, it would sound self-centered and selfish.

Since I am writing about how you can become a confident woman, I want to restate that I am not talking about self-confidence. I don't want you to have confidence in yourself unless that confidence is first rooted in God. If our confidence is a fruit of us being first rooted in God, we have the right kind of confidence that produces true boldness.

As Paul said, "We are self-confident in His confidence."

Those of us who think we are bold should ask ourselves if we have confidence or conceit. Bill Crawford said, "The difference between self-confidence and conceit is as simple as love and fear. Jesus was self-confident . . . Hitler was afraid."

Be sure your confidence is rooted in the Lord.

———————————

Lord, I am confident today because my confidence is rooted and grounded in You. On my own, I will fall on my face. My trust is in You. Amen.

Boast in the Lord

"Let not the wise man glory in his wisdom, let not the mighty man glory in his might, nor let the rich man glory in his riches; but let him who glories glory in this, that he understands and knows Me, that I am the LORD, exercising lovingkindness, judgment, and righteousness in the earth, for in these I delight," says the LORD.
—JEREMIAH 9:23–24 NKJV

Good parents teach their children not to brag, and it is right to do so. No one enjoys a braggart who is in love with herself and believes she is the answer to all of humanity's problems. Some people think they know so much that it is obvious they know nothing at all. We have not even begun to have knowledge until we know that we don't know anything compared to what we need to know.

In teaching our children not to brag, we should not teach them that it is wrong to acknowledge the positive aspects of who they are. If you go and apply for a job but understate your skills due to fear of sounding conceited, you probably won't get the job. Be confident, but let your confidence be rooted in God. We are what we are due to His grace and mercy.

Confidence breeds confidence. When someone presents herself in a confident manner, it causes me to have confidence that she can do what needs to be done.

You are God's creation; that's reason for confidence.

———————————

Lord, I glory in the fact that I know You, and that You are the Lord over the earth. Thank You for what You're doing in my life. Amen.

Put on Humility

Clothe (apron) yourselves, all of you, with humility [as the garb of a servant, so that its covering cannot possibly be stripped from you, with freedom from pride and arrogance] toward one another. For God sets Himself against the proud (the insolent, the overbearing, the disdainful, the presumptuous, the boastful)—[and He opposes, frustrates, and defeats them], but gives grace (favor, blessing) to the humble.
               —1 PETER 5:5

I remember complimenting a friend on doing a fine job of grilling for a dinner party. He was a very godly man and immediately responded that it was not him but the Lord. In my opinion, it would have been much better if he had said, "Thank you for the compliment," and in his own prayer time thanked God for helping him. When someone compliments us, we should graciously receive it. Take each compliment that you receive as a rose, and at the end of the day take the entire bouquet and offer it back to God, knowing that it came from Him.

If I were to paraphrase 1 Peter 5:5, it would say, "All of you should put on humility. Wear it as a garment and never let it be stripped from you. Live with freedom from pride and arrogance toward one another, because God sets Himself against the proud and haughty (the presumptuous and boastful), and He opposes and even frustrates and defeats them, but He helps the humble."

Lord, I clothe myself in humility and ask You to strip away any arrogance or pride from my life. Help me to live in freedom. Amen.

Divine Protection

Like snow in summer and like rain in harvest, so honor is not fitting for a [self-confident] fool.   —PROVERBS 26:1

The book of Proverbs has much to say about self-confidence. A fool is always taking some kind of beating from the devil because he opens the door through self-confidence. God is our defense and protection, but our confidence must be in Him and not in us. When we are wholly trusting in God for all of our strength in all the affairs of life, we experience a divine protection that is amazing.

The self-confident man or woman may experience a financial beating. They make bad deals, get cheated, invest in stocks that become worthless, and all because they moved in their own knowledge rather than seeking the wisdom of God.

The fool may experience a mental beating. Self-confident people must worry, reason, be anxious, and have fear. They depend on themselves to solve their problems, so they have to figure things out.

Fools also experience emotional beating. Nothing really works out right when people lean on themselves. Nothing is more frustrating than doing your very best to solve problems and yet always failing. We begin to think something is wrong with us, and God is merely hindering our success in the hopes that we will eventually wear ourselves out and come to Him for help.

You can save a lot of time and energy by going to God first.

Lord, I want to live in the shelter of Your wings and protection. I root my confidence in You alone and lean on You for help. Amen.

Humble and Bold

*Be strong (confident) and of a good courage, for you shall cause this
people to inherit the land which I swore to their fathers to give them.
Only you be strong and very courageous, that you may do according
to all the law which Moses My servant commanded you. Turn
not from it to the right hand or to the left, that you may prosper
wherever you go.*   —JOSHUA 1:6–7

Not only is it possible to be humble and bold, it is impossible to be
truly bold without humility. Joshua was a man who was both. God
told him to finish the job Moses started and take the Israelites into the
Promised Land. Immediately after giving Joshua the command, God
announced to him, "No man shall be able to stand before you all the
days of your life. As I was with Moses, so I will be with you; I will not
fail you or forsake you" (Joshua 1:5).

Joshua's confidence rested in the fact that God was with him, and
because of that he was able to go forward to do something that he probably felt unqualified to do. Joshua must have felt fear because the Lord
repeatedly told him to "fear not," which means "don't run!"

God told Joshua that if he would be strong, confident, and full of
courage, he would cause the people to inherit the land that God had
promised them.

**Lord, what an amazing promise this is! I receive it as my own.
Help me to know Your Word and to be absolutely faithful to it.
Amen.**

Boldness or Pride?

I, Wisdom [from God], make prudence my dwelling, and I find out knowledge and discretion. The reverent fear and worshipful awe of the Lord [includes] the hatred of evil; pride, arrogance, the evil way, and perverted and twisted speech I hate.

—PROVERBS 8:12–13

A confident woman takes action. I have heard that there are two types of people in the world: the ones who wait for something to happen and the ones who make something happen. Some people are naturally shy, while others are naturally bold, but with God on our side we can live in the supernatural, not the natural. We all have something to overcome. A naturally bold person has to overcome pride, excessive aggression, and false confidence, while the naturally shy must overcome anxiety, timidity, the temptation to withdraw from challenges, and low confidence.

A bold person can often be assertive to the point of being rude. What some people think is boldness is, in reality, pride—which is one of the things God's Word says that He hates. It seems that bold people just naturally assume they are right about most things, and they don't mind telling other people just how right they are. And, while confidence is a good thing, egotism is not. Thank God we can benefit from our strengths and overcome our weaknesses through His help.

Lord, I want to make something happen through my life, but with the confidence that comes through Your strength. I humble myself under Your mighty hand and refuse to trust in myself alone. Amen.

No Excuses

But the Lord said to me, Say not, I am only a youth; for you shall go to all to whom I shall send you, and whatever I command you, you shall speak. Be not afraid of them [their faces], for I am with you to deliver you, says the Lord.   —JEREMIAH 1:7–8

Jeremiah was a very young man who was given a very big job. God told him that he had been called as a prophet to the nations. He was to be a mouthpiece for God. The thought of it frightened Jeremiah, and he began to make all kinds of excuses about why he could not do what God was asking. He was looking at himself, and he needed to look at God. He was also looking at people and wondering what they would think and do if he took the bold step God was encouraging him to take. God told him to just remember that He was with him and that is all he needed.

Remember that God wants us to face things. Whatever you run from will always be waiting for you somewhere else. Our strength to conquer is found in pressing forward with God. The Lord told Jeremiah in the final verse of chapter one that the people would fight against him, but they would not prevail for one simple reason: "I am with you."

Whatever you're facing, God is facing it with you.

————————

Lord, help me take my eyes off my circumstances and place them on You. Whatever You want for my life, I can do it because of Your presence with me. Amen.

Giants Fall

And again there was war at Gath, where was a man of great stature who had twenty-four fingers and toes, six on each hand and each foot. He also was born to the giant. And when he reproached and defied Israel, Jonathan son of Shimea, David's brother, slew him.

—1 CHRONICLES 20:6–7

God wants us to stretch our faith muscles and stand against fear. He wants us to say, "No! Fear is not going to rule in my life." As we learn to use prayer to confront and combat the small fears, He'll help us learn to tackle the bigger fears too.

Don't let fear freeze you into paralysis. Hannah Hurnard, author of *Hinds' Feet on High Places*, was once paralyzed by fear. Then she heard a sermon on scarecrows that challenged her to turn her fear into faith.

The preacher said, "A wise bird knows that a scarecrow is simply an advertisement. It announces that some very juicy and delicious fruit is to be had for the picking. There are scarecrows in all the best gardens. . . . If I am wise, I too shall treat the scarecrow as though it were an invitation. Every giant in the way which makes me feel like a grasshopper is only a scarecrow beckoning me to God's richest blessings." He concluded, "Faith is a bird that loves to perch on scarecrows. All our fears are groundless."

———————

Lord, there's no giant of fear that can stand when I approach it with faith. I stand against the fear in Your name, and I trust You to lead me to overcome it. Amen.

Choose Boldness

And they were all filled (diffused throughout their souls) with
the Holy Spirit and began to speak in other (different, foreign)
languages (tongues), as the Spirit kept giving them clear and loud
expression. . . . For the promise [of the Holy Spirit] is to and for you
and your children, and to and for all that are far away.

—ACTS 2:4, 39

Jesus promised His disciples that after His death and resurrection He would send His Holy Spirit to fill them with real power. They would experience true boldness that would be rooted and grounded in their faith in Him. Peter, along with others, received this power from on high on the day of Pentecost, and Acts 2 finds Peter preaching boldly in the streets of Jerusalem, no longer caring one bit about what anyone thought. Peter saw himself as the pretender and sinner that he was. He repented, was forgiven, and was filled with holy boldness that can come only from God.

Ask God to help you and He will. You don't have to pretend to be brave; if you are frightened, tell God how you feel. If you are worried, give those worries to God. After all, He knows anyway. You can say you feel fear, but I also encourage you to say that you won't let it stop you from going forward. I challenge you to say, "I feel fear, but I choose boldness!"

———————

Lord, only You can provide me with the boldness that comes from the Holy Spirit. I ask You to fill me now with Your presence that I might be truly brave. Amen.

Opposition Will Come

*For a wide door of opportunity for effectual [service] has opened
to me [there, a great and promising one], and [there are] many
adversaries.*   —1 CORINTHIANS 16:9

Quitting is not an option for the confident woman. She must decide
what she wants or needs to do and make up her mind that she will finish her course. You will experience some opposition no matter what
you attempt to do in life. Remember that the whole goal of fear is to
stop you. Fear wants you to run, to withdraw, and to hide. The apostle
Paul said that when doors of opportunity opened to him, opposition
often came with it. Confidence believes that it can handle whatever
comes its way; it doesn't fear what has not happened yet.

The apostle Paul was given a job to do, and he was determined to
do it even though he knew that it meant imprisonment and suffering.
He kept his eyes on the finish line, not on what he knew he would
go through. He said he wasn't moved by the opposition, but that his
goal was to finish his course with joy. Enjoyment is not possible if we
are afraid all the time. Fear brings present torment concerning future
situations that may not happen anyway. Paul knew that whatever did
happen, God would be faithful to strengthen him so that he might
patiently endure it.

**Lord, no matter what I face today, I am determined to stay
the course and not retreat. Strengthen me for the battle that I
might finish my course. Amen.**

Eyes on the Prize

*We are hedged in (pressed) on every side [troubled and oppressed in
every way], but not cramped or crushed; we suffer embarrassments
and are perplexed and unable to find a way out, but not driven
to despair; we are pursued (persecuted and hard driven), but not
deserted [to stand alone]; we are struck down to the ground, but
never struck out and destroyed.*   —2 CORINTHIANS 4:8–9

If we stare at our giants too much, the fear of them will overtake us.
Keep your eyes on the prize, not the pain. In the Bible, Paul explains
how they were pressed on every side and troubled and oppressed in
every way. They could see no way out, but they refused to give up.
He made his mind up that no matter what happened, he was going
to finish his course. Paul explained that they did not get discouraged
because they looked not at the things they could see but to the things
they could not see.

If we stare at our problems too much, think and talk about them too
much, they are likely to defeat us. We don't deny the existence of problems, we don't ignore them, but we do not permit them to rule us. Any
problem you have is subject to change. All things are possible with God!

Glance at your problems but stare at Jesus.

———————

**Lord, if Paul could endure through all the adversity he faced,
by Your grace I can make it through whatever I face. Help me
to see beyond the problems to You. Amen.**

Be Tenacious

*David said to Saul, Let no man's heart fail because of this Philistine;
your servant will go out and fight with him.... David said, The Lord
Who delivered me out of the paw of the lion and out of the paw of the
bear, He will deliver me out of the hand of this Philistine. And Saul
said to David, Go, and the Lord be with you!*

—1 SAMUEL 17:32, 37

When David came against the giant Goliath, he did not stand for hours looking at the giant wondering how to win the battle. The Bible says that he ran quickly to the battle line, all the time talking about the greatness of God and declaring his victory ahead of time. David did not run away from his giant; he courageously ran toward him.

Robert Schuller said, "If you listen to your fears, you will die never knowing what a great person you might have been."

If David had run from Goliath, he would never have been king of Israel. He was anointed by God to be king twenty years before he wore the crown. During those years he faced his giants and proved that he had the tenacity to endure difficulty without quitting.

Did David feel any fear as he approached Goliath? I think he did. In David's writings he never claimed to be free from the feelings of fear. He talked about being afraid, but he chose to be confident!

———————

Lord, I have some bears and lions and giants that I need to face. Help me to be tenacious and take them on in Your name. Amen.

Run Your Race

Do you not know that in a race all the runners compete, but [only] one receives the prize? So run [your race] that you may lay hold [of the prize] and make it yours. Now every athlete who goes into training conducts himself temperately and restricts himself in all things. . . . We [do it to receive a crown of eternal blessedness] that cannot wither. —1 CORINTHIANS 9:24–25

Paul said that we are each running a race and that we should run it to win. Winning requires preparation, training, sacrifice, and a will to press past opposition. It often requires failing many times but continuing, always keeping on, despite any opposition we may encounter along the way. Cowards quit, but confidence and courage finish.

When we make decisions that we know inside our heart aren't the best decisions, such as always choosing the easy way, it bothers our conscience. We may try to ignore the voice of conscience, but it whispers to us that we have not done our best. So when you are faced with decisions that plague or wear you down, be confident in your ability that you will see success. Say "It shall be done!"

Are you tempted to give up on something right now? Don't! Finishing your race will build your confidence. You will trust yourself more, and that is important. Winners don't always take first place, but they must finish the race.

Lord, I want to give You my very best today and run my race with joy and confidence. I will sacrifice whatever is necessary to finish my course. Amen.

A Clear Conscience

*Let us all come forward and draw near with true (honest and
sincere) hearts in unqualified assurance and absolute conviction
engendered by faith (by that leaning of the entire human personality
on God in absolute trust and confidence in His power, wisdom, and
goodness), having our hearts sprinkled and purified from a guilty
(evil) conscience and our bodies cleansed with pure water.*

—HEBREWS 10:22

I have learned from experience that a guilty conscience hinders the
flow of confidence. Confidence is faith in God and a belief that because
He is helping you, you can succeed in whatever you need to do. However, if we feel guilty, we will shrink back from God rather than boldly
expecting Him to assist us. We will give up rather than face our challenges in life because we feel bad about ourselves.

If you want to walk confidently, strive to keep your conscience clear
of offense toward God and man. Even quitting when you know you
should keep going will bother your conscience. God did not give us
His Holy Spirit so we could be in bondage to fear. He did not send the
power of His Spirit into our lives so we could be weak-willed, wimpy, or
the type of person who gives up when the going gets tough. Remember:
God gave us a spirit of power, love, and a sound mind (2 Timothy 1:7).

***

**Lord, thank You that through the blood of Jesus I can come to
You with a clear conscience. Help me to walk in power, love,
and sound mind today. Amen.**

Free from Condemnation

Therefore, [there is] now no condemnation (no adjudging guilty of wrong) for those who are in Christ Jesus, who live [and] walk not after the dictates of the flesh, but after the dictates of the Spirit. For the law of the Spirit of life [which is] in Christ Jesus . . . has freed me from the law of sin and of death. —ROMANS 8:1–2

A woman we will call Stacie asked to be interviewed for the new job in her company. Something vague was bothering her, though, and when the time came for the interview, her confidence had disappeared. The minute her supervisor realized that Stacie was unsure of herself, she lost confidence in her also and quickly filled the position with someone else.

Stacie began praying about what had happened to her confidence and remembered making personal unnecessary phone calls during working hours, knowing it was against company policy. She also took extra-long lunch hours on days when her supervisor was out of the office. Her conscience bothered her, but she reasoned that she deserved a few perks.

The Bible tells us that reasoning leads us into deception that is contrary to the truth. The truth was plain and simple. Stacie's actions were wrong! She was stealing from her company and even though she tried to ignore her conscience, deep down inside she felt guilty. She learned that confidence and condemnation don't work well together.

———————

Lord, search my heart for any reasonings I hold that are deceptions. I want to be completely free from the law of sin and death and condemnation. Amen.

Serving Him

He began to speak freely (fearlessly and boldly) in the synagogue;
but when Priscilla and Aquila heard him, they took him with
them and expounded to him the way of God more definitely
and accurately.   —ACTS 18:26

Priscilla and her husband, Aquila, had a church in their home (1 Corinthians 16:19), and since she is mentioned equally with him, she must
have pastored the church alongside him (Acts 18:2–26). Interestingly,
her name is listed first, which some scholars say may indicate that she
had a larger pastoral role than her husband. Obviously, Priscilla played
a significant role in speaking about Christ within the church.

When Luke mentions the travels of Jesus, he also mentions the
twelve men who were with Him, and some women (Luke 8:1–3). Is it
possible that these women had a publicly recognized role similar to
that of the men? At least one biblical scholar believes they did. These
women provided for Jesus from their belongings, according to Luke.
Women ministered both to and with Jesus. The same Greek word that
is translated *deacon* and applied to seven men in the New Testament
is also applied to seven women. They are Peter's mother-in-law; Mary
Magdalene; Mary, the mother of James and Joses; Salome, the mother
of Zebedee's children; Joanna, the wife of Chuza; Susanna; and Martha, the sister of Mary and Lazarus.

Clearly, God uses women! How will He use you?

———————————

**Lord, whatever role You have for me in Your service, I want
to minister with You and for You. Use my heart and soul and
hands and voice for Your honor. Amen.**

Take Courage

Do not be afraid of the enemy; [earnestly] remember the Lord and imprint Him [on your minds], great and terrible, and [take from Him courage to] fight for your brethren, your sons, your daughters, your wives, and your homes. —NEHEMIAH 4:14

All of us, at one time or another, wish we had more courage. Think about the courage that Jochebed, the mother of Moses, showed. She defied Pharaoh's order to kill all of the Hebrew boys and hid her son for three months before finally placing him in a basket, praying and trusting that God would provide. Her daughter, Miriam, exhibited great courage when she watched her little brother's makeshift boat float right to Pharaoh's daughter. Instead of hiding or running away, she approached the princess with boldness and offered to get a Hebrew nurse (Moses' mother) to help care for the child.

Courage means to be brave, bold, and adventurous. It's a quality like that in Jochebed and Miriam's example that allows a person to encounter danger and challenge with firmness and resolve. We all need courage. Courage comes from God, while fear is what Satan tries to give us. In the Bible we see the phrase "take courage." Courage is available, the same way fear is, but we can choose to reject fear and take courage.

———————

Lord, I choose to reject the fears that will arise today. I look to You and "take courage" for all the challenges that are before me. Imprint upon my mind the constant remembrance of who You are and what You can do for me. Amen.

Don't Take In Criticism

Now Miriam and Aaron talked against Moses [their brother]
because of his Cushite wife, for he had married a Cushite woman.
And they said, Has the Lord indeed spoken only by Moses? Has He
not spoken also by us? And the Lord heard it. Now the man Moses
was very meek (gentle, kind, and humble).

—NUMBERS 12:1–3

Sometimes the people who are criticized the most are the ones who try to do something constructive with their lives. It amazes me how people who do nothing want to criticize those who try to do something. After many years of suffering over the criticisms of people and trying to gain their approval, I finally decided that if God is happy with me, that is enough.

Each time someone criticizes you, try making a positive affirmation about yourself to yourself. Don't just stand by and take in everything anyone wants to dump on you. Establish independence! Have your own attitude about yourself and don't be defeated by criticism.

During Winston Churchill's last year in office, he attended an official ceremony. Several rows behind him two gentlemen began whispering. "They say Churchill is getting senile." "They say he should step aside and leave the running of the nation to more dynamic and capable men." When the ceremony was over, Churchill turned to the men and said, "Gentlemen, they also say he is deaf!"

If God is happy with you, that's enough!

———————————

Lord, at the end of the day, I want You to be happy with the way I lived, whether others criticize me or not. If You are happy with me, that's enough! Amen.

Encourage One Another

Therefore encourage [admonish, exhort] one another and edify
[strengthen and build up] one another.
—1 THESSALONIANS 5:11

The Duke of Wellington, the British military leader who defeated Napoleon at Waterloo, was not an easy man to serve under. He was brilliant, demanding, and not one to shower his subordinates with compliments. Yet even Wellington realized that his methods left something to be desired. In his old age a young lady asked him what, if anything, he would do differently if he had his life to live over again. Wellington replied, "I'd give more praise."

Because we all encounter difficulty while we are running our race and trying to reach our goals, we all need encouragement. The more we get, the easier it is to stay on track and avoid wasting days or weeks in depression and despair. One of the best ways I know to get something I want or need is to give some of it away. God's Word teaches us to sow and then we shall reap. If a farmer plants tomato seeds, he will get a harvest of tomatoes. You can be the channel that God uses to keep someone confidently pressing toward success rather than giving up. If we plant encouragement in the lives of other people, we will reap a harvest of encouragement in our own.

———————————

Lord, help me to not take others for granted but rather to find as many ways as possible to encourage them. I want to be a channel of blessing to others, and I trust that the encouragement I need will return to me. Amen.

Whose Approval?

Many even of the leading men (the authorities and the nobles)
believed and trusted in Him. But because of the Pharisees they did
not confess it, for fear that [if they should acknowledge Him] they
would be expelled from the synagogue; for they loved the approval
and the praise and the glory that come from men [instead of and]
more than the glory that comes from God.   —JOHN 12:42–43

You might be trapped in a religious boat, going to church, bored, just waiting till it gets over, playing a bunch of silly religious games, playing up to all the right people so you can be in the right social group at church. That's not the way God wants you to live. He wants you to be full of zeal and radically in love with Him! If you want God to do something in your life, you have to be willing to step out of the boat.

It's pretty sad when we care more about what people think than we do about what God thinks. I would rather get criticized, gossiped about, put out of the group, or anything than live one more day of my life unhappy and miserable. Jesus is passing by, and I'm getting out of the boat. Will you join me? Let's agree: "I will follow Him. I will not stay in prison any longer; I will be free."

———————————

Lord, I will follow You, no matter what that means. I will not play religious games in order to keep others' approval. I want the glory that comes from You alone. Amen.

Take Responsibility

[So] they summoned them and imperatively instructed them not to
converse in any way or teach at all in or about the name of Jesus.
But Peter and John replied to them, Whether it is right in the sight
of God to listen to you and obey you rather than God, you must
decide (judge). But we [ourselves] cannot help telling what we have
seen and heard.   —ACTS 4:18–20

What is your boat? Is it a boat of passivity and indecision? Is there
something crying out in you, "I wish I had a life...had some friends...
could lose some weight...could have some fun...could get out of debt.
I want to be free!" Well, get up and get out of the boat. Get going. Stop
whining and moaning about it. You are the only one who can do anything about it. Take responsibility for your life.

You can pray until you're blue in the face for God to make it happen
miraculously, but what if God is saying you have to confront it yourself
and deal with it yourself? Are you too afraid to do it? Perhaps you feel
that if you make no decisions, you can't be wrong. And if you make no
decisions, you think you have no responsibility. But you have to stay in
the boat and take the consequences.

———————

Lord, I hate being lulled into passivity and staying trapped
when You are calling me to action. I will take responsibility
for my life today and start turning my wishes into reality.
Amen.

Change the Culture

So Hilkiah the priest, Ahikam, Achbor, Shaphan, and Asaiah went to Huldah the prophetess, the wife of Shallum son of Tikvah, the son of Harhas, keeper of the wardrobe—now she dwelt in Jerusalem, in the Second Quarter—and they talked with her. She said to them, Thus says the Lord, the God of Israel: Tell the man who sent you to me . . .
—2 KINGS 22:14–15

Harriet Beecher Stowe (1811–1896) wrote what is probably the best-selling American novel of the nineteenth century, *Uncle Tom's Cabin*. A daughter of the famous preacher Lyman Beecher, she took an early interest in theology and works for social improvement. Having come in contact with fugitive slaves and learned what life was like for a black in the South, she was encouraged to write a book about the evils of slavery. The resulting classic sold over three hundred thousand copies in a year—a sales number absolutely unheard of at the time.

At a time in our country's history when politics and cultural change were still very much a man's world, Harriet stood up to misguided and misinformed cultural and racial notions of the day and worked hard to ensure that people everywhere could experience freedom, regardless of their skin color. She was also credited with even bigger things. President Abraham Lincoln, when meeting her during the Civil War, reportedly said, "So you're the little woman who wrote the book that started this great war!"

———————

Lord, I can change the culture of my life by the choices I make and the way I live every day. Help my words to reflect Your Word. Amen.

Take a Stand

Blessed and happy and enviably fortunate and spiritually
prosperous (in the state in which the born-again child of God enjoys
and finds satisfaction in God's favor and salvation, regardless of his
outward conditions) are those who are persecuted for righteousness'
sake (for being and doing right), for theirs is the kingdom of heaven!
—MATTHEW 5:10

In our world today most people compromise rather than take a stand for what is right. Jesus said we would be persecuted for righteousness' sake, and most people are not up for that. Jesus also promised a reward; however, the majority of people want reward without commitment. If we do what God has asked us to do, we will get what He promised us we could have. Salvation is free, and its only condition is to "believe," but the benefits of being a Christian do come with conditions. God simply said, "If you will, I will." Most Christians live far below their God-ordained destiny and privileges because they compromise rather than take a stand.

Take a stand. If you are the only one you know who is willing to do what is right, it may be a lonely walk, there may be persecution along the way, but the rewards are worth it. You will have the satisfaction of knowing that you lived your life fully and completely and refused to let fear be your master.

Lord, I am willing to join with You and stand up for what I know is right. My destiny lies with You, and I choose Your kingdom above all. Amen.

We Are His Hands

If one member suffers, all the parts [share] the suffering; if one
member is honored, all the members [share in] the enjoyment of it.
Now you [collectively] are Christ's body and [individually] you are
members of it, each part severally and distinct [each with his own
place and function].   —1 CORINTHIANS 12:26–27

Some individuals pass quietly and fearfully through life and never do anything to make the world a better place. They are so concerned with self-preservation that they never reach out to those around them who are crying out for help. Think about the neighbor who just found out she has terminal cancer or the family you heard about at church who is in danger of losing their home because the husband lost his job. The bank is ready to foreclose on their loan, and they really have nowhere to go. They are desperate and don't know what to do. Everyone tells them that God will provide, but no one is doing anything to help.

We must realize that God works through people. We are His hands, feet, arms, mouth, eyes, and ears. God does miracles, but He does them through people with uncommon courage. Those who forget about themselves long enough will notice that God has placed someone in their path who is hurting and needy. We pray for God to use us, and when He tries, we are often too busy to be bothered.

Where does God want you to be His hands and feet?

Lord, help me to be Your hands and to reach out to those in need around me. Help me to do all that I can. Amen.

Deny Yourself

*And Jesus called [to Him] the throng with His disciples and said
to them, If anyone intends to come after Me, let him deny himself
[forget, ignore, disown, and lose sight of himself and his own
interests] and take up his cross, and [joining Me as a disciple
and siding with My party] follow with Me [continually, cleaving
steadfastly to Me].*   —MARK 8:34

Jesus said if we want to be His disciples, we will forget about ourselves, lose sight of ourselves and all of our own interests. The minute
we hear that, fear strikes our hearts and we hear loudly in our heads,
"What about me? If I forget myself, who is going to take care of me?"
My beloved, do not be afraid, God Himself will take care of you. Everything you do for other people will come back to you many times over,
with joy. If you are willing to give yourself away, you will have a much
better life than you ever would have had trying to keep yourself.

Are you using the resources you have in the service of God and man?
Be courageous. Forget about yourself and start doing all you can to help
others. Get a new goal. "Put smiles on faces." Encourage, edify, lift up,
comfort, help, give hope, relieve pain, and lift burdens.

**Lord, You called me to a life far bigger than my own interests.
Help me to forget about myself and follow You wherever You
lead. My greatest pleasure is to be Your disciple. Amen.**

Put Smiles on Faces

*For whoever is bent on saving his [temporal] life [his comfort and
security here] shall lose it [eternal life]; and whoever loses his
life [his comfort and security here] for My sake shall find it [life
everlasting]. For what will it profit a man if he gains the whole world
and forfeits his life?*   —MATTHEW 16:25–26

We must all make sure that we are not like the rich man in the Bible
who had so much that all of his barns were full with no room for more.
Instead of giving any of it away, he decided that he would tear down
the barns he had and just build bigger ones and collect more stuff for
himself. I think he was the dumbest man in the Bible.

He could have decided that he would use what he had to bless
others, but he must have been a fearful, selfish man, who only had
room in his life for himself (Luke 12:16–20). God called the man a fool
and said, "This very night they [the messengers of God] will demand
your soul of you; and all the things that you have prepared, whose will
they be?" The man was going to die that night and all he would leave
behind was "stuff." He could have added to many lives and put smiles
on thousands of faces. Instead, he fearfully and selfishly only cared
about himself.

Where can you reach out and share the blessings God has given you?

————————

**Lord, my barns may not be full, but I still can give in such
a way that others are blessed. Help me to give of my "stuff."
Amen.**

Running Over

Give, and [gifts] will be given to you; good measure, pressed down, shaken together, and running over, will they pour into [the pouch formed by] the bosom [of your robe and used as a bag]. For with the measure you deal out [with the measure you use when you confer benefits on others], it will be measured back to you.

—LUKE 6:38

When God created Adam and Eve, He blessed them, told them to be fruitful and multiply, and to use all the vast resources of the earth that He gave them in the service of God and man. Are you being fruitful? Is your life causing increase? When you get involved with people and things, do they increase and multiply? Some people only take in life, and they never add anything. I refuse to be that kind of person. I want to make people's lives better.

Women are sensitive to the needs of others. I believe God gives you and me an ability to be touched by the infirmities of others for the express purpose of helping. Women are experts in bringing comfort. Courageous women are givers. Don't selfishly and fearfully pass through this life, but do everything you can, every way you can, for everyone that you can, as often as you can. If that is your goal, you will be one of those rare individuals who actually makes the world a better place.

———————

Lord, help me to use the gifts You've given me in the service of others. Make me to be fruitful in others' lives. Amen.

Looking Forward

Listen to and obey My voice, and I will be your God and you will
be My people. . . . But they would not listen to and obey Me or
bend their ear [to Me], but followed the counsels and the stubborn
promptings of their own evil hearts and minds, and they turned
their backs and went in reverse instead of forward.

—JEREMIAH 7:23–24

I believe you are going to act on these devotional readings and begin living boldly and fearlessly as a confident woman. It doesn't matter how you lived before now; this is a new beginning. Every day God's mercy is new, and it is available for all of us today. Don't look back; look forward!

Be decisive, follow your heart, and don't be overly concerned about what other people think of you and your decisions. Most of them are not thinking about you as much as you might imagine that they are anyway.

Don't live constantly comparing yourself with others; be your unique self. (See 2 Corinthians 10:12.) Celebrate who God has made you to be. There is only one who has the unique traits and skills that make up who you are. Enjoy the fact that God knew what He was doing, and rely on the thought that surely God said the same thing about you as He did when He called the world into creation: "And it was good."

———————————

Lord, I will look forward today, and I will follow Your voice and obey. I take hold of Your mercy and rejoice in who You've made me to be. Amen.

Be Glad

Be glad then, you children of Zion, and rejoice in the Lord, your God; for He gives you the former or early rain in just measure and in righteousness, and He causes to come down for you the rain, the former rain and the latter rain, as before. And the [threshing] floors shall be full of grain and the vats shall overflow with juice [of the grape] and oil.   —JOEL 2:23–24

So many times our outward appearance shows the way we're feeling inside. But it can also work the other way! When we look confident on the outside, we can feel more confident on the inside. When you walk, stand upright. Don't slump your shoulders and hang your head down. You are full of the life of God, so act like it!

Live with passion, zeal, and enthusiasm. Don't just try to "make it" through the day. Celebrate the day. Say, "This is the day the Lord has made, I will rejoice and be glad in it" (see Psalm 118:24). Don't dread the day; attack the day. Know what you want to accomplish today and go for it.

You go, girl—you start talking and walking with confidence! It is time for you to look up, not down. It is time for you to expect great things to happen in your life.

———————————

Lord, I want to live this day passionately and to celebrate Your life in me. This is the day You have made, and I want to bring You glory in it. Amen.

Smile

I smiled on them when they had no confidence, and their depression did not cast down the light of my countenance. I chose their way [for them] and sat as [their] chief, and dwelt like a king among his soldiers, like one who comforts mourners.   —JOB 29:24–25

It only takes seventeen muscles to smile, but forty-three to frown. In other words, you work a whole lot harder looking sour than looking happy! So make it a point to smile more. Smile a lot. The more you smile, the better you will feel. Your smile not only makes you appear and feel more confident, it gives others confidence. They feel approved of and accepted when we smile at them. We actually say more with our body language than we do with words. I can often tell if a person is confident just by the way they carry themselves and by the look on their face. Some people always look unsure and even frightened, while others appear confident and at ease.

You may think that you cannot do anything about the way you look, but you can. I started out as a person who rarely smiled. I had a perpetual solemn look. I had lost hope; I had a negative attitude; I was fearful, and it showed on my face and in the way I carried myself. I started making changes by just smiling. Now I smile a lot.

Make it a point to smile several times a day and see how it changes how you feel.

Lord, whether I feel like it or not, I will smile today and bring cheer to those I meet. I will rejoice and be glad. Amen.

Love and Respect

*However, let each man of you [without exception] love his wife as
[being in a sense] his very own self; and let the wife see that she
respects and reverences her husband [that she notices him, regards
him, honors him, prefers him, venerates, and esteems him; and
that she defers to him, praises him, and loves and admires him
exceedingly].*
—EPHESIANS 5:33

We see in God's Word that God established how authority should
flow from Him to man and then to woman. The Bible states that the
husband is the head of the wife as Christ is the Head of the church.
The woman is to submit to her husband as is fitting in the Lord. However, that was never intended to include abuse, control, manipulation,
or mistreatment of any kind. In fact, man is instructed in God's Word
to love his wife as he loves his own body; to nurture her and treat her
kindly and tenderly (Ephesians 5:21–33).

God has established lines of authority that allow an orderly, peaceful existence. He expects us to submit to and respect one another. If
a married couple can handle themselves the way God intended, their
relationship will be wonderful and unbelievably fruitful. However,
pride destroys most relationships. It's the great "I" factor. Selfish, self-
centered people do whatever they must to get their own way, including
abusing those they were intended to nourish and protect.

Lord, I trust You to help me to be strong in all of my relationships, to show respect and honor appropriately. I humble
myself before You. Amen.

A Happy Heart

A glad heart makes a cheerful countenance, but by sorrow of heart the spirit is broken....A happy heart is good medicine and a cheerful mind works healing, but a broken spirit dries up the bones.
—PROVERBS 15:13; 17:22

Most women are concerned about their looks, and a smile is an inexpensive way to improve your looks instantly. Ziggy said, "A smile is a facelift that is in everyone's price range."

When you were born, you were crying and everyone around you was smiling; live your life in such a way that when you die, you will be smiling and everyone else will be crying.

You may be familiar with Joel Osteen, a pastor from Houston, Texas. He not only pastors the largest church in the United States, but he is also on television in many parts of the world. Joel is known as "the smiling preacher." He literally smiles all the time. I have eaten with him several times, and I am still trying to figure out how he can eat and smile at the same time, but he does it. He is a great pastor and teacher of God's Word, but I believe one of the main things that helps his popularity is his smile. People want to feel better, and anytime we smile at them it helps them do that. A smile reassures people and puts them at ease.

Lord, Your love and grace bring the deepest happiness to my heart. I receive it from You, and I ask You to pour it out to others through my smiles and care. Amen.

The Power of Words

Death and life are in the power of the tongue, and they who indulge in it shall eat the fruit of it [for death or life].

—PROVERBS 18:21

According to the Bible, the power of life and death is in the tongue, and we often have to eat our words.

I wonder how many times in our lives we say, "I'm afraid..." "I'm afraid I'll get that flu that is going around." "I'm afraid my kids will get in trouble." "I'm afraid it's going to snow, and I'm afraid to drive in it, if it does." "With the way prices are going up, I'm afraid I won't have enough money." "I'm afraid if I don't go to that party, people will think badly of me." "I'm afraid we won't get a good seat at the theater." "I'm afraid someone will break into my house while I'm out of town." If we heard a recording of every time in our life we have said "I'm afraid," we would probably be amazed that our lives are going as well as they are.

If we really understood the power of words, I think we would change the way we talk. Our talk should be confident and bold, not fearful. Fearful talk not only affects us in an adverse way, but it affects those around us.

Don't underestimate the power of words.

Lord, show me the ways I need to change the way I talk. Help me to break the bad habits I've adopted and the negative words I repeat over and over. Amen.

Speak God's Word

Let the words of my mouth and the meditation of my heart be
acceptable in Your sight, O Lord, my [firm, impenetrable] Rock and
my Redeemer.   —PSALM 19:14

Don't speak negatives such as "I just don't have any confidence" or "I'll never overcome my fears." Say what you want, not what you have. Anything God says you can have, you can have. But you will need to get into agreement with Him. David said, "My confidence is in the Lord," and you can say the same thing. Paul said, "We can do all things through Christ Who strengthens us." So you can say, "I can do whatever God tells me to do in life, because Christ will give me strength." God says in His Word that He did not give us a spirit of fear, so we can say, "I will not fear. God has not given me a spirit of fear." I'm sure you get the idea by now.

Romans 12 teaches us that though God has a good plan for our lives, we must totally renew our minds and learn how to think right before we will see it come to pass.

As you speak God's Word out loud, you renew your own mind.

Lord, teach me Your Word that I might speak Your Word.
Help me to align my thoughts with Your thoughts and may my
words be acceptable in Your sight. Amen.

A Turning Point

*I have learned in any and all circumstances the secret of facing every
situation, whether well-fed or going hungry, having a sufficiency
and enough to spare or going without and being in want. I have
strength for all things in Christ Who empowers me [I am ready for
anything and equal to anything through Him Who infuses inner
strength into me; I am self-sufficient in Christ's sufficiency].*

—PHILIPPIANS 4:12–13

What is in your heart comes out of your mouth (Matthew 12:34), and
what you keep in your mouth affects your heart. It is a cycle. What
comes first—is it thoughts or words? It really doesn't matter because
they affect each other, and both must be corrected in order for us to
enjoy the life Jesus died to give us.

Stop saying "I'm depressed," "I'm discouraged," "I'm ready to give
up," or "Nothing good ever happens to me." All talk of that type is
totally useless. They are words that cannot add to your life, but they
can certainly prevent you from living.

If you have considered yourself to be a person with low self-esteem,
no confidence, cowardly, timid, shy, and fearful, this can be a turning
point for you. However, you will have to be persistent. It is not what we
do right one or two times that makes a difference in our lives; it's what
we do right consistently.

———————————

**Lord, in my thoughts and my words, I want to always confess
that You are my sufficiency. Help me to be ready for anything
because You empower me. Amen.**

The Encourager

However, I am telling you nothing but the truth when I say it is profitable (good, expedient, advantageous) for you that I go away. Because if I do not go away, the Comforter (Counselor, Helper, Advocate, Intercessor, Strengthener, Standby) will not come to you [into close fellowship with you]; but if I go away, I will send Him to you [to be in close fellowship with you]. —JOHN 16:7

What we make happen for someone else, God will make happen for us. Do you sometimes find yourself wishing you had more encouragement, maybe from your family or friends or boss? But how often do you encourage others? If you're not sure, then make an extra effort right away. You can be the channel that God uses to keep someone confidently pressing toward success rather than giving up.

Did you know that the Holy Spirit is called "The Encourager"? The Greek word *parakletos* is translated as the words "Holy Spirit" and includes comfort, edification, and encouragement as part of its definition. Through the Holy Spirit, Jesus sent us a Comforter, a Helper, a Strengthener, an Edifier, and an Encourager, and He sent Him to be in close fellowship with us. He lives inside of those who are believers in Jesus Christ. Let God encourage you through His Spirit. He will never tell you that you're not going to make it. He will never tell you that your case is hopeless.

Lord, thank You for coming to dwell inside of me through the Holy Spirit. I open my heart to Your encouragement, comfort, and edification today. Amen.

Free Access to God

And, beloved, if our consciences [our hearts] do not accuse us [if they do not make us feel guilty and condemn us], we have confidence [complete assurance and boldness] before God.   —1 JOHN 3:21

Some people are unable to pray boldly because their consciences bother them. There are things they need to repent of and commitments they need to make to do things differently. If that is the case with you, then just do it. If something is wrong in your life, don't spend the rest of your days feeling bad about it . . . do something about it!

Ephesians 3:20 tells us that God is able to do exceedingly, abundantly, above and beyond all that we could ever dare to hope, ask, or think. Are you daring in prayer? Are you expecting enough? The devil wants us to believe we must go to God with head hung low, telling Him how terrible we are. He wants us to believe that we dare not ask for too much, because after all, we don't deserve anything. Satan is afraid of bold, daring, confident, fearless, and expectant prayer.

I love the Scripture I am about to quote, so please take time to look it over carefully. "In Whom, because of our faith in Him, we dare to have the boldness (courage and confidence) of free access (an unreserved approach to God with freedom and without fear)" (Ephesians 3:12).

Lord, I am challenged to rise up and be more daring in prayer. I truly believe that You are able to do abundantly more than I have ever dared to ask or think. Amen.

Examine Yourself

Examine yourselves as to whether you are in the faith. Test yourselves. Do you not know yourselves, that Jesus Christ is in you?
—2 CORINTHIANS 13:5 NKJV

The Bible tells us to examine ourselves, and I wholeheartedly agree that we need to do so. We should examine ourselves to see if we have sin, and if so, we should sincerely repent, then move on to living without that sin in our lives.

There is a great difference between examination and condemnation. Examination helps us prove to ourselves that we are in Christ and He is in us, and that in Him we have been set free from sin. Condemnation keeps us mired in the very sin we feel condemned about. It does not deliver us—it traps us! It weakens us and saps all our spiritual strength. We give our energy to feeling condemned rather than living righteously.

There is such a thing as excessive self-examination, and I personally believe it opens the door for much of the unbalance we see today in this area among God's children. To be overly introspective and continually examining our every move opens a door to Satan. In the past I experienced multiple problems in this area, and I know for a fact that you and I will never be confident in prayer until the problem is dealt with thoroughly and completely.

Examine, but don't condemn. God has forgiven confessed sin so you can move forward. He isn't dwelling on it; why should you?

———————

Lord, I ask You to search my heart and expose any sin in my life. I refuse to get trapped in endless introspection and condemnation. Set me free from all sin. Amen.

Confidence in Prayer

*Therefore He is able also to save to the uttermost (completely,
perfectly, finally, and for all time and eternity) those who come to
God through Him, since He is always living to make petition to God
and intercede with Him and intervene for them.*

—HEBREWS 7:25

I believe a lot of people are dissatisfied with their prayer life, and I can
relate because I felt that way myself for a lot of years. I was committed
to praying every morning, but at the end of my prayer time, I always felt
vaguely frustrated. I finally asked God what was wrong with me, and
He responded in my heart by saying, "Joyce, you don't feel that your
prayers are good enough." It was right back to the old condemnation
thing all over again. I was not enjoying prayer because I had no confidence that my prayers were acceptable.

God had to teach me some lessons about praying in faith, about
understanding that the Holy Spirit was helping me in prayer, and that
Jesus was interceding along with me (Romans 8:26). If two of the Per-
sons of the Godhead were helping me, surely my imperfect prayers were
perfected by the time they arrived at the throne of God the Father.

When you pray, remember who's helping you.

Lord, help me to understand how You come alongside me
and help me as I pray. I believe my prayers are good enough
because You perfect them. Amen.

Simple, Believing Prayer

And when you pray, do not heap up phrases (multiply words, repeating the same ones over and over) as the Gentiles do, for they think they will be heard for their much speaking. . . . For your Father knows what you need before you ask Him.

—MATTHEW 6:7–8

We must develop confidence in simple, believing prayer. We need the confidence that even if we simply say, "God, help me," He hears and will answer. We can depend on God to be faithful to do what we have asked Him to do, as long as our request is in accordance with His will. We should know that He wants to help us because He is our Helper (Hebrews 13:6).

Too often we get caught up in our own words concerning prayer. Sometimes we try to pray so long, loud, and fancy that we lose sight of the fact that prayer is our conversation with God. The length or loudness or eloquence of our prayer is not the issue; it is the sincerity of our heart and the confidence we have that God hears and will answer us that is important.

Sometimes we try to sound so devout and elegant that we get lost. We don't even know what we are trying to pray about. If we could ever get delivered from trying to impress God, we would be a lot better off.

Simple prayer from the heart is what impresses God.

———————

Lord, free me from the belief that my prayers must be eloquent and just right. Keep reminding me that what You really want from me is a heartfelt conversation. Amen.

Pray without Ceasing

*Be unceasing in prayer [praying perseveringly]. Thank [God] in
everything [no matter what the circumstances may be, be thankful
and give thanks], for this is the will of God for you [who are] in
Christ Jesus.*   —1 THESSALONIANS 5:17–18

If we don't understand simple, believing prayer, that instruction can
come down upon us like a very heavy burden. We may feel that we are
doing well to pray thirty minutes a day, so how can we possibly pray
without ever stopping? We need to have such confidence about our
prayer life that prayer becomes just like breathing, an effortless thing
that we do every moment we are alive. We don't work and struggle at
breathing, unless we have a lung disorder, and neither should we work
and struggle at praying. I don't believe we will struggle in this area if we
really understand the power of simple, believing prayer.

If we don't have confidence in our prayers, we will not pray very
much, let alone pray without ceasing. Obviously the terminology
"without ceasing" does not mean that we must be offering some kind of
formal prayer every moment twenty-four hours a day. It means that all
throughout the day we should be in a prayerful attitude. As we encounter each situation or as things come to our mind that need attention, we
should simply submit them to God in prayer.

———————

**Lord, develop a prayerful attitude in me. Help me to make
prayer as simple as breathing. Whatever comes my way, let me
bring it to You in prayer. Amen.**

Secret Prayer

You must not be like the hypocrites, for they love to pray standing in the synagogues . . . that they may be seen by people. . . . But when you pray, go into your [most] private room, and, closing the door, pray to your Father, Who is in secret; and your Father, Who sees in secret, will reward you in the open.   —MATTHEW 6:5–6

Although some prayers are public prayers or group prayers, most of our prayer life is secret and should be that way. In other words, we don't have to broadcast how much we pray and everything we pray about.

"Secret prayer" means a number of things. It means that we do not broadcast to everyone we know our personal experiences in prayer. We pray about the things and people God places on our hearts, and we keep our prayers between us and Him unless we have a really good reason to do otherwise.

There is nothing wrong with saying to a friend, "I have been praying for the youth of our nation a lot lately" or "I have been praying for people to enter into a more serious relationship with God." Sharing of this type is simply part of friendship, but there are things God places on our heart to pray about that we should keep to ourselves.

"Secret prayer" means that we do not make a display of our prayers to impress people. Some things are better kept between us and God!

Lord, I yearn to grow closer to You through secret prayer. I know that You see me and hear me. Draw close and speak to my heart. Amen.

Keys to Heaven

I will give you the keys of the kingdom of heaven; and whatever you bind (declare to be improper and unlawful) on earth must be what is already bound in heaven; and whatever you loose (declare lawful) on earth must be what is already loosed in heaven.

—MATTHEW 16:19

Since we are spiritual as well as physical beings, we are able to stand in the physical realm and affect the spiritual realm. This is a very definite privilege and advantage. For example, if I have a grandchild who is experiencing difficulties in school, I can go into the spiritual realm through prayer and bring about action that will cause change in that situation. "God is a Spirit" (John 4:24), and every answer we need to every situation is with Him.

Jesus told Peter that He would give him the keys of the kingdom of heaven (Matthew 16:19). Keys unlock doors, and those keys can represent various types of prayer and the power of binding and loosing. Jesus was speaking about the power of faith, and we know that one way faith is released is through prayer. In Jesus' name we can bind (hinder) the devil, and in His name we can loose angels by requesting that they be dispatched from heaven to provide protection for ourselves or for others. (See Matthew 26:53; Hebrews 1:7,14.) The act of prayer binds evil and looses good.

———————————

Lord, thank You for the keys to Your Kingdom. Give me wisdom on how to use them in my daily life and to become an effective servant of Yours. Amen.

Pray about It

We ... have not ceased to pray and make [special] request for you, [asking] that you may be filled with the full (deep and clear) knowledge of His will in all spiritual wisdom [in comprehensive insight into the ways and purposes of God] and in understanding and discernment of spiritual things. —COLOSSIANS 1:9

Trisha was haunted by an unreasonable fear that her husband, Bob, would get involved with another woman and leave her. Her fear made her suspicious, and she frequently accused her husband of things that made no sense to him at all. Over time, Trisha's behavior slowly but surely eroded Bob's respect for her. He never gave her one reason to distrust him and could not understand what her problem was. To be honest, she didn't understand it either until she began to pray about it. God revealed to her that her fear was the fruit of a sudden change in her own life when as a child her father left her mother for another woman.

Having understanding about where the fear came from helped Trisha to resist it. She began reading and educating herself about the nature of fear. For quite some time she still had some of the same thoughts and feelings, but she was now able to reason with herself because she had knowledge. As time went by, the fear went with it, and Bob and Trisha's relationship healed.

Where does your fear spring from? Knowing the answer is a step toward healing.

_____

Lord, I need insight into Your ways and purposes and to discern the truth about my life. I depend on You for revelation to help me understand my problems and overcome them. Amen.

The Prayer of Petition

For this reason I am telling you, whatever you ask for in prayer,
believe (trust and be confident) that it is granted to you, and you
will [get it].   —MARK 11:24

This prayer is by far the most often used. When we petition God, we ask for something for ourselves. When we pray for others, we are interceding. Most of us, sorry to say, are overly interested in ourselves. For that reason, we frequently exercise our right to petition God. It is, of course, not wrong to ask God to do things for us, but our petitions should be well balanced with praise and thanksgiving.

It is important to petition God about our future—to pray and ask Him for His help in allowing us to succeed at being ourselves. Our success won't come through personal struggle or vain effort. It will only come as a result of God's grace. You and I must add our effort to His grace, but effort without grace is useless. Grace comes as a result of asking for it. Asking is praying the prayer of petition.

You and I can be bold in petitioning God for any type of need in our lives. We are not restricted to a certain number of requests per day. We can feel at ease talking to God about anything that concerns us.

———————————

Lord, You call me into Your presence, and I come to You as my Father with my requests. I am confident that You are listening and that You will grant the desires of my heart. Amen.

The Prayer of Praise and Thanksgiving

Speak out to one another in psalms and hymns and spiritual songs,
offering praise with voices [and instruments] and making melody
with all your heart to the Lord, At all times and for everything giving
thanks in the name of our Lord Jesus Christ to God the Father.

—EPHESIANS 5:19–20

Praise is a narration or a tale in which we recount the good things about an individual, in this case, God. We should praise the Lord continually. By continually, I mean all throughout the day. We should praise Him for His mighty works, the things He has created, and even the things He is yet to do in each of our lives.

We should also thank Him always, in good times and especially in difficult ones. When prayers of petition outweigh prayers of praise and thanksgiving in our prayer life, I believe it says something about our character.

Greedy people ask, ask, ask, and rarely ever appreciate what they have already received. I do not believe that God will release us into the fullness of all that He has planned for us until we become thankful for what we have already been given.

Powerful living comes through thanksgiving. One of the ways we can "pray without ceasing" is by being thankful all day long, praising God for His goodness, mercy, loving-kindness, grace, and His long-suffering and patient nature.

Lord, You alone are worthy of my praise and thanksgiving,
and I give You mine. Teach me more about Your character that
I might worship You more throughout my day. Amen.

The Prayer of Intercession

And I sought a man among them who should build up the wall and stand in the gap before Me for the land, that I should not destroy it, but I found none.   —EZEKIEL 22:30

To intercede means to stand in the gap for someone else. If there is a breach in people's relationship with God, we have the privilege of placing ourselves in that breach and praying for them. If they have a need, we can intercede for them and expect to see them comforted and encouraged while they wait. We can also expect a timely breakthrough for them concerning their need being met.

Praying for others is equivalent to sowing seed. We all know that we must sow seed if we are to reap a harvest (Galatians 6:7). Sowing seed into the lives of other people is one sure way to reap a harvest in our own life. Each time we pray for someone else, we are assuring our own success.

Help someone else succeed by praying for them. If you want your ministry to succeed, pray for someone else's ministry. If you want your business to succeed, pray for someone else's business. If you need a breakthrough over some bad habit that is hindering you and holding you back, pray for someone else who has a need in a similar area.

Lord, lead me into a life of intercession for others. I ask You by Your Spirit to put people upon my heart to pray for, and I ask You to help me to be faithful to do so. Amen.

The Prayer of Commitment

Casting the whole of your care [all your anxieties, all your worries, all your concerns, once and for all] on Him, for He cares for you affectionately and cares about you watchfully.   —1 PETER 5:7

When we are tempted to worry or take the care of some situation in life, we should pray the prayer of commitment. For example, if I have done my best to get to an appointment on time, and due to circumstances beyond my control it appears I am going to be late, I have learned to pray the prayer of commitment. I say, "Lord, I am giving this situation to You; do something to make things work out right." I find that when I do that, things do work out all right. Either the Lord gives me favor with those I am supposed to meet and they totally understand, or I arrive and find they were also running behind and were concerned I would have to wait for them.

In order to succeed at being ourselves, we must continually be committing ourselves to God, giving to Him those things that appear to be holding us back. Only God can take proper care of those types of situations.

God intervenes in our situations when we commit them to Him. Commit to the Lord your children, your marriage, your personal relationships, and especially anything you may be tempted to be concerned about.

———————————

Lord, I commit into Your hands and care everything that is going on in my life. I desire that You may be glorified today and forever. Amen.

The Prayer of Consecration

Also I heard the voice of the Lord, saying, Whom shall I send? And who will go for Us? Then said I, Here am I; send me.

—ISAIAH 6:8

In the prayer of consecration, we dedicate our lives and all that we are to Him. In order for God to use us, we must consecrate ourselves to Him.

When we truly consecrate ourselves to the Lord, we lose the burden of trying to run our own lives. I would rather voluntarily follow God than struggle to get Him to follow me. He knows where He is going, and I know I will reach my destination safely if I allow Him to lead.

I consecrate myself to God in prayer on a regular basis. I say, "Here I am, Lord. I am Yours; do with me as You please." Then sometimes I add, "I hope I like what You choose, Lord, but if I don't, Your will be done and not mine."

Consecration and/or dedication to God is the most important aspect of succeeding at being ourselves. We don't even know what we are supposed to be, let alone know how to become whatever it is. But as we regularly keep our lives on the altar in consecration to God, He will do the work that needs to be done in us, so He may do the work He desires to do through us.

———————

Lord, I gladly consecrate myself—body, soul, and spirit—to You today. Take my life, shape my life, and use my life for Your glory. Amen.

Shake It Up

And He Who is seated on the throne said, See! I make all things new.   —REVELATION 21:5

Although I want to be dependable and faithful, I don't always want to be predictable. Sometimes I get bored with myself, and I have to ask God for a creative idea to shake up my life a little.

Doing something outrageous means different things to different people. For one it might mean climbing Mount Everest and to another it might mean a clothing style change. I have always liked lots of glitz and everything very fancy. My children kept trying to get me to keep up with changing styles and I firmly resisted for quite a while. They kept saying, "C'mon Mom, start styling." At first I told them, "I can't dress like that; I am sixty-two."

Then God told me to stop making decisions based on my age, and I decided I would do something outrageous, something totally unexpected, and change my dress code. My children finally convinced me that just because I was in my sixties, I didn't have to dress like it. They wanted me to wear jeans, boots, and belts hanging on my hips. One day I made a decision that I was going to shock them, so I changed my wardrobe style. I have decided that from now on I am going to dress up-to-date no matter how old I am.

Where will you shake up your life?

———————————

Lord, keep me fresh and new and alive in my attitudes and perspectives. Help me to shake it up today and break out of my rut. Amen.

Joy and Peace

May the God of your hope so fill you with all joy and peace in believing [through the experience of your faith] that by the power of the Holy Spirit you may abound and be overflowing (bubbling over) with hope.   —ROMANS 15:13

I remember an evening when I was feeling strongly dissatisfied and discontented. I went to my promise box, a little container filled with Scriptures that help recall God's promises whenever there is a need. Well, I felt I needed something, but I was not sure what it was. I had no peace or joy and was absolutely miserable. I pulled out a card with Romans 15:13 printed on it, and it was indeed "a word in season" for me. My problem was simple—I was doubting instead of believing. I was doubting God's unconditional love, doubting that I could hear from Him, doubting His call on my life, doubting that He was pleased with me. I was filled with doubt. When I saw the problem, I got back into faith and out of doubt. My joy and peace returned immediately.

I have found the same thing to be true again and again in my life. When joy and peace seem to be gone, I check my believing—usually it is gone also. It stands to reason then that doubting ourselves will also steal our joy and peace and confidence.

Confess your doubt—don't let it rob you.

———————————

Lord, I ask You to fill me with the joy and peace that come through placing my faith in You. Cause hope to overflow through my life by the power of Your Spirit and heal me of my doubt. Amen.

Contentment

*John answered, A man can receive nothing [he can claim nothing,
he can take unto himself nothing] except as it has been granted to
him from heaven. [A man must be content to receive the gift which is
given him from heaven; there is no other source.]*   —JOHN 3:27

John the Baptist's disciples were getting concerned that Jesus was baptizing too, and that everyone was leaving their master and flocking to Him. They went to John with this report. Had John not been secure in himself and in his calling, he may have become fearful and jealous. He may have felt led to compete with Jesus in order to maintain his ministry. But John's attitude was, "I can only do what I have been divinely authorized and empowered to do, so I must be content with that gift and calling."

Because of my background, I was always comparing myself with other people, frequently jealous of their possessions and abilities. I tried to keep up with everyone else. Often I felt pressured and frustrated, because I was operating outside my gifts and calling. When I finally realized that I could not do anything unless God had ordained and anointed it, I started relaxing and saying, "I am what I am. I can't be anything unless God helps me. I am just going to concentrate on being the best me I can be."

God doesn't want you to be like someone else; He wants you to be the best *you* can be.

———————

Lord, help me to find that place of being content with who I am and what I have. By Your grace I want to be the best me I can be. Amen.

More Than Conquerors

Yet amid all these things we are more than conquerors and gain a surpassing victory through Him Who loved us.

—ROMANS 8:37

We need to have a sense of triumph. Paul assures us that through Christ Jesus we are more than conquerors. We must believe that truth gives us the confidence that we already have the victory before we even face the challenges that come our way in life.

Sometimes our confidence is shaken when trials come, especially if they are lengthy. We should have so much confidence in God's love for us that no matter what comes against us, we know deep inside that we are more than conquerors. If we are truly confident, we have no need to fear trouble, challenges, or trying times, because we know they will pass.

Whenever a trial of any kind comes against you, always remember: This too shall pass! Be confident that during the trial you will learn something that will help you in the future.

Without confidence we are stifled at every turn. Satan drops a bomb, and our dreams are destroyed. Eventually we start over, but we never make much progress. We start and get defeated, start and get defeated, start and get defeated, over and over again. But those who are consistently confident, those who know they are more than conquerors through Jesus Christ, make rapid progress.

Lord, because You are in my life, I have confidence that I can triumph over trials. I choose to believe in Your love and the victory You won for me on the cross. Amen.

Your Potential

But Jesus looked at them and said, With men this is impossible, but all things are possible with God.   —MATTHEW 19:26

Insecurity, self-doubt, and fear can totally prevent us from ever reaching our full potential. But if our confidence is in Christ rather than in ourselves, we are free to develop our potential because we are free from the fear of failure.

As Christians, our number one job is the development of personal potential. Merriam-Webster's Collegiate Dictionary (11th edition) defines *potential* as "existing in possibility: capable of development into actuality." It defines *potentiality* as "ability to develop or come into existence." In other words, where there is potential, all the parts necessary for success are there, but they are not yet put into action. They still need something to propel them, something to empower and motivate them to be developed.

Potential cannot manifest without form. There must be something for it to be poured into, something that will cause it to take shape and become useful. For instance, when you are offered a promotion, you are being offered a form in which to pour your potential. You will never see it take shape unless you do something to exercise it. You have potential, but it needs to be developed.

What stands in the space between potential and manifestation? I believe it is three things: time, determination, and hard work!

———————

Lord, I know that You have placed great potential inside of me, and I ask Your help in reaching mine. All things are possible with You. Amen.

Develop Your Gift

For God's gifts and His call are irrevocable. [He never withdraws them when once they are given, and He does not change His mind about those to whom He gives His grace or to whom He sends His call.]   —ROMANS 11:29

If we don't develop our potential, it won't get developed, because no one else can do it for us. Find out what you want to do and begin to train yourself for it. If you know you can write great songs, develop your gift; arrange your life so you can write songs. If you know you can lead worship, then practice, learn music, sing with all your mind and heart, and believe. Begin leading worship, even if you start with only you and the cat or you and your children. If you know you have a talent for business, an ability to make money, then study, pray, go to school, and step out.

Whatever your gift and calling, entrust it to the Lord and be relentless in your pursuit of reaching your full potential. In some way we should improve ourselves every day. We should go forward, letting go of what lies behind, including past mistakes and past victories. Even hanging on to the glory of past victories can prevent us from being all God wants us to be in the future. Never be satisfied with being anything less than all you can be.

———————————

Lord, I recognize that I am responsible to develop and use the talents You have placed within me. Give me wisdom on the best way to go about it. Amen.

Through Disappointments

No temptation has overtaken you except such as is common to man;
but God is faithful, who will not allow you to be tempted beyond
what you are able, but with the temptation will also make the way
of escape, that you may be able to bear it.

—1 CORINTHIANS 10:13 NKJV

People will disappoint you. Life will disappoint you. Things will happen that you did not expect to happen, and you have to believe in the power of God and be able to say, "I can do whatever I need to do through Christ Who strengthens me." God will never allow more to come to us than we can bear, so it's foolish to say, "I can't stand this. I can't do this." We don't always understand why, but we know God has His reasons, and we can get through it.

Nobody can keep you unhappy if you don't want to be unhappy. Stop giving somebody else the responsibility for your joy. If you'll start to do what you can do and stop worrying about what you can't do, God can get involved and make some miraculous things happen in your life. I know that hurts are deep and painful, but we have to be very careful about just sitting in our boat and nursing our wounds for too long. There's a time to grieve, and there's a time you have to move on.

Lord, my joy is found in You, and I can't rely upon others or life to bring me happiness. Help me to live in the strength You give. Amen.

Free from Legalism

Look out for those dogs [Judaizers, legalists], look out for those mischief-makers, look out for those who mutilate the flesh. For we [Christians] are the true circumcision, who worship God in spirit and by the Spirit of God and exult and glory and pride ourselves in Jesus Christ, and put no confidence or dependence [on what we are] in the flesh and on outward privileges and physical advantages and external appearances.   —PHILIPPIANS 3:2–3

This passage destroys any reason to believe that our confidence can be in anything we can do or have done. It clearly tells us that our confidence cannot be "in the flesh," but instead must be "in Christ Jesus." It also warns us to beware of legalists.

It is freeing to finally see that our worth and value are not based on what we do, but on who we are in Christ. God has assigned value to us by allowing Jesus to die for us. By the very act of Christ's death on the cross, and the suffering He endured, God the Father is saying to each one of us, "You are very valuable to Me, and I will pay any price to redeem you and see that you have the good life I originally intended for you."

Once you and I have our "who" straightened out, then and only then can we begin to effectively pray about our "do."

Lord, I confess that my value is based upon what Jesus had done for me on the cross alone. Thank you for making me so valuable to you. Amen.

Off the Treadmill

But to him who does not work but believes on Him who justifies the ungodly, his faith is accounted for righteousness, just as David also describes the blessedness of the man to whom God imputes righteousness apart from works. —ROMANS 4:5–6 NKJV

If we spend years on the performance/acceptance treadmill, it is hard to get off it. It becomes a way of living. It affects our thoughts, perceptions, and decisions. We can become so addicted to feeling good about ourselves only when we perform well that we willingly endure a life of misery. It is a cycle of trying and failing, trying harder and failing again, feeling guilty and rejected, trying again and failing again, and on and on.

God does not want us on the performance/acceptance treadmill. He wants us to feel good about ourselves whether we perform perfectly or not. He doesn't want us to be filled with pride, but He certainly did not create us to reject ourselves. This is where a revelation concerning our "who" and our "do" is so valuable. We should be able to separate the two and take an honest look at both. If we perform poorly, we can be sorry and hope to do better the next time. We can try to improve our performance (our "do"), but our worth and value (our "who") cannot be determined by our performance.

Lord, thank You for providing me with a way off the treadmill of trying to gain Your acceptance. By faith through grace I stand in Your complete acceptance and righteousness. Amen.

Trust God's Grace

I do not set aside the grace of God; for if righteousness comes through the law, then Christ died in vain.

—GALATIANS 2:21 NKJV

I discovered years ago that every time I became frustrated it was because I was trying to do something myself, in my own strength, instead of putting my faith in God and receiving His grace (help). Receiving a revelation of God's grace was a major breakthrough for me. I was always "trying" to do something and leaving God out of the loop. I tried to change myself and my husband and children, tried to get healed, tried to prosper, tried to make my ministry grow, and tried to change every circumstance in my life that I did not like. I was frustrated because none of my trying was producing any good results.

God will not permit us to succeed without Him. If He did, we would take the credit that is due Him. If we could change people, we would be changing them to suit our purposes, which would steal their freedom to make their own choices. I finally learned to pray for what I thought needed to be changed and let God do it His way in His timing. When I began trusting His grace, I entered His rest. Grace is always flowing to us in every situation, but it must be received by faith.

Lord, give me the understanding of Your grace that frees me from doing things in my own strength. Help me to do my part and rest in the fact that You will do the rest. Amen.

First Steps

What time I am afraid, I will have confidence in and put my trust
and reliance in You. By [the help of] God I will praise His word;
on God I lean, rely, and confidently put my trust; I will not fear.
                                                        —PSALM 56:3–4

Life changed greatly for me when I finally understood that even if I am shaking as a result of fear, I am not behaving cowardly as long as I keep pressing forward to do whatever it is the fear is trying to get me not to do.

A woman attended one of my conferences and testified that it was the first time she had gone out of her home in thirty-five years. As a child, she was abused, and although she married and had children, she decided that life would be safer if she stayed inside where no one could hurt her. She managed different ways of getting the things she needed. Eventually, she started watching my daily television program and discovered that I had also been sexually abused by my father. She decided that if I could speak boldly in front of thousands of people, she could go out of her house. Her decision to come to my conference was the first step for her in confronting her fear. She did something afraid. She had to take one step before she could take two.

Take that first step; the next one will be easier.

Lord, if others can make it through their fears, I can as well. Show me the first steps I need to take that will lead to freedom. Amen.

God's Promise

No man shall be able to stand before you all the days of your life. As I was with Moses, so I will be with you; I will not fail you or forsake you. —JOSHUA 1:5

I often think of Joshua and how he must have felt when God told him that he was to take Moses' place and lead the Israelites into the Promised Land. Moses was an amazing leader. Who would want to try to fill his shoes?

God told Joshua that he would succeed, not because of anything he had in the natural, but because He was with him. Moses was successful only because God was with him. God told Joshua that the same thing would hold true for him if he believed. God kept encouraging Joshua to be strong and confident, to take courage and not be afraid. In other words, He kept telling him to believe!

God asks you and me to put our faith in Him and to believe that we can do whatever He asks us to do. He is mighty to uphold us and make us stand. He will support us and keep us from failing. His strength is readily available to us. We receive it through believing in it and the promise God has made to give it to us. The Lord will be strong in us—we will experience victory in our lives!

———————

Lord, I draw my confidence from Your promise to be with me. I am strong and will succeed because of Your presence. Amen.

From Strength to Strength

Blessed (happy, fortunate, to be envied) is the man whose strength is in You, in whose heart are the highways to Zion. Passing through the Valley of Weeping (Baca), they make it a place of springs; the early rain also fills [the pools] with blessings. They go from strength to strength [increasing in victorious power]; each of them appears before God in Zion. —PSALM 84:5–7

I have discovered that when I am unhappy, I am tempted to start blaming my unhappiness on some circumstance or person in my life who is not giving me what I feel I need. Satan wants us to think that nothing will ever change, that things will only get worse. He wants us to inventory every disappointing thing that has ever happened in our lives and think about how mistreated we have been. We can either be angry or we can look to God to meet our need.

We will absolutely never fulfill our destinies and succeed at being all God has planned for us if we don't think according to the Word of God. Even if I have negative circumstances, I can stay happy by having right thoughts toward them. That's why we need to constantly keep our minds and hearts focused on Him and not on our circumstances. When our strength is in God, even the difficult places in life can be turned into blessings.

Lord, I draw my strength from You today. Help me to keep my eyes on You and see the difficult places turned into pools of blessings. Amen.

Quiet Inner Confidence

*And the effect of righteousness will be peace [internal and external],
and the result of righteousness will be quietness and confident trust
forever.*   —ISAIAH 32:17

Through the years, many people tried to hold me back from God's call
on my life. There were those who did not understand what I was doing
and why I was doing it, so they judged me falsely. At times their criticism and judgment made me want to "sit down" and forget about my
vision from God.

But I had a big God standing up on the inside of me, and "sitting
down" was not an option to me. He caused me to stand up on the
inside and be determined to go forward no matter what others thought,
said, or did. It was not always easy, but I learned from my experience
that being frustrated and unfulfilled due to being out of the will of God
is more difficult than pressing through all the opposition.

Standing up on the inside does not mean being rebellious or having
an aggressive attitude toward those who don't understand us. It means
having a quiet inner confidence that takes us through to the finish line.
It is knowing inside that despite what is happening on the outside,
everything is going to be all right because God is on the scene, and
when He is present nothing is impossible.

Lord, Your presence in my life changes everything about me.
Help me to stand up alongside You for all that You want me to
do and say and be. Amen.

More Than Enough

*Now to Him Who, by (in consequence of) the [action of His] power
that is at work within us, is able to [carry out His purpose and] do
superabundantly, far over and above all that we [dare] ask or think
[infinitely beyond our highest prayers, desires, thoughts, hopes, or
dreams].*   —EPHESIANS 3:20

When the things we are facing in our lives loom so big in our eyes
that our mind goes "tilt," we need to think in the spirit. In the natural,
many things are impossible. But in the supernatural, spiritual realm,
with God nothing is impossible. God wants us to believe for great
things, make big plans, and expect Him to do things so great it leaves
us with our mouths hanging open in awe. James 4:2 tells us we have
not because we ask not! We can be bold in our asking.

Sometimes in my meetings people will approach the altar for prayer
and sheepishly ask if they can request *two* things. I tell them they can
ask God for all they want to, as long as they trust Him to do it His way,
in His timing.

When you pray, do it standing up on the inside. What I mean is, do
it respectfully, yet aggressively and boldly. Recall that God said He is
the Almighty God (Genesis 17:1); in other words, "more than enough."

**Lord, open my spiritual eyes to see what it means to pray to
the Almighty God who is "more than enough." I come humbly
and boldly with expectancy of great things. Amen.**

Pit to Palace

Then Pharaoh said to Joseph, "Inasmuch as God has shown you all this, there is no one as discerning and wise as you. You shall be over my house, and all my people shall be ruled according to your word; only in regard to the throne will I be greater than you."

—GENESIS 41:39–40 NKJV

Joseph was sold into slavery by his brothers who hated him. They actually threw him into a pit and intended to leave him there to die. A pit is a ditch, a trap, a snare. It refers to destruction. Satan always wants to bring us into the pit. They ended up selling him to slave traders, and he became the slave of a wealthy ruler in Egypt. Even though he was sold as a slave, he believed he could do great things. Everywhere Joseph went, God gave him favor. He even found favor in prison where he spent many years for an offense he did not commit. Ultimately, he ended up in the palace, second in command to Pharaoh, the ruler over all Egypt.

Joseph had a right attitude. Without a right attitude, a person can start in the palace and end up in the pit. Some, it seems, have great opportunities given to them, and they do nothing with their lives, while others who get a very bad start in life overcome all obstacles and succeed.

Wouldn't you rather start out in a pit and end up in a palace?

———————————

Lord, whatever obstacles stand in my way today, You are greater. Thank You for the favor You have given me to keep rising up and overcoming. Amen.

You Are Not Alone

And even he who is brave, whose heart is as the heart of a lion, will utterly melt.   —2 SAMUEL 17:10

We are all brave in some areas and fearful in others. The pendulum may swing one way or the other, but we all have some of both. For example, a woman we will call Theresa was timid and shy, and yet was very brave when it came to facing pain and tragedy. She had cancer at the age of thirty-two and endured surgery and painful radiation and chemotherapy treatments. Theresa also had three miscarriages before she finally gave birth to a healthy child. She bore these difficulties graciously, bravely, and with little complaint.

Janice, a friend of Theresa's, was bold and aggressive and appeared to be fearless until she suddenly lost her job of twenty years and her 401(k) retirement program to corporate fraud. She faced tragedy but did not handle it graciously. She displayed fear that amazed those who knew her.

It's important for us to realize that we are not alone in our battles with fear. The devil wants nothing better than to convince you that there is something really wrong with you and that other normal people don't have the same kinds of problems. Don't let him do it; all of us experience fear.

Lord, You know me inside and out. You see my strengths and weaknesses. I trust You to be working and equipping me to face the challenges of today and tomorrow. Help me to be brave, knowing that You are with me. Amen.

A Blameless Heart

*For the eyes of the Lord run to and fro throughout the whole earth
to show Himself strong in behalf of those whose hearts are blameless
toward Him.*   —2 CHRONICLES 16:9

God does not say He is looking for someone with a perfect performance, but rather someone with a perfect heart—a heart that desires to
please Him, a heart that is grieved over sin and evil, a heart that believes
in Him and His willingness and ability to forgive and restore. God
knows we cannot manifest perfection. It is acceptable to be needy!

God is a God of hearts. He sees and cares about our attitude of heart
even more than our performance. I have said many times that I believe
God would rather have a believer who has a good heart and a less than
perfect performance than one who has a perfect performance but an
impure heart. It is possible to be very religious and to keep all the rules
but to have a heart that is far from God.

For example, Jesus had much to say to the Pharisees of His day. They
had a polished performance, kept the laws, followed all the rules and
regulations, and were proud of it. They also had a judgmental attitude
toward others, did not walk in love, and showed no mercy. Jesus called
them whitewashed tombs full of dead men's bones (Matthew 23:27).

Walk in love; walk in mercy.

**Lord, my performance is far from perfect, but in my heart
I desire to please You in everything. Draw me close to Your
heart today that I may be like You. Amen.**

Do It Joyfully

But the fruit of the [Holy] Spirit [the work which His presence within accomplishes] is love, joy (gladness), peace, patience (an even temper, forbearance), kindness, goodness (benevolence), faithfulness, gentleness (meekness, humility), self-control (self-restraint, continence). Against such things there is no law [that can bring a charge].... If we live by the [Holy] Spirit, let us also walk by the Spirit.   —GALATIANS 5:22, 25

It has become a game with me to try to beat the joy-sucker of dread at his own game. I want to prove to the devil that I can enjoy everything I do and that his tactics to steal my joy just won't work anymore. Greater is He that is in me than he who is in the world (1 John 4:4). I believe it glorifies God when we refuse to live in fear, worry, dread, or any other relatives of theirs.

When I find myself in a situation I would rather not be in, whether it is waiting or doing an unpleasant task, I make a decision that I will do it joyfully and not dread it, and then I exercise self-control. I use those faith muscles that God has given to me as well as to every person on the planet. If we allow fear in our lives, it breeds more fear, but if we practice walking in faith, it becomes easier to do it again and again.

Lord, thank You for giving me everything I need to walk in faith and overcome what the enemy throws at me. I will live joyfully because You walk with me. Amen.

Real Freedom

And you will know the Truth, and the Truth will set you free.
—JOHN 8:32

There is only one thing that will set us free, and that is the truth. Yet that is the one thing we have a hard time dealing with.

It was difficult for me to face the fact that I was insecure, I didn't like myself, and I needed God's help and healing in my life. If I had refused to face the truth, I would still be in bondage. I would still be trying to please people, addicted to approval in order to keep a position that I probably would not even like. As it is, I am free. I know who I am in Christ apart from what I do. I want to please people, but I am not devastated if they are not pleased with me. As long as I know my heart is right, that is sufficient. If I am doing the best I can and people don't approve, what they think will have to be between them and God.

I want approval, but I am not addicted to it. I enjoy it, but if I have to live without it, I can. I went through the pain of facing truth and change, and it brought me freedom. The only way out of bondage is to go through what we need to go through as we move toward freedom.

Lord, help me to face the truth about my life that I might be set free from any bondages that hold me back. Help me to change what needs to go. Amen.

Hold the Line

Samuel said, What have you done? Saul said, Because I saw that the people were scattering from me, and that you did not come within the days appointed, and that the Philistines were assembled at Michmash, I thought, The Philistines will come down now upon me. . . . So I forced myself to offer a burnt offering.

—1 SAMUEL 13:11–12

Saul caved in to the stress that fear brought and lost his confidence in God. I believe we often get involved in things just because we are afraid of being left out. We are afraid we won't know what is going on or that someone else will gain control of a situation if we are not there to speak for ourselves. We want our children to be like all the other children, so we let them get involved in far too many things because we are afraid they will be rejected.

Because of the abuse in my home and all the secrets I had to keep, I always felt left out. I was afraid my children would go through the same pain I did, so anything they wanted to do, I thought we should find a way to do it. It's the kind of stress that some moms allow to push them to buy a $150 pair of tennis shoes for their child just because "everyone has them." If that describes you, it's time to say no.

Lord, it's so easy to cave in when stress pushes my buttons. Help me to remain confident in You and to be able to say no. Amen.

Develop Your Character

Withstand him; be firm in faith [against his onset—rooted, established, strong, immovable, and determined], knowing that the same (identical) sufferings are appointed to your brotherhood (the whole body of Christians) throughout the world.

—1 PETER 5:9

We may look at other people and think they never have to go through anything difficult, but we all go through different things. Some people have gone through devastating things that nobody knows anything about. Some people have learned the art of suffering silently. They know only God can help them, so they don't bother telling everyone they meet what they are going through.

It is not wrong to share our troubles with a friend or counselor, but the point is that we cannot assume others are not having challenges in life just because they don't look depressed or don't talk about their problems. We all get hurt at times, and we all have the same opportunity either to let it make us bitter or to let it make us better. How can injustices make us better? For one thing, they help us develop character. Doing what is right when we don't have feelings supporting us builds strong character in us. Intelligence and talents are God's gifts, but character is developed. We need to move beyond hurt and be willing to give ourselves away and lay down our lives for others (John 15:13).

———————

Lord, help me to get my eyes off of my troubles and to reach out and help those around me who are hurting. Give me discernment and compassion to truly make a difference. Amen.

Anger

*When angry, do not sin; do not ever let your wrath (your
exasperation, your fury or indignation) last until the sun goes down.
Leave no [such] room or foothold for the devil [give no opportunity
to him].* —EPHESIANS 4:26–27

We all get angry, but we must be careful to understand why we are
angry. Many people who become frequently angry have a root of insecurity in their lives that wipes out their confidence. Those who are easily offended and touchy are insecure. They must be treated well to feel
good about themselves. And if not, they get angry.

God never tells us not to feel anger, but He does give instructions
on how we process our anger. When we stay angry, we open a door for
the devil to work in our lives. Most of the ground gained by Satan in
the Christian's life is gained through bitterness, resentment, and unforgiveness. People who easily fly into a rage always make a bad landing.
When our emotions are out of control, so is our life. Anger makes our
mouth work faster than our mind. We end up saying and doing things
we are sorry for later.

Staying angry and harboring unkind feelings toward others is disobedience. We must realize sustained anger is sin. If we don't look at it
for what it is, we may be tempted to hang on to it.

What are you hanging on to today?

_____

**Lord, help me to understand my anger and to never let it be
sustained and destroy my confidence. May I be quick to forgive others and keep my life in control. Amen.**

Is It Mistreatment?

He who is slow to anger is better than the mighty, he who rules his [own] spirit than he who takes a city.   —PROVERBS 16:32

People who lack confidence often perceive they are being mistreated when in actuality that is not the case at all. I can remember feeling mistreated and angry when Dave did not agree with me about minor issues. His opinion, which he certainly was entitled to have, was merely different than mine, but I was so insecure I felt rejected. As they say, "I made mountains out of molehills." I would turn a minor incident into a tragedy because I was so touchy. When I did not get my way, I felt mistreated and became angry. When I was corrected in even a minor way, I responded with anger and felt I was being treated unfairly. The truth is I was very angry because I was very insecure.

My point is this: It is possible to believe you are being treated unfairly when that is not the case at all. The way I processed people's reactions to me was totally out of balance because of my past abuse. I could not correctly discern when I was genuinely being mistreated compared to when people were simply being honest with me about their own feelings.

—————————

Lord, I need to be discerning whenever I am processing people's reactions to me. Help me to be secure enough in Your love to receive truth from others who are being honest with me. Amen.

The Real Enemy

But if your enemy is hungry, feed him; if he is thirsty, give him drink; for by so doing you will heap burning coals upon his head. Do not let yourself be overcome by evil, but overcome (master) evil with good.   —ROMANS 12:20–21

Placing blame is a problem, but placing blame in the wrong place is even worse. The Bible says our warfare is with the devil, not with people (Ephesians 6:12). We desire revenge when people hurt us, but if the devil is really the one behind all of our pain, how can we get him back?

The Bible also states we overcome evil with good. Satan is evil, and the way to get back at him is to aggressively be good to everyone we meet, including our enemies. It is not natural to pray for one's enemies or to bless them. It is not the response the devil expects or hopes for. When we do become angry and bitter, we play right into his hands. We open a door for him to walk through and allow him to gain access to many areas of our lives through an unforgiving attitude. Our joy is adversely affected, as is our health, our peace, our prayer life, our sleep habits, our confidence, et cetera. Unity and agreement produce power, so it stands to reason that disagreement and disunity produce powerlessness.

Choose power today.

———————————

Lord, I need to see the real enemy who's behind the evil that comes my way. Help me to overcome it by doing good to others, even to those whom I perceive to be my enemies. Amen.

Live in Harmony

Fill up and complete my joy by living in harmony and being of the same mind and one in purpose, having the same love, being in full accord and of one harmonious mind and intention.

—PHILIPPIANS 2:2

Paul was aware of God's wonderful plan for His children. He wanted everyone to receive the best God had for them, and he knew that would be impossible if they did not live in harmony. We are repeatedly taught in Scripture to live in peace. In the Bible, Jesus Himself is called the "Prince of Peace" (Isaiah 9:6).

God has clearly instructed Dave and me that we must keep strife out of our lives and ministry if we want to be successful at what He has called us to do. In order to do so, we must be generous with forgiveness. We must refuse to let bitterness take root in our hearts (Hebrews 12:15). We cannot allow ourselves to be offended or remain angry. This means we cannot follow our feelings; we must press past feelings and do what God asks us to do.

Sometimes God asks us to let something go and not even mention it; at other times He requires us to confront and communicate openly about situations. Communication often clears up confusion and brings balance to situations that cause conflict. Lack of confrontation opens the door for greater misunderstanding and strife.

Ask God for the wisdom you need to know on when to confront and when to let go.

Lord, help me to be generous with forgiveness and keep strife out of my life. Show me when to be quiet and when to confront, and give me strength for both. Amen.

Boundaries

Do not be so deceived and misled! Evil companionships
(communion, associations) corrupt and deprave good manners and
morals and character.   —1 CORINTHIANS 15:33

Just as a person puts up a fence around his property to keep intruders out, so you must establish limits and margins—invisible lines you draw in your life to protect yourself from being used and abused. If you had a privacy fence around your yard, and on a sunny afternoon you looked out into your yard and saw your neighbors sunbathing while their children played without permission, what would you do? You would probably be very forceful in letting them know that your yard is off limits to them for such activities without your permission.

You need to be just as forceful in letting people know you expect them to respect the limits and margins you have erected around your personal life.

It is important to realize that God has given you authority first and foremost over your own life. If you don't accept and exercise that authority, you may spend your life blaming others for things you should be doing something about. You should make your own decisions according to what you believe God's will is for you. On Judgment Day, God will not ask anyone else to give an account of your life; He will ask only you!

———————

Lord, I recognize my responsibility to put boundaries around my life and not allow others to adversely affect me. Help me to be wise about the limits I place around my personal life. Amen.

Speak the Truth

Rather, let our lives lovingly express truth [in all things, speaking truly, dealing truly, living truly]. Enfolded in love, let us grow up in every way and in all things into Him Who is the Head, [even] Christ (the Messiah, the Anointed One).   —EPHESIANS 4:15

People-pleasing behavior often leads people to tell lies because they fear people won't accept the truth. They say yes with their mouth while their heart is screaming no. They may not want to do something, but they act as if they do for fear of displeasing someone. If they ever do say no, they usually make an excuse rather than tell the truth that they just don't want to do what they are being asked to do. They may not feel it is the right thing for them to do.

We don't want to be rude, but neither do we want to be liars. Most people pleasers are not honest about their desires, feelings, and thoughts. They tell people what they want to hear, not what they need to hear. A healthy relationship demands honesty. We should be able to say to people, "I don't have peace about making that commitment right now," and they should graciously receive that answer, but it rarely happens. Some people may not want to hear the truth, but that does not relieve us of the responsibility to speak the truth.

Speak the truth in love today.

———————

Lord, help me to speak and live the truth in all that I do. I don't want to be rude, but I refuse to be dishonest or to resort to half-truths to avoid the real truth. Amen.

Manifest His Glory

To them God willed to make known what are the riches of the glory
of this mystery among the Gentiles: which is Christ in you, the hope
of glory. —COLOSSIANS 1:27 NKJV

We can only realize and experience the glory of God in our lives because of Christ in us. He is our hope of seeing better things.

The glory of God is His manifested excellence. As the children of God, we have a blood-bought right to experience the best God has planned for us. Satan furiously fights the plan of God in each of our lives, and his primary weapon is deception. When we are deceived, we believe something that is not true. Even though it is not true, it seems true for us because that is what we believe.

When we look at ourselves and our own abilities, we feel defeated, but remembering that Christ is in us is our hope of realizing the glory. It keeps us encouraged enough to press on toward better things. We limit ourselves when we look to ourselves alone and fail to see Jesus. We can be excellent people with excellent attitudes, excellent thoughts, and excellent words. God's glory can be manifested in us and on us, but only as we believe it is possible. Start expecting more of His glory in your life. He is waiting to manifest His glory—to you and through you!

Lord, I ask You to shine Your glory through my life. You are my only hope of glory, and I live to manifest You to others in all I say and do. Amen.

Satisfaction

I have seen all the works that are done under the sun, and behold, all is vanity, a striving after the wind and a feeding on the wind.
—ECCLESIASTES 1:14

We all want to feel satisfied. We all want contentment. We all want to know we are loved and accepted for who we are. We may think acceptance and approval from people will make us feel complete. However, the Bible teaches us that when we trust in man to give us what only God can give, we live under a curse; but when we trust in the Lord, we are blessed (Jeremiah 17:5–8). The joy, peace, and fulfillment we seek come from being filled with God, and nothing else. They do not come from having a certain person in our lives, or from money, position, power, fame, accomplishments, or anything else.

If you don't believe me, try all the other things. You will ultimately come to the same conclusion that you are bankrupt as a person, that nothing you have tried has given you a sense of fullness and completeness. Read the book of Ecclesiastes, which was written by Solomon. He was a man who tried virtually everything to find this kind of deep inner completeness and satisfaction. Nothing he tried worked until he came full circle and realized that what he truly wanted had been available all the time. He wanted God (Ecclesiastes 12:13)!

Lord, show me the subtle and not so subtle ways that I look for satisfaction in something other than in You. What I really want is You. Amen.

Exercising Authority

For it is disgraceful for a woman to talk in church [for her to usurp and exercise authority over men in the church].

—1 CORINTHIANS 14:35

Part of the problem in Corinth was that women may have been usurping authority over men, which is a wrong attitude that some women who teach or preach can develop. They may think their position allows them to exercise authority over people. I cannot be responsible for what other women do, but as for me, I can honestly say that when I teach God's Word, I don't see myself exercising authority over men or women. I use the gift of communication that God has given me to fulfill the call on my life to teach. I want to help people understand God's Word so they can easily apply it to their daily lives. When I hold a public meeting, I believe I have authority over that meeting and that I am responsible to keep order, but I have never felt that I was taking authority over people. It is difficult to know exactly what was going on when Paul wrote this letter, but we cannot take this verse to mean that women were forever forbidden to speak in church. We must look at all of the other Scriptures that clearly indicate that God regularly used women.

Lord, I am not interested in having authority over any other person, but I do want the confidence that comes from having the authority of Your Word working in and through my life. Amen.

Give Thanks

We should not tempt the Lord [try His patience, become a trial
to Him, critically appraise Him, and exploit His goodness] as
some of them did—and were killed by poisonous serpents; nor
discontentedly complain as some of them did—and were put out
of the way entirely by the destroyer (death).

—1 CORINTHIANS 10:9–10

Every time something didn't go right for the Israelites in the wilderness, they complained, criticized, tried God's patience, and exploited His goodness. When we don't open our mouths and give thanks, but instead complain and murmur, we are exploiting the goodness of God, because no matter what is going on in our lives, God is still good.

I am not trying to say that if we complain about something, God is going to cause us to perish. But how many doors do we open for the devil in our lives through murmuring? How many times do we ask God to give us something, and after He gives it to us, we start complaining because we have to take care of it? This kind of wilderness mentality keeps us living in the wilderness when we could be living in the Promised Land. In Philippians 2:14, we are told to do "all things" without complaining—that means everything. We can accomplish anything and always be a winner as long as we have a godly attitude and exercise control over our mouth daily.

Lord, I say with all my heart that You are good and Your mercies are new every morning. Keep me from a wilderness mentality and complaining about what is going on in my life. Amen.

No Immunity

Then Jezebel sent a messenger to Elijah, saying, So let the gods do to me, and more also, if I make not your life as the life of one of them by this time tomorrow. Then he was afraid and arose and went for his life.   —1 KINGS 19:2–3

Are some people cursed to be afraid while others are blessed with being brave? We recognize that we are born with different temperaments. We don't choose them; God chooses them to help us fulfill our purpose in life. Some people are just naturally more aggressive, brave, and daring than others. But I personally don't believe anyone is totally immune from fear. Even Elijah, who appeared to be the bravest of all, was afraid of Jezebel.

Some people do a better job than others of hiding their fears. They may not even admit to themselves that they have fears, but the reality is that Satan attacks everyone with fear. We can overcome it! If it weren't possible to overcome fear, God would not have instructed us in His Word to "fear not!"

The way to develop confidence is to do the thing you fear and get a record of successful experiences behind you. Henry Ford said, "One of the greatest discoveries a man makes, one of his great surprises, is to find he can do what he was afraid he couldn't do."

———————————

Lord, thank You for the victories You've given me already. I look to You to keep moving me forward to overcome what I've not believed I could do. Amen.

Radical Blessings

If you will listen diligently to the voice of the Lord your God, being watchful to do all His commandments which I command you this day, the Lord your God will set you high above all the nations of the earth. And all these blessings shall come upon you and overtake you if you heed the voice of the Lord your God.

—DEUTERONOMY 28:1–2

Anyone who wants to live in the radical, outrageous, chase-you-down-the-street-and-overtake-you blessings of God has to do something to receive them. We must realize that the blessing package described in Deuteronomy 28:1–14 is conditional. They come from a willingness to obey God whether He tells us to do something in our heart or in His Word.

If we struggle with why God isn't blessing us, it may be because God has already told us the things we need to do to get our life in order and to receive the radical blessings. We really don't need to whine and complain about doing what God tells us to do because anything that He tells us to do, He gives us the ability to do. The problem may be that we just haven't done what He has told us to do. Perhaps more than ever we need to get up and get going. Sometimes we have to go through in obedience and just keep moving forward.

Lord, search my heart and show me any area where I am not doing what You have shown me. Make it clear in my heart, and I will be quick to obey. Amen.

Practice the Truth

I assure you, most solemnly I tell you, A servant is not greater than his master, and no one who is sent is superior to the one who sent him. If you know these things, blessed and happy and to be envied are you if you practice them [if you act accordingly and really do them]. —JOHN 13:16–17

I remember a woman who attended one of my conferences. It was a banquet, and the people who attended were sitting at tables together having a meal. This woman was sitting with a group of ladies. At the end of the conference, she came to me and said, "As I listened to all those ladies talk about their problems and their breakthroughs, about what God had done for them, where they came from and where they are now, I realized that many of them have gone through the same thing I went through, which was abuse in childhood. Every single thing that God has spoken to those ladies, He has spoken to me over the years. Everything that He has told them to do, He has also told me to do. The only difference is, they did it, and I didn't."

The woman received a great revelation that day. Her problems were no worse than many other people. What she needed to do was begin doing what God told her to do.

———

Lord, remind me of the truths You've shown me that I've failed to put into practice. Forgive me for the times I haven't responded to the light You've given me. Amen.

Watch Your Step

And having shod your feet in preparation [to face the enemy with the firm-footed stability, the promptness, and the readiness produced by the good news] of the Gospel of peace.   —EPHESIANS 6:15

In warfare, soldiers protect their feet so they can stand and fight the enemy. Paul tells us that we must walk in peace in order to defeat Satan's attacks. To have peace in your life, you have to be a peacemaker and a peace maintainer. You can't just wait for peace to fall upon you. The psalmist instructs us to pursue, inquire for, crave, and go after peace (Psalm 34:14). If you want peace badly enough, you will make whatever changes you need to make to see that you get it. For instance, if you're stressed out all the time and exceeding your limits, you need to cut a few things out of your life and restore your peace.

Satan is an expert at stealing our joy and getting us upset so we lose our peace and he can overpower us. When we are being aggravated by the devil, we are to remain constant and fearless (Philippians 1:28). Keep your eyes on God and trust in Him, and He will take care of the situation. When the enemy is coming against us, the most powerful thing we can do is refuse to let it upset us and instead walk in peace.

———————————

Lord, thank You for the peace You've given me through the good news of the Gospel. Help me to walk in peace and joy, constant and fearless. Amen.

The Confident Woman Devotional

Let God Be God

*Why, when I came, was there no man? When I called, why was
there no one to answer? Is My hand shortened at all, that it cannot
redeem? Or have I no power to deliver? Behold, at My rebuke I dry
up the sea, I make the rivers a desert.* —ISAIAH 50:2

We can worry about hundreds of different things—from what people
think of us to what will happen to us as we age. How long will we be
able to work? Who will take care of us when we get old if we are not
able to care for ourselves? What happens if the stock market crashes?
What if gas prices go up? What if I lose my job? Quite often, worry
does not even have a basis or a nugget of truth to it. There is no known
reason to even think about the things that worry and then frighten us.
Worry can even become a bad habit. It is just what we do! Some people
fret over something all the time. If they don't have problems of their
own, they worry about other people and their problems.

The only answer is to "stop worrying and place your trust in God."
He has the future all planned, and He knows the answer to everything.
His Word promises us that He will take care of us if we trust in Him.

**Lord, my future is in Your hands. In reality, I can't truly con-
trol anything. I humble myself before You and cast my cares
into Your hands. Thank You for Your care. Amen.**

Pray about Everything

So do not worry or be anxious about tomorrow, for tomorrow will have worries and anxieties of its own. Sufficient for each day is its own trouble.   —MATTHEW 6:34

Someone once said that "Worry is interest paid on trouble before it falls due." Trying to solve tomorrow's problems today only steals the energy God has prearranged for you to enjoy today. Don't waste your time worrying! It is vain and useless. Don't be like the bassoon player who went up to his conductor and nervously said that he could not reach the high E-flat. His conductor just smiled and replied, "Don't worry. There is no E-flat in your music tonight." Many of our worries are like that—unfounded and unnecessary.

Worry is the end of faith, and faith is the end of worry. You can only be a confident woman once you remove fear and worry from your life, and it starts with prayer. Prayer opens the door for God to get involved and meet our needs. The apostle Paul said we are to be anxious for nothing, but in all things, by praying, we will experience the peace of God (Philippians 4:6–7). He didn't say in "some" things; he didn't say in "one" thing, but he said in "everything." Prayer must replace our worry.

Lord, I open the door and invite You into all the affairs of my life. I have needs that only You can meet, and I know it's useless to worry about them. Today I commit my needs to You and will rest my faith in You. Amen.

Power for Living

So be subject to God. Resist the devil [stand firm against him], and he will flee from you. —JAMES 4:7

It is not going to do us one bit of good to try to resist the devil if we are not going to submit to God, because the power to resist the devil is found in submitting to God. If you want to keep Satan under your feet, you have to walk in obedience. Don't have any known disobedience, any purposeful disobedience in your life.

Do I ever disobey God? Yes, but I don't do it on purpose. I might lose my temper and say something that I shouldn't. But as soon as God starts dealing with me about it, I do what He says. I have a reverential fear of God in my life, and I think we need a lot more of that. I believe that God is God, and I believe He means business. If He tells me to do something, He means it, and when He tells me not to do something, He means it. Yes, we live under grace, but grace is not an excuse to sin; grace is the power to live a holy life. Disobedience is one of Satan's favorite entrances by which to gradually draw us into a web of sin that is devastating for us in the end.

Lord, I know that there is power for living today as I submit my life to You. Thank You for the grace that empowers me to walk in obedience. Amen.

Love One Another

I give you a new commandment: that you should love one another.
Just as I have loved you, so you too should love one another. By
this shall all [men] know that you are My disciples, if you love one
another [if you keep on showing love among yourselves].

—JOHN 13:34–35

You can defeat Satan with a good, strong, healthy love walk. Not enough Christians concentrate on walking in love. We concentrate on prosperity, healing, success, our breakthrough, how to change our family, how to get a loved one saved. But Jesus said we need to concentrate on walking in love.

I am talking about treating people with excellence. I am talking about meeting needs. I am talking about how we talk *about* one another and how we talk *to* one another. I am talking about not being rude. Walking in love means being a blessing to somebody else.

It is impossible to keep Satan under our feet while leading a selfish lifestyle that always reverts back to "What about me—me, me, me, me?" One of the first things the Bible says about love is that it is not selfish or self-seeking. Love does not do the right thing to get something; love simply does the right thing because it is the right thing to do. It not only blesses others; it blesses the one doing the loving.

Lord, I pray that Your love would be so concentrated in my heart that I might love others as You love me. Make me a source of blessing to others and a victor over the enemy. Amen.

Free from Entanglements

Take [with me] your share of the hardships and suffering [which you are called to endure] as a good (first-class) soldier of Christ Jesus. No soldier when in service gets entangled in the enterprises of [civilian] life; his aim is to satisfy and please the one who enlisted him.   —2 TIMOTHY 2:3–4

When God gives us something to do, He places a call on our lives. One of the things that we must not do is get so caught up in our own needs that we stop doing what God has given us to do. We have a tendency to get entangled in things that we must avoid. We are in the world but must resist becoming worldly or loving the world and the things in it in an excessive manner.

Entanglements will get us off course and prevent us from completing the call of God on our lives. Sometimes we even get entangled in other people's problems. Although we certainly want to get involved and help people, we must not get out of balance. There is a difference between godly involvement and entanglements. We can even get entangled in our own needs. We can stay so busy trying to provide for ourselves that we miss God's will. We should all occasionally take an inventory of our activities and make sure we are giving ourselves to God's priorities.

———————————

Lord, there is no end to the distractions and entanglements that come my way every day. Help me to stay focused on Your will and priorities. Amen.

The Power of Knowledge

[And I pray] that the participation in and sharing of your faith may produce and promote full recognition and appreciation and understanding and precise knowledge of every good [thing] that is ours in [our identification with] Christ Jesus [and unto His glory].
—PHILEMON 1:6

The renewing of the mind is the most important thing a person needs to do after receiving Jesus Christ as their Savior. Jesus died for our sins, and He wants us to enjoy the life He has provided. God's Word teaches us that He has provided a good plan for each person, yet they will never experience it unless they know about it and also know how to access it (Romans 12:2). People perish and their lives are destroyed for a lack of knowledge (Hosea 4:6). Knowledge and understanding are power when applied properly.

Many fears are the result of something that happened in the past and that we fear will happen again. If a person's mother died of cancer, she might fall prey to a fear that she will die the same way. She could become paranoid and fear that every little ache, pain, or strange feeling in her body is cancer. Fear that you will suffer causes suffering already while you are in fear. Don't be afraid that your life will end; instead, believe that it's just beginning.

———————

Lord, I believe that You have a good plan for my life and that I can access it every day. I look to You regarding every aspect of my life and ask You to be Lord and King. Amen.

Godly Character

And not only that, but we also glory in tribulations, knowing that tribulation produces perseverance; and perseverance, character; and character, hope. Now hope does not disappoint, because the love of God has been poured out in our hearts by the Holy Spirit who was given to us. —ROMANS 5:3–5 NKJV

God wants to restore all of our character to godliness. Habit is actually character. Habits are formed by discipline or the lack of discipline. Our character is basically what we do over and over. It is what other people have come to expect of us, such as being on time or how we respond in a certain circumstance. Over time, habits become part of our character.

We should not get legalistic about our character issues, but we do need to make an effort to develop character in those areas where we know we have problems. Changes in character come about by developing new habits. We need to commit ourselves to changing these faulty habits every time we confront them.

Godly character has much to do with discipline and the habits we form. Just as you can develop the habit of being on time, you can develop the habit of listening or giving to other people. You can choose to be kind and gentle, to watch your words, to pray and give thanks. It's about all of your life being shaped into the image of Christ.

Lord, You see my character flaws and weaknesses, and yet You still love me. Help me to discipline myself in those areas that still need changing. Amen.

Leave a Mark

Then [Joseph] *dreamed still another dream and told it to his brothers, and said, "Look, I have dreamed another dream. And this time, the sun, the moon, and the eleven stars bowed down to me." So he told it to his father and his brothers; and his father rebuked him and said to him, "What is this dream that you have dreamed? Shall your mother and I and your brothers indeed come to bow down to the earth before you?"*   —GENESIS 37:9–10 NKJV

Joseph was a dreamer; he made big plans. The devil does not want us to have dreams and visions of better things. He wants us to sit around and be "do-nothings."

I challenge you to make up your mind right now to do something great for God. No matter where you started, you can have a great finish. If people have mistreated and abused you, don't waste your time trying to get revenge—leave them in God's hands and trust Him to bring justice in your life.

Know what you want out of life, what you want to do. Don't be vague! To be confident means to be bold, open, plain, and straight-forward—that does not sound like a vague, sheepish, fearful individual who is uncertain about everything. Decide to leave your mark in this world. When you depart from this earth, people should know that you have been here.

———————

Lord, I desire to live in such a way that Your name is lifted up through my life. Bless others through me and may they see You through my witness. Amen.

The Test of Character

He was guilty of no sin, neither was deceit (guile) ever found on His lips. When He was reviled and insulted, He did not revile or offer insult in return; [when] He was abused and suffered, He made no threats [of vengeance]; but He trusted [Himself and everything] to Him Who judges fairly. —1 PETER 2:22–23

One definition of *charisma* is "great personal magnetism; charm," but *character* is "moral or ethical strength, integrity." There are a lot of people who have charisma, but no character. We see this all the time in life.

Our character is revealed by what we do when nobody is watching. This is a key to walking in confidence with God. Many people will do the right thing when somebody is watching them, but they won't do the right thing when nobody sees but God. As Christians, our commitment should be, "I am going to do the right thing simply because it is right."

Character is also seen when we do the right thing to others even though the right thing is not yet happening to us. As demonstrated by Jesus, one test of our character is, will we treat somebody right who is not treating us right? Will we bless someone who is not blessing us? It all comes down to what's in our heart, whether we trust Him Who judges fairly.

———————————————

Lord, how You responded to those who reviled and mistreated You was amazing . . . and humbling. May Your Spirit keep reshaping my spirit and character that I might reflect the same. Amen.

Cooperation Required

For I know the thoughts and plans that I have for you, says the Lord,
thoughts and plans for welfare and peace and not for evil, to give you
hope in your final outcome.   —JEREMIAH 29:11

The most important thing is not how we start but how we finish. Some people get started with a bang, but they never finish. Others are slow starters, but they finish strong.

God has a plan for each of us. It is our destiny. But it is a possibility, not a "positively." Even if someone prophesies over us wonderful things in the name of the Lord, what is being prophesied is the heart, the will, and the desire of God for us. It doesn't mean it is positively going to happen, because if we don't cooperate with God, it is not going to come to pass. We have a part to play in seeing that plan come true.

I challenge you to cooperate with God every single day of your life to develop your potential. Every day you should learn something new. Every day you should grow. Every day you should be a bit further along than you were the day before. We must each discover our God-given gifts and talents, what we are truly capable of, and then put ourselves to the task of developing those gifts, talents, and capabilities to their fullest extent.

Lord, I am thrilled that You have a plan for my life. That I have a destiny is amazing. I want to cooperate with You today and make that a reality. Amen.

Be Still

Let be and be still, and know (recognize and understand) that I am
God. I will be exalted among the nations! I will be exalted in the
earth! The Lord of hosts is with us; the God of Jacob is our Refuge
(our High Tower and Stronghold). Selah [pause, and calmly think of
that]!   —PSALM 46:10–11

One of the reasons so many of us are burned-out and stressed-out
is that we don't know how to be still—to "know" God and "acknowledge" Him. When we spend time with Him, we learn to hear His voice.
When we acknowledge Him, He directs our paths. If we don't spend
time being still, getting to know Him, and hearing His voice, we will
operate from our own strength in the flesh.

We need to learn to be quiet inside and stay in that peaceful state so
that we are always ready to hear the Lord's voice. Many people run from
one thing to the next. Because their minds don't know how to be still,
they don't know how to be still. At one time, I felt I had to find something to do every evening. I had to be involved and on the go, being a
part of whatever was going on. I didn't want anything to go on that I
didn't know about. I was not a human being; I was a human doing.

Which are you?

———————————

Lord, teach me how to be still before You and actually "know"
that You are God. Help me to be quiet inside and hear Your
voice. Amen.

Hand to the Plow

Jesus said to him, No one who puts his hand to the plow and looks back [to the things behind] is fit for the kingdom of God.

—LUKE 9:62

God does not want us living in the past. He knows that even if we could go back and re-create everything just as it was in days gone by, it would still not be the same. Do you know why? Because that was then, and this is now. Yesterday is gone; it is lost in the recesses of time. This is now. We have a now God. We are a now people, and we must live a now life—one day at a time.

So often people lose their joy because they had something in the past that made them joyful that is now gone. Many are pining away for the move of God that was, or a relationship that was but is not anymore. It is too bad it no longer exists, but it doesn't, and there is nothing you or I can do about it. Instead, we must learn to live in the present. God is moving now—let's enjoy now! Thank God we can press on to what He has in store for us, but in the meantime we need to keep our hand to the plow and quit looking back to what once was and will never be again.

Lord, it's so easy to stay stuck in the past and what was. I put my hand to the plow today and look ahead to what You're doing now. Amen.

In His Time

You yourselves are my witnesses [you personally bear me out] that
I stated, I am not the Christ (the Anointed One, the Messiah), but
I have [only] been sent before Him [in advance of Him, to be His
appointed forerunner, His messenger, His announcer]. He must
increase, but I must decrease.... [He must grow more prominent;
I must grow less so.   —JOHN 3:28, 30

John the Baptist had a clear understanding of his calling, and he was content to fulfill it, even when it meant the diminishing of his role. As Christians we must be *content*. If I can never preach as well as some other preacher, I have to be content to preach the best I can. You and I cannot go beyond the grace of God in our lives. We cannot receive a gift from God just because we want one. The Holy Spirit gives us gifts according to His will for us, and we must be satisfied with what He gives.

Sometimes even though God wants to confer a gift upon us, it is not yet time for it to be bestowed. Until God says, "Now!" we can struggle and fuss and complain and quarrel, but we will still not get it. We won't get it until He gives it, so we may as well learn to be content with such things as we have.

———————————

Lord, give me a clear sense of my calling so I can be the best I can be and yet not be fussing over what I am not. I simply want to serve You. Amen.

Be a Fighter

Fight the good fight of the faith; lay hold of the eternal life to which you were summoned and [for which] you confessed the good confession [of faith] before many witnesses.

—1 TIMOTHY 6:12

You and I are to fight the good fight of faith in our daily lives as we struggle against spiritual enemies in high places and in our own mind and heart. One part of fighting is being able to recognize the enemy, knowing when things are wrong. As long as we are passive, Satan will torment us. Nothing is going to change about our situation if all we do is sit and wish things were different. We have to take action. Too often we don't move against the enemy when he comes against us with discouragement or fear or doubt or guilt. We just draw back into a corner somewhere and let him beat us up.

You and I are not supposed to be punching bags for the devil; instead, we are supposed to be fighters. Now, the devil wants us to fight in the natural with everybody around us. But God wants us to forget all the junk that Satan stirs up within us to get us riled up against other people. Instead, He wants us to fight against the spiritual enemies who try to war over our lives and steal our peace and joy.

———————

Lord, give me discernment to never get distracted by my frustrations with people and lose sight of the spiritual battle I am in. I confess Jesus as my Lord and Victor today. Amen.

Victory over Frustrations

Catch us the foxes, the little foxes that spoil the vines, for our vines have tender grapes. —SONG OF SOLOMON 2:15 NKJV

Besides the huge disappointments that occur when we fail to get the job or promotion or house we wanted, little disappointments can create frustration, which in turn may lead to bigger problems that can produce a great deal of damage. For example, suppose someone is supposed to meet you for lunch and fails to show up, and then you make a special trip downtown to buy a discounted item only to find it is sold out. These minor frustrations can add up to cause a lot of grief. That's why we have to know how to handle them and keep them in perspective. Otherwise, they can get out of hand and be blown up all out of proportion.

We have to be on our guard against the little foxes that destroy the vineyards, because all together they can do just as much damage as the serious disappointments that often accompany or follow them. We must learn to do as Paul did in the book of Acts 28 when the serpent attached itself to his hand—he simply shook it off! Practice dealing quickly with disappointments as they come, and they will not pile up into a mountain. Victory is not the absence of problems; it is the presence of God's power.

Lord, help me to deal quickly with the frustrations and disappointments I face. You are greater than anything life can throw at me today. Amen.

Covenant Rights

And [the cripple] bowed himself and said, What is your servant, that you should look upon such a dead dog as I am?

—2 SAMUEL 9:8

Mephibosheth was the grandson of King Saul and the son of Jonathan, who had been a covenant friend to David. Crippled as a youth, Mephibosheth had a poor self-image, a dead-dog image. Instead of seeing himself as the rightful heir to his father's and grandfather's legacy, he saw himself as someone who would be rejected.

When David sent for Mephibosheth, he fell down before the king and displayed fear. Mephibosheth's response is an important example of the kind of poor self-image that causes us to operate in fear instead of faith. We look at what is wrong with us instead of what is right with Jesus. He has taken our wrongness and given us His righteousness (2 Corinthians 5:21). We have a covenant with God, sealed and ratified in the blood of Jesus Christ. We need to walk in the reality of that truth.

David told Mephibosheth not to fear, that he intended to show him kindness. David blessed him for Jonathan's sake. He gave him servants and land and provided for all of his needs (2 Samuel 9:13).

I relate Mephibosheth's lameness to our own weaknesses. We may also fellowship and eat with our King Jesus—even though we have faults and weaknesses. What a gift!

———————————

Lord, thank You for bringing me into a covenant relationship through the blood of Jesus. I praise You for bringing me to Your table where I can fellowship with You. Amen.

Run to Him

For by the death He died, He died to sin [ending His relation to it] once for all; and the life that He lives, He is living to God [in unbroken fellowship with Him]. Even so consider yourselves also dead to sin and your relation to it broken, but alive to God [living in unbroken fellowship with Him] in Christ Jesus.

—ROMANS 6:10–11

The devil delights in reminding us daily of all our mistakes from the past. One morning I was spending my time with the Lord, thinking about all the areas in which I had failed, when the Lord spoke to my heart: "Joyce, are you going to fellowship with Me or with your problems?" It is our fellowship with God that helps and strengthens us to overcome our problems. Our relationship and fellowship is to be with God, not with our sins.

How much do you fellowship with your sins, failures, and weaknesses? Whatever time it is, it is wasted. When you sin, admit it, ask for forgiveness, and then continue your fellowship with God. We are alive to God, living in unbroken fellowship with Him. Don't let your sins come between you and the Lord. Even when you sin, God still wants to spend time with you, hear and answer your prayers, and help you with all of your needs. He wants you to run to Him, not away from Him!

Lord, I want to live in unbroken fellowship with You. I consider my relationship with sin to have been broken at the cross and behind me. Amen.

Be Courageous

Then came the daughters of Zelophehad . . . before Moses, Eleazar
the priest, and the leaders, . . . saying, Our father died in the
wilderness . . . and he had no sons. Why should the name of our
father be removed from his family because he had no son? Give to
us a possession among our father's brethren.

—NUMBERS 27:1–4

Rosa Parks (1913–2005) was the unknown seamstress who started
the modern American Civil Rights Movement. On December 1, 1955,
in the city of Montgomery, Alabama, she refused to move to the back of
the bus after a white man got on board and wanted to sit in a front seat.
Rosa's mother believed "you should take advantage of the opportunities, no matter how few they were." Rosa said that her lifelong acquain-
tance with fear made her determined and gave her courage to appeal
her conviction during the bus boycott that followed her arrest and
conviction. The U.S. Supreme Court ruled that segregation on buses
was unconstitutional. Parks was the first woman to receive the Martin
Luther King Jr. Nonviolent Peace Prize.

Rosa refused to live in fear; she was determined to have what was
rightfully hers, and her determination sparked government reform
for all.

From Rosa's life, we see that if one person is courageous enough to
step out and attempt to do something about a problem, other people
with the same desire will also come forward.

———————

Lord, help me to always have the courage to not allow others
to take what is rightfully mine. Help me to confront what is
wrong with the truth of Your Word. Amen.

From the Inside Out

They tie up heavy loads, hard to bear, and place them on men's shoulders, but they themselves will not lift a finger to help bear them. —MATTHEW 23:4

You and I pressure ourselves and other people when we have unrealistic expectations. We often expect more out of people than they are able to give us. Continued pressure on people we are in relationship with will ultimately cause the collapse of that relationship. God does not want us or others to live under this kind of pressure.

I remember the years I furiously tried to change my husband, Dave, and each of our children in different ways. Those were frustrating years, because no matter what I tried, it didn't work! We cannot change people by pressuring them or by nagging them. Only prayer and God's love will work.

As humans, all of us require space, or freedom, to be who we are. We want to be accepted and loved as we are. We don't want people giving us the message, even subtly, that we must change in order to be "in." I am not saying that we must accept sin and wrong behavior in other people and merely put up with it. I am saying that *the way to change is prayer, not pressure!* For change to be lasting, it must come from the inside out. Only God can cause that type of heart change.

––––––––––––

Lord, I have tried to change loved ones, and it's always failed. Show me how to pray for them and to release them into Your hands. Amen.

Be a Servant

For you, brethren, were [indeed] called to freedom; only [do not let your] freedom be an incentive to your flesh and an opportunity or excuse [for selfishness], but through love you should serve one another. —GALATIANS 5:13

Jesus said, in essence, "If you love Me, you will obey Me" (see John 14:21). To say "I love Jesus" and walk in disobedience is deception. Words are wonderful, but a full love walk must be much more than words. Jesus also instructed us that if we are not feeding the hungry, giving water to the thirsty, clothing the naked, caring for the sick, and visiting those in prison, we are not doing anything for Him (Matthew 25:34–45).

I definitely love my husband, but the fulfillment of love must find some service to flow through. How can I say I love my husband if I never want to do anything for him? It is very easy to slide into an "everybody wait on me" attitude, but I am determined to swim upstream, against the pull of my flesh, and to be a servant and a blessing everywhere I go. Serving others sets them free to love. It disarms even the most hateful individual. The whole purpose in being a servant is to show others the love of God that He has shown us so that they too can share in it—and then pass it on.

Lord, Your call is clear that through love I am to serve the people who surround me. Help me to share Your love and be a blessing today. Amen.

Glorious Freedom

So if the Son liberates you [makes you free men], then you are really and unquestionably free.   —JOHN 8:36

Some people say children are gullible, meaning they believe anything, no matter how ridiculous it sounds. But children are not gullible; they are trusting. It is children's nature to trust unless they have experienced something that teaches them otherwise. And another thing we all know about children is that they can enjoy just about anything, even turning work into games.

Our heavenly Father wants us to know that we are His precious little ones and to put our complete faith in Him to care for us. He wants us to take His hand and lean on Him, continually asking for His help. Everything that God calls us to do, He must help us do. He is ready, waiting, and more than willing. But we must come humbly as little children—sincere, unpretentious, honest, open—knowing that without Him, we can do nothing.

As God's children we were never intended to live in bondage of any kind. We should be experiencing glorious freedom and liberty—freedom to enjoy all that God has given us in Christ. He has given us life, and our goal should be to enjoy it. Seek to become and remain childlike with all the simplicity of a child. It will enhance the quality of your life in a most amazing way.

———————

Lord, I come to You as Your child and ask You to set me free from any sin or bondage. Take my hand and lead the way. Amen.

Celebrate Life

The thief comes only in order to steal and kill and destroy. I came that they may have and enjoy life, and have it in abundance (to the full, till it overflows).   —JOHN 10:10

It is possible to live our lives blandly going through the motions of working, accomplishing, doing, but to never truly enjoy life. This is true of unbelievers as well as believers who have not learned to enjoy the life God has given them. Jesus gave us life so we can derive pleasure from being alive, not just so we can go through the motions until He comes back for us or takes us home.

We need to learn how to celebrate in God's joy, to live life "to the full." Enjoying life is a decision that is not based on enjoyable circumstances. It is an attitude of the heart, a decision to enjoy everything because everything—even little, seemingly insignificant things—has a part in God's overall "big picture."

Doubt and unbelief are thieves of joy, but simple childlike believing releases the joy that is resident in our spirit because the Holy Spirit lives there. As we believe that it is God's will for us to experience continual joy, we will discover a power that lifts us above our life circumstances. We will be free to leave our problems in God's hands while we enjoy His blessings.

Lord, I don't want to miss out on the fullness of joy that You have for me today. Help me to live life to the full and leave my problems in Your care. Amen.

Celebrate the Positive

For we all often stumble and fall and offend in many things. And if anyone does not offend in speech [never says the wrong things], he is a fully developed character and a perfect man, able to control his whole body and to curb his entire nature.   —JAMES 3:2

Our thoughts and words about ourselves are tremendously important. In order to overcome the negative thinking and speaking that have been such a natural part of our lifestyle for so long, we must make a conscious effort to *meditate on and speak positive things about ourselves.* We need to get our mouth in line with what the Word of God says about us. Positive confession of the Word of God should be an ingrained habit of every believer. If you have not yet begun to develop this important habit, start today. Begin thinking and saying good things about yourself: "I am the righteousness of God in Jesus Christ. I prosper in everything I lay my hand to. I have gifts and talents, and God is using me. I operate in the fruit of the Spirit. I walk in love. Joy flows through me."

We can appropriate the blessings of God in our lives if we will continually and purposefully speak about ourselves what the Word of God says about us. We will receive positive results.

———————

Lord, I will make the positive confession of Your Word an ingrained habit of my life. Help me to get my mouth in line with the truth of what You have done for me. Amen.

Unforgiveness

And whenever you stand praying, if you have anything against anyone, forgive him and let it drop (leave it, let it go), in order that your Father Who is in heaven may also forgive you your [own] failings and shortcomings and let them drop. But if you do not forgive, neither will your Father in heaven forgive your failings and shortcomings.   —MARK 11:25–26

One of the greatest reasons why prayer isn't answered among Christians is *unforgiveness*. Jesus gave His disciples a command to forgive, and then He told them plainly that if they did not forgive, neither would their Father in heaven forgive them their failings and shortcomings. He was blunt with them, because He knew what a stumbling block unforgiveness would be for their spiritual life.

It is important to note that forgiveness and having faith to move mountains comes in the same context. There is no power in speaking to a mountain if the heart is full of unforgiveness. Yet this problem is rampant among God's children. If there is anything that will short-circuit God from answering our prayers, it's a heart full of unforgiveness and bitterness toward others. You can't go into your prayer closet and expect God to move mountains for you or on behalf of others when you've hardened your heart with unforgiveness. Extend abundant mercy and forgiveness just as God forgave you in Christ.

———————

Lord, help me to always remember what it cost You to forgive me, and yet You freely forgave me. I want my heart to be like Yours and to extend mercy to others as well. Amen.

It Is a New Day

Let us then fearlessly and confidently and boldly draw near to the throne of grace (the throne of God's unmerited favor to us sinners), that we may receive mercy [for our failures] and find grace to help in good time for every need [appropriate help and well-times help, coming just when we need it]. —HEBREWS 4:16

We see from this Scripture the attitude we should live with. Fearless! Confident! Bold! We cannot ask fearfully and expect to receive. We come in that way because we know with assurance that God is faithful, He is good, and He wants to meet our needs. We don't need to act as if God is a miser whose arm we must twist to convince Him to help us. He is waiting to hear your cry!

Many of the wrong attitudes toward women over the centuries have either changed or they are in the process of being changed. We are sorry for the women who lived in the past and did not know the freedom we enjoy today. We still have a way to go, but as the saying goes, "We've come a long way, baby!" It is a new day. There are no hindrances. The door is wide open for you to realize your dreams. Walk confidently into your future and never look back! You go, girl!

———————

Lord, I want to live fearlessly and confidently, knowing that You are faithful and will always meet my needs. Thank You for open doors and a bright tomorrow. Amen.

About the Author

JOYCE MEYER is one of the world's leading practical Bible teachers. A #1 *New York Times* bestselling author, she has written more than eighty inspirational books, including *Power Thoughts, Never Give Up!*, the entire Battlefield of the Mind family of books, and two novels, *The Penny* and *Any Minute*, as well as many others. She has also released thousands of audio teachings, as well as a complete video library. Joyce's *Enjoying Everyday Life*® radio and television programs are broadcast around the world, and she travels extensively conducting conferences. Joyce and her husband, Dave, are the parents of four grown children and make their home in St. Louis, Missouri.

Joyce Meyer Ministries
U.S. & Foreign Office Addresses

Joyce Meyer Ministries
P.O. Box 655
Fenton, MO 63026
USA
(636) 349-0303
www.joycemeyer.org

Joyce Meyer Ministries—Canada
P.O. Box 7700
Vancouver, BC V6B 4E2
Canada
(800) 868-1002

Joyce Meyer Ministries—Australia
Locked Bag 77
Mansfield Delivery Centre
Queensland 4122
Australia
(07) 3349 1200

Joyce Meyer Ministries—England
P.O. Box 1549
Windsor SL4 1GT
United Kingdom
01753 831102

Joyce Meyer Ministries—South Africa
P.O. Box 5
Cape Town 8000
South Africa
(27) 21-701-1056

Other Books by Joyce Meyer

*Study Guide available for this title

Joyce Meyer Spanish Language Titles

Las Siete Cosas Que Te Roban el Gozo
(Seven Things That Steal Your Joy)
Empezando Tu Dia Bien (Starting Your Day Right)
La Revolución de Amor (Love Revolution)
Come la Galleta . . . Compra los Zapatos
(Eat the Cookie . . . Buy the Shoes)
Pensamientos de Poder (Power Thoughts)

By Dave Meyer

Life Lines